D1715443

EMERGING BUSINESS
ONLINE

EMERGING BUSINESS ONLINE

Global Markets and the Power of B2B Internet Marketing

LARA FAWZY AND LUCAS DWORSKI

Vice President, Publisher: Tim Moore
Associate Publisher and Director of Marketing: Amy Neidlinger
Executive Editor: Jeanne Glasser
Editorial Assistant: Pamela Boland
Development Editor: Herb Schafner
Operations Manager: Gina Kanouse
Senior Marketing Manager: Julie Phifer
Publicity Manager: Laura Czaja
Assistant Marketing Manager: Megan Colvin
Cover Designer: Chuti Prasertsith
Managing Editor: Kristy Hart
Project Editor: Betsy Harris
Copy Editor: Keith Cline
Proofreader: Water Crest Publishing, Inc.
Indexer: Lisa Stumpf
Senior Compositor: Gloria Schurick
Manufacturing Buyer: Dan Uhrig

© 2011 by Lara Fawzy and Lucas Dworski
Published by Pearson Education, Inc.
Publishing as FT Press
Upper Saddle River, New Jersey 07458

FT Press offers excellent discounts on this book when ordered in quantity for bulk purchases or special sales. For more information, please contact U.S. Corporate and Government Sales, 1-800-382-3419, corpsales@pearsontechgroup.com. For sales outside the U.S., please contact International Sales at international@pearson.com.

Company and product names mentioned herein are the trademarks or registered trademarks of their respective owners.

Printed in the United States of America

First Printing October 2010

ISBN-10: 0-13-706441-1
ISBN-13: 978-0-13-706441-0

Pearson Education LTD.
Pearson Education Australia PTY, Limited.
Pearson Education Singapore, Pte. Ltd.
Pearson Education North Asia, Ltd.
Pearson Education Canada, Ltd.
Pearson Educación de Mexico, S.A. de C.V.
Pearson Education—Japan
Pearson Education Malaysia, Pte. Ltd.

Library of Congress Cataloging-in-Publication Data

Fawzy, Lara, 1981-

  Emerging business online : global markets and the power of B2B internet marketing / Lara Fawzy, Lucas Dworski.

    p. cm.

  ISBN 978-0-13-706441-0 (hbk. : alk. paper) 1. Marketing—Developing countries. 2. Internet marketing—Developing countries. I. Dworski, Lucas, 1980- II. Title.

  HF5415.12.D44F39 2011

  658.8'72—dc22

                                  2010028146

I would like to thank God for my ability to see, think, and write this book and for listening to my prayers.

I want to thank my family, especially my mother Nagat Barakat for always believing in me and providing me with more than what words could ever describe; my uncle Mustafa Barakat for encouraging me to be brave, daring, and innovative; and my sisters Amal Fawzy and Sandra Fawzy for supporting and encouraging me—in spite of all the time this book took away from them, they constantly encouraged me. I'd like to dedicate this book to my amazing young nephews Hicham Bakkali and Omar Shareef Bakkali, my rays of sunshine, energy, and motivation.

I would like to extend my thanks to coauthor and great friend, Lucas Dworski, for supporting, inspiring, and shaping my ideas and for his amazing contributions, dedication, and hard work. It was a great day when we created the concept of the ebocube model. I thoroughly enjoyed working with him on this project and admire his intelligence, decisiveness, and incredible knowledge.

—Lara Fawzy

First of all, I would like to thank my coauthor Lara Fawzy, a tremendous business partner and great friend, a person without whom this book wouldn't be published. I admire your dedication and determination, your hard work on this project, your intelligence, and your "out of the box" thinking that made it possible to define the ebocube business model and finalize the book. Thanks!

I would like to thank my family and friends who supported me during this challenging time.

Special thanks goes to my mother Wanda Anna Dworska, to whom I would like to dedicate this book and the hours of hard work spent working on it.

—Lucas Dworski

Contents

Acknowledgments

Thanks to the following people who contributed information to our book:

- Local marketing Internet communication managers, marketing operation managers, database marketing managers, business development managers, local agencies and sales teams in emerging markets who took the time to provide us with information, research, and interviews, which gave us deep local knowledge and understanding of emerging markets; you really did help us strengthen our model and insight on these huge and diverse markets. You truly believed in our model and shared our vision in defining it and publishing it.

- FT Press for enabling us to publish this book; we consider this to be a great achievement. In particular, we'd like to thank Jeanne Glasser, Executive Editor and our editor and mentor, for spurring us on when we hit the "writing wall" and for seeing the potential in our project. We'd like to thank Betsy Harris, Project Editor, for fantastically managing the production of our book! We'd also like to thank Keith Cline, Copy Editor, for adding the magic touches to our copy. We'd also like thank Mindy Reed from The Author's Assistant for originally editing our manuscript.

- The many colleagues and friends who supported us through writing this book have our sincere gratitude.

- James Cronk, Director, Financial Services Industries for Emerging Markets for taking the time to provide us with valuable strategic insight into market trends split by industry in emerging markets; the challenges, your view on long-term trends, and your senior experience and knowledge of these markets were invaluable, especially in this time of great uncertainty.

- Companies penetrating emerging markets—we'd like to thank the various companies that allowed us to test the ebocube model and realize the real-life challenges in executing online campaigns in emerging markets, as well as the global corporate that we both originally worked for that provided us with our advanced experience and training in online marketing in emerging markets.

- Rebecca Bell Ellis, Senior Vice President for Acceleration, for providing us both with customer relationship management (CRM) training that inspired our model and for also providing us with huge encouragement and sharing with us your experience in CRM gained over your 25-year career.

- The Internet was also a great tool for validating our knowledge.

About the Authors

Lara Fawzy is currently an Online Campaign Marketing Manager, for Cisco's African region (based in Cairo, Egypt). Lara is also Director and founder of her own firm, ebocube, and conducts online marketing training in the African region. She has worked for Cisco Systems in various roles, including online customer relationship marketing for emerging markets (based in the UK). In this role, she worked closely with local marketing teams, sales teams, and agencies across emerging markets. She also created and executed online marketing campaigns using complex data segmentation and tracked and reported on campaigns through advanced customer relationship management tools.

As a Marketing Operations Manager with Cisco in Cairo, she worked closely with the African and Gulf marketing teams, strengthening her experience and knowledge of emerging markets.

Previously, Lara worked for O2, Telefonica, as a Campaign Manager, launching the high-profile Apple iPhone 3G in the UK business market and helping to redesign the company website.

Lara is a qualified Chartered Marketer. She graduated from University of London, Royal Holloway, School of Management, with a Management BSc, specializing in marketing. Her degree was largely based on Harvard research; she studied management models and theories by leading management and marketing gurus such as Michael Porter, Philip Kotler, and Peter Drucker.

Lucas Dworski is originally from Poland, Central Eastern Europe. He has more than a decade's experience in marketing, including international marketing. Lucas has worked and lived in Germany, the UK, Netherlands, and Poland. He's passionate about global marketing, particularly in emerging markets. Lucas's experience is specialized in customer relationship management and complex online localized international campaigns.

Lucas has worked and consulted for global international American corporations such as Cisco and Computer Associates CA, as well as many smaller companies. Lucas has experience in campaign management and campaign execution for a wide number of countries (more than 130) in emerging markets. He has executed campaigns that have been fully measurable, trackable, and localized for local market needs. Lucas also has in-depth experience in database management, having worked in customer relationship management for several years.

Introduction

We live in an age of information overload, significantly facilitated by the Internet. Anyone from almost anywhere can send, access, and post information across the globe in a matter of seconds. As applications and technologies continue to evolve, our ability to leverage the Internet will continue to impact the way we work and live.

The ubiquity of media connectivity also generates understandable worries about losing the benefits of face-to-face collaboration and "the human touch." Without question, people will continue to gather and meet for business, social, and family reasons. This is in our cultural and biological DNA and will never change. Millions of people around our world dismissed aspects of email, social media, or even cell phones decades ago, only to eventually understand how they complemented or improved existing practices and connections. We should adapt and use new technologies when they serve our common interests and humanity.

A new-generation technology prompted the authors to write this book, a technology that, like social media and email before it, can become a part of the daily lives of millions of people. That technology is telepresence, the next generation of videoconferencing technology. Telepresence uses the Internet to transfer conference calls as well as high-definition images and presentations. It can provide life-size images and surround sound and can thus create the illusion that all the attendees are in the same room.

Holographic videoconferencing is an application that beams three-dimensional images of people into a room. This is but one example of existing and emerging technologies that present an effective and responsible alternative to world leaders and business executives who currently fly around the world and ride in limousines to meeting locations. Digital and information technologies are allowing businesses in emerging markets to dramatically upgrade their business processes and operations.

As billions of people now access the Internet, emerging nations and markets are increasing their investments in these technologies to give people greater access (and speed) to information. This book explores how and why the Internet and related technologies are redefining how we conduct business globally. We identify the most salient new ideas shaping the global information marketplace, and explore how these offer government and private sector managers a new generation of digitally based management and communication tools.

It's a Small World After All

The world is smaller. Distance and time no longer present insurmountable barriers to doing business on a global scale. The Internet reduces the need to travel for meetings, and it speeds up the flow of information. Co-authoring this book models the effectiveness of virtual communication. Although we reside in two different countries, interactive web conferencing tools enabled us to edit the chapters and exchange information as effectively as working face to face. We were able to share our desktops so that each one could view the document in real time as it was being edited.

Web conferencing tools allowed for the use of Voice over Internet calls, which let us talk for free or at the charge of the monthly subscription and Internet connection. We conducted research by recording Internet conference calls and then playing back the information.

We pitched the manuscript to FT Press using web conferencing tools to share presentations and creative ideas. The FT Press editors are based in America and Australia; one of us is in Africa, and the other is in Europe: four continents, connected virtually.

Both of us hold professional positions with global organizations and take part in virtual teams focused on emerging markets (EMs). Therefore, we've seen firsthand the transformational effect of web applications that enable us to share work, participate in telemeetings, and otherwise communicate with clients, vendors, and partners. Among other professional duties, we are often tasked with executing and managing online marketing campaigns for EMs. From these successes, we have perfected the ebocube (emerging business online) model.

The ebocube Model

Global corporations, private and nongovernmental organizations, small businesses, and entrepreneurs have tapped the Internet and computer reporting tools to do business in and with EMs. These organizations are learning as they go, experimenting with various digital and reporting tools and techniques. Professionals share information and ideas through informal means, but no firm or consultant has created a robust, well-defined Internet business strategy. In this early stage of transacting twenty-first century business activity through digital means, we still lack tested practices based on metrics and methods to measure return on investment. We are addressing that need with this book and the ebocube model, a framework to articulate, measure, and guide the process of Internet-based marketing and business development. This book lays out the multitude of reasons to use the Internet and ebocube model.

Emerging Markets

Many books and journals explain the benefits of the Internet. This book goes further, introducing you to an innovative Internet marketing and sales model defined for business-to-business (B2B) marketing in emerging markets. We call the model *ebocube*.

The term *emerging market* describes a region of the world with relatively recent industrial and technological change and now experiencing rapid economic growth. Goldman Sachs popularized the acronym BRIC (Brazil, Russia, India, and China)[1] to identify countries that many economists believe to be economically powerful in terms of current and future growth. However, our consideration of EMs encompasses more than just the BRIC countries. For the purpose of the ebocube model, we've researched regions and countries in Asia, Latin America, the Middle East and Africa, Russia and the Commonwealth of Independent States, and Central Eastern Europe. We have also worked with all these regions.

Even though developing markets are experiencing recessionary effects from the global financial crisis, many countries remain in a robust growth position. Growth will continue to come from EMs for the next "10 to 15 years, not only during this current recession," states James Cronk, Director, Financial Services Industries for Emerging Markets, for a global IT company. The CEO of our previous employer, Cisco Systems Inc., said in a speech that "emerging markets are on fire," referring to sales growth coming from these markets. Although he made that remark before the onset of the recession, economic indicators show that his conclusion still holds true.

EMs are generally characterized by large populations, as is obvious with China and India. Whereas some of these markets remain politically and economically unstable, many other EM nations have through reform successfully stabilized their economies and normalized their trade practices. EMs (130 countries and counting) comprise more than two-thirds of the global land mass. Most are rich in natural resources (in large part because their slow industrial and economic development has left their resources untapped) and host diverse industries, including manufacturing, oil and gas, agriculture, and more. Some EM nations have the potential to leapfrog developed markets because they are not slowed by *legacy* technologies. Japan, for example, became an advanced economy post World War II by leapfrogging technology developed by countries like the UK after the Industrial Revolution, among other factors. India leapfrogged landline telephony to become a mobile, wireless economy. Although we could debate whether some of the countries mentioned previously are still emerging economies, the strategies outlined in our book still apply.

When trading in these economies, risks and uncertainty exist, just as in any international market where businesses deal with unknowns. Some EMs we discuss in this book are politically unstable or otherwise risky, and therefore they are less predictable than developed economies, which have stable, established economic and political environments.

Emerging Markets + the Internet = the ebocube Model

ebocube stands for *emerging business online,* with *cube* referring to a visual framework of our three-phase model. The Internet underpins this model.

Internet penetration in EMs is growing, with businesses in those markets being particularly early and enthusiastic adopters. The Internet helps bridge the travel, time zone, and cost barriers necessary to successfully market and communicate business products in EM nations. The Internet makes it easier to penetrate EMs, enabling commerce at the click of a button.

Senior executives in developed economies, working in B2B organizations, small and large, are asking the following questions:

- How can we get ahead of competitors in emerging markets?
- How can our business mitigate risks when we enter risky, high-growth emerging markets?
- How can we measure marketing activities and sales-related results in these markets?

The ebocube model defines an end-to-end integrated marketing process. The authors and our colleagues have tested this model and processes across these markets. We developed ebocube for B2B marketers in developed economies targeting EMs. However, we predict that EM professionals will also use the model to market to domestic markets and to other EMs. EMs are already leveraging the power of the Internet through innovative business models to generate commerce—the Chinese site AliBaba.com, a leading online global market place for small businesses, demonstrates this.

During the dotcom boom, many companies went bust because they didn't know how to really leverage the Internet (even with all the hype!). Similarly, in recent years, social media has excited interest in the business world and also confused or even intimidated marketers. However, most companies don't yet know what they want to achieve with social media and how they will measure results or return on marketing investment. Many companies currently use social media to just post information, thus failing to engage customers and partners in sustainable relationships.

Digital applications, new technologies, and a dizzying universe of websites make for a daunting combination for marketers in developed markets and EMs. Global business managers and staff desperately need flexible and adaptable frameworks that demystify sales and marketing practices as relationships criss-cross digital, business, and national borders. The ebocube closes the loop between marketing and sales in EMs.

The ebocube is, of course, a digital model, so it has modest environmental impact. It is built to provide electronic customer relationship management (CRM) capabilities, based on metrics, data, and business intelligence.

B2B Model

We developed the ebocube as a B2B model to address the needs of global professionals over the next decades as B2B commerce shapes standards and establishes precedents. We have built ebocube to suit B2B buying cycles and requirements because these are much more predictable environments than consumer markets in relatively fragile and unequal (wealth-wise) nations. We share decades of frontline experience working in B2B in dozens of EMs.

Data, Reporting, and the ebocube

Fundamental to the ebocube is company (firmographic) and customer data. We rely on contact and company data to market effectively and directly to businesses. Digital conduits aligned with database marketing can be described as electronic customer relationship management (eCRM)—that is, using Internet tools to interact with contacts to build a commercial relationship.

Three Phases of the ebocube

- **Phase one, the dashboard and the datacube:** This phase focuses on reporting on marketing, sales, and company or contact data for the businesses you're targeting in EM. It measures what's working (or not working) and which market is generating the highest return on marketing investment (ROMI). The datacube also represents the quality of contact data to leverage an eCRM strategy. The ebocube means business decisions are not based on instinct or assumption, but on numbers and business intelligence.

- **Phase two, campaign and data planning:** Using the ebocube commercial cycle (contact buying cycle/decision-making process and data life cycle), phase two discusses the proposition used, messaging, the incentive, localization, budgeting, and integrating media mix (online and offline) to achieve ebocube commercial cycle goals.

- **Phase three, marketing operations demonstration:** In phase three, you budget, plan, execute, track, and measure campaigns to feed the dashboard with meaningful metrics, and feed your company database, which can be represented in the datacube. Phase three closes the loop on marketing, data, and sales in EMs.

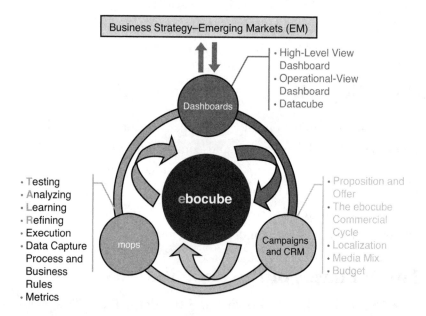

Figure I.1   The ebocube model

Endnotes

[1] Wikipedia, "BRIC," http://en.wikipedia.org/wiki/BRIC.

1

Emerging Markets

Upon completion of this chapter, you should be able to

- Identify emerging market regions and nations that promise potential economic growth
- Explain why emerging markets are significant for business expansion
- Recognize the dynamism of economic superpower status
- Discuss how outsourcing by Western companies has transformed emerging markets
- Distinguish the different modes of Internet connectivity in emerging markets
- Describe the business life cycle in developed versus emerging markets
- Understand that your marketing strategies must be tailored to the specific culture/population of the emerging market

Brazil, Russia, India, and China comprise what is referred to as the BRIC markets. These countries are central to our research because they are the world's fastest-growing economies, are home to billions of people, and are poised to dominate the world economy in the twenty-first century.

The acronym BRIC derives from Goldman Sachs circa 2001. Goldman Sachs asserts that by 2050 the combined economies of the BRIC nations could eclipse the combined economies of the current richest four countries of the world. The BRIC countries cover a quarter of the earth's land mass and, currently, are home to more than

40% of the world's population.[1] Despite the current recession, these countries economies are expanding. The weakening U.S. dollar and British pound are also helping companies from developed countries increase their sales in emerging markets (EMs). Some economists even assert that the BRIC nations may potentially lead global economic growth, and these same economists link global economic recovery to the success of the BRIC economies.

Our ebocube model includes a number of EMs beyond the BRIC quartet, with their inclusion based on the scope of the business opportunities in those EM nations. In terms of your own business strategy in these countries (including whether your product will sell there), you need to research each country and assess the opportunity potential, size/profitability of the business segment, and the stability and size of your targeted industries. With ebocube, you can virtually test the response to marketing campaigns and generate sales leads in these different markets.

Geographic Regions

In this book, our focus on EMs includes the big four (BRIC) and a number of other countries that have attracted significant investor attention in recent years. We perceive opportunities in less-well-documented regions (e.g., Central and Eastern Europe, the Middle East and Africa, Russia and the Commonwealth of Independent States, Latin America [LatAM], and Asia). Some of the countries we discuss have yet to generate the attention that billion-plus population markets guarantee. Nonetheless, their growth is notable, and they present myriad opportunities for growing businesses.

Historically, the EM nations we cover in this book were not open to global trade (or, if they were, they were difficult to enter and penetrate). Traditionally, they have been considered (and sometimes still are considered) high-risk environments and politically unstable. These are just factors to consider, not absolutes impervious to change.

Asia

EMs in the Asia region range from China to Vietnam. We have focused our research on China, Hong Kong, India, Indonesia, Korea, Malaysia, the Philippines, Singapore, Taiwan, Thailand, and Vietnam.

China is the most populous country in the world (India is second), so China naturally receives a lot of media attention. But it's not the only game in the region. The Asian countries mentioned previously are mostly untapped EMs and represent a huge potential for sales and growth for your business.

In India, English is the most important language for national, political, and commercial communication. Hindi is the most widely *spoken* language and the primary tongue of 41% of the Indian people; there are 14 other official languages in India![2] For the purpose of business-to-business (B2B) marketing, English is widely acceptable.

Table 1.1 lists the EMs in the Asia region and provides a few important pieces of information for those wanting to exploit business opportunities in these individual countries and the region as a whole.

TABLE 1.1 Emerging Markets in the Asia Region

Country	ISO Code	Region	Language	Domain	Time Zone
Bhutan	BT	Asia	Dzongkha	.bt	GMT +6
Brunei	BN	Asia	Malay	.bn	GMT +8
Burma	MM	Asia	Burmese	.mm	GMT +6.5
Cambodia	KH	Asia	Khmer	.kh	GMT +7
China	CN	Asia	Standard Mandarin	.cn	GMT +8
East Timor	TL	Asia	Tetum, Portuguese	.tl	GMT +9
Hong Kong	HK	Asia	Chinese, English	.hk	GMT +8
India	IN	Asia	Hindi, English	.in	GMT +5.5
Indonesia	ID	Asia	Indonesian	.id	GMT +7 to +9
Laos	LA	Asia	Lao	.la	GMT +7
Macau	MO	Asia	Chinese, Portuguese	.mo	GMT +8

TABLE 1.1   Emerging Markets in the Asia Region

Country	ISO Code	Region	Language	Domain	Time Zone
Malaysia	MA	Asia	Malay	.ma	GMT +9
Maldives	MV	Asia	Divehi (Mahl)	.mv	GMT +5.5
Mongolia	MN	Asia	Mongolian	.mn	GMT +7 to +8
Nepal	NP	Asia	Nepali	.np	GMT +4.75
North Korea	KP	Asia	Korean	.kp	GMT +9
Philippines	PH	Asia	Filipino, English	.ph	GMT +8
Singapore	SG	Asia	English, Malay	.sg	GMT +8
South Korea	KR	Asia	Korean	.kr	GMT +9
Sri Lanka	LK	Asia	Sinhala, Tamil	.lk	GMT +5.5
Taiwan	TW	Asia	Standard Mandarin	.tw	GMT +8
Thailand	TH	Asia	Thai	.th	GMT +7
Vietnam	VN	Asia	Vietnamese	.vn	GMT +7

Central Eastern Europe

The term *Central and Eastern Europe* (CEE) is now in widespread use, after replacing *Eastern Bloc,* and describes the former Communist countries in Europe (after the Iron Curtain collapse).[3] Table 1.2 lists the countries in CEE, languages, time zones, and country domain codes. Why is this information (in this table and the other tables in this chapter) important? Because in the United Kingdom, we might want to access http://ebocube.co.uk, whereas people in Poland may want to access http://ebocube.pl.

The countries in the CEE region (even neighboring countries) differ significantly in terms of culture, language, religion, economics, and politics. You must factor in these differences to any of your business plans in the region.

TABLE 1.2 Emerging Markets in the CEE Region

Country	ISO Code	Region	Language	Domain	Time Zone	EU Member
Albania	AL	CEE	Albanian	.al	GMT +1	
Bosnia and Herzegovina	BA	CEE	Bosnian	.ba	GMT +1	
Bulgaria	BG	CEE	Bulgarian	.bg	GMT +2	Yes
Croatia	HR	CEE	Croatian	.hr	GMT +1	
Czech Republic	CZ	CEE	Czech	.cz	GMT +1	Yes
Estonia	EE	CEE	Estonian	.ee	GMT +2	Yes
Hungary	HU	CEE	Hungarian	.hu	GMT +1	Yes
Latvia	LV	CEE	Latvian	.lv	GMT +2	Yes
Lithuania	LT	CEE	Lithuanian	.lt	GMT +2	Yes
Macedonia	MK	CEE	Macedonian	.mk	GMT +1	
Poland	PL	CEE	Polish	.pl	GMT +1	Yes
Romania	RO	CEE	Romanian	.ro	GMT +2	Yes
Serbia	RS	CEE	Serbian	.rs	GMT +1	
Slovakia	SK	CEE	Slovak	.sk	GMT +1	Yes
Slovenia	SI	CEE	Slovenian	.sl	GMT +1	Yes
Turkey	TR	CEE	Turkish	.tr	GMT +2	

The CEE region includes 16 different languages and hundreds of dialect variations. Therefore, you can't approach all these countries in the same manner, with the same message and timing. Assumptions you make about each country could lead to poor response. They could even result in devastating mistakes that cause you to offend the local culture and thus damage your reputation. You need to understand and account for these differences in phase two of the ebocube: campaign and data planning.

The CEE region includes economically, politically, socially, and technologically mature countries such as Poland, the Czech Republic, and Turkey. It also includes more fragile and vulnerable developing markets, such as Serbia, Albania, and Croatia. Some CEE countries are relatively new members of the European Union (e.g., Bulgaria, the Czech Republic, Estonia, Hungary, Latvia, Lithuania, Poland, Romania, Slovakia, and Slovenia[4]), whereas the rest of the CEE nations are not members of EU. This discrepancy makes the launch of campaigns in this region even more challenging because you must follow a specific country's laws and sometimes E.U. legislation, too.

Latin America and the Caribbean

Latin America (LatAM) is a culturally diverse region spanning two continents and offers developed economies huge growth opportunities across many different sectors. The Caribbean islands, including Barbados, St. Lucia, and the Bahamas, are widely known for their tourism industry. LatAM is home to Brazil, the *B* in BRIC. Brazil offers huge potential; it has a large population and abundant natural resources.

Mexico also offers opportunities for massive growth and serves as a gateway between the United States and LatAM. A number of languages are spoken across the region (see Table 1.3). As in other regions previously discussed, the cultures across the LatAM region are unique and diverse. B2B initiatives must factor in the dynamism of the population/culture in this region. Such cultural consideration in initiatives is called *localization* and must be addressed in phase two of ebocube. The vast majority of Latin Americans are Roman Catholic. However, membership in the Catholic Church in Latin America is declining while membership in other Christian religions is increasing, particularly in Guatemala, Brazil, and Puerto Rico.[5]

TABLE 1.3   Emerging Markets in LatAM and the Caribbean Region

Country	ISO Code	Region	Language	Domain	Time Zone
Anguilla	AI	LatAM	English	.ai	GMT –4
Antigua and Barbuda	AG	LatAM	English	.ag	GMT –4
Argentina	AR	LatAM	Spanish	.ar	GMT –3
Aruba	AW	LatAM	Dutch	.aw	GMT –4
Bahamas	BS	LatAM	English	.bs	GMT –5
Barbados	BB	LatAM	English	.bb	GMT –4
Belize	BZ	LatAM	English	.bz	GMT –6
Bermuda	BM	LatAM	English	.bm	GMT –4
Bolivia	BO	LatAM	Spanish	.bo	GMT –4
Brazil	BR	LatAM	Portuguese	.br	GMT –3/4/5
Cayman Islands	KY	LatAM	English	.ky	GMT –5
Chile	CL	LatAM	Spanish	.cl	GMT –4
Colombia	CO	LatAM	Spanish	.co	GMT –5
Costa Rica	CR	LatAM	Spanish	.cr	GMT –6
Cuba	CU	LatAM	Spanish	.cu	GMT –5
Dominica	DM	LatAM	English	.dm	GMT –4
Dominican Republic	DO	LatAM	Spanish	.do	GMT –4
Ecuador	EC	LatAM	Spanish	.ec	GMT –5
El Salvador	SV	LatAM	Spanish	.sv	GMT –6
Falkland Islands (Malvinas)	FK	LatAM	English	.fk	GMT –4
French Guiana	GF	LatAM	French	.gf	GMT –3
Grenada	GD	LatAM	English	.gd	GMT –4
Guadeloupe	GP	LatAM	French	.gp	GMT –4
Guatemala	GT	LatAM	Spanish	.gt	GMT –6
Guyana	GY	LatAM	English	.gy	GMT –4
Haiti	HT	LatAM	French	.ht	GMT –5
Honduras	HN	LatAM	Spanish	.hn	GMT –6
Jamaica	JM	LatAM	English	.jm	GMT –5
Martinique	MQ	LatAM	French	.mq	GMT –4
Mexico	MX	LatAM	Spanish	.mx	GMT –6
Montserrat	MS	LatAM	English	.ms	GMT –4

TABLE 1.3   Emerging Markets in LatAM and the Caribbean Region

Country	ISO Code	Region	Language	Domain	Time Zone
Netherlands Antilles	AN	LatAM	Dutch	.an	GMT –4
Nicaragua	NI	LatAM	Spanish	.ni	GMT –6
Panama	PA	LatAM	Spanish	.pa	GMT –5
Paraguay	PY	LatAM	Spanish	.py	GMT –4
Peru	PE	LatAM	Spanish	.pe	GMT –5
Puerto Rico	PR	LatAM	Spanish	.pr	GMT –4
Saint Kitts and Nevis	KN	LatAM	English	.kn	GMT –4
Saint Lucia	LC	LatAM	English	.lc	GMT –4
Saint Pierre and Miquelon	PM	LatAM	French	.pm	GMT –3
Saint Vincent and the Grenadines	VC	LatAM	English	.vc	GMT –4
Suriname	SR	LatAM	Dutch	.sr	GMT –3
Trinidad and Tobago	TT	LatAM	English	.tt	GMT –4
Turks and Caicos Islands	TC	LatAM	English	.tc	GMT –5
Uruguay	UY	LatAM	Spanish	.uy	GMT –3
Venezuela	VE	LatAM	Spanish	.ve	GMT –4.5
Virgin Islands, British	VG	LatAM	English	.vg	GMT –4
Virgin Islands, U.S.	VI	LatAM	English	.vi	GMT –4

The Middle East and Africa

The Middle East has been a center of world affairs for all of recorded history.[6] The region is home to Egypt, one of the world's earliest and longest-lasting civilizations and a rapidly emerging hotspot for outsourcing. The Middle East and Africa (MEA) region is also home to the Emirates, Qatar, and Saudi Arabia, where they control the world's largest oil reserves (along with Libya).

South Africa is also in the MEA region. The South African economy received a significant boost as the country prepared to host the 2010 FIFA World Cup. That boost came in the form of government spending before the competition and from increased tourism and after the World Cup.

South Africa borders Namibia, Botswana, Zimbabwe, Mozambique, Swaziland, and Lesotho; and its well-developed road and rail links provide reliable ground transportation deep into sub-Saharan Africa.[7]

The Middle East is the geographic origin of three of the world's major religions: Christianity, Islam, and Judaism. Arabic is a major language spoken in the Middle East, although English is also spoken, especially among the middle and upper class, and it's a well-accepted business language; in fact, business is often taught in English. In various African nations, many people speak French. Keep this in mind if you have a French website. You might want to check where your traffic is coming from. Could it be French-speaking Africa (see Table 1.4)? Africa is the world's second largest (in land mass) and second most-populous continent (after Asia). Nigeria alone has a population of 140 million and is often called the "Giant of Africa." The MEA countries in Africa differ in culture from the countries in the Gulf.

TABLE 1.4 Emerging Markets in the MEA Region

Country	ISO Code	Region	Language	Domain	Time Zone
Afghanistan	AF	MEA	Dari (Persian)	.af	GMT +4.5
Algeria	DZ	MEA	Arabic, French, Tamazight	.dz	GMT +1
Angola	AO	MEA	Portuguese	.ao	GMT +1
Bahrain	BH	MEA	Arabic	.bh	GMT +3
Benin	BJ	MEA	French	.bj	GMT +1
Botswana	BW	MEA	English, Tswana	.bw	GMT +2
British Indian Ocean Territory	IO	MEA	English	.oi	GMT +6
Burkina Faso	BF	MEA	French	.bf	GMT
Burundi	BI	MEA	Kirundi, French	.bi	GMT +2
Côte D'Ivoire	CI	MEA	French	.ci	GMT
Cameroon	CM	MEA	French, English	.cm	GMT +1
Cape Verde	CV	MEA	Portuguese	.cv	GMT −1

TABLE 1.4   Emerging Markets in the MEA Region

Country	ISO Code	Region	Language	Domain	Time Zone
Central African Republic	CF	MEA	Sango, French	.cf	GMT +1
Chad	TD	MEA	French, Arabic	.td	GMT +1
Comoros	KM	MEA	Comorian, Arabic, French	.km	GMT +3
Congo (Bazzaville)	CG	MEA	French	.cg	GMT
Congo, the Democratic Republic of the	CD	MEA	French	.cd	GMT +1/2
Djibouti	DJ	MEA	Arabic, French	.dj	GMT +3
Egypt	EG	MEA	Arabic	.eg	GMT +2
Equatorial Guinea	GQ	MEA	Spanish, French, Portuguese	.gq	GMT +1
Eritrea	ER	MEA	Arabic, English, Tigrinya	.er	GMT +3
Ethiopia	ET	MEA	Amharic	.et	GMT +4
French Southern Territories	TF	MEA	French	.tf	GMT +5
Gabon	GA	MEA	Franch	.ga	GMT +1
Gambia	GM	MEA	English	.gm	GMT
Ghana	GH	MEA	English	.gh	GMT
Guinea	GN	MEA	French	.gn	GMT
Guinea-Bissau	GW	MEA	Portuguese	.gw	GMT
Iran	IR	MEA	Persian	.ir	GMT +3.5
Iraq	IQ	MEA	Arabic, Kurdish	.iq	GMT +3
Jordan	JO	MEA	Arabic	.jo	GMT +2
Kenya	KE	MEA	Swahili, English	.ke	GMT +3
Kuwait	KW	MEA	Arabic	.kw	GMT +4
Lebanon	LB	MEA	Arabic	.lb	GMT +2
Lesotho	LS	MEA	Sesotho, English	.ls	GMT +2
Liberia	LR	MEA	English	.lr	GMT
Libyan Arab Jamahiriya	LY	MEA	Arabic	.ly	GMT +2

TABLE 1.4   Emerging Markets in the MEA Region

Country	ISO Code	Region	Language	Domain	Time Zone
Madagascar	MG	MEA	Malagasi, French, English	.mg	GMT +3
Malawi	MW	MEA	English	.mw	GMT +2
Mali	ML	MEA	French	.ml	GMT
Mauritania	MR	MEA	Arabic	.mr	GMT
Mauritius	MU	MEA	English	.mu	GMT +4
Mayotte	YT	MEA	French	.yt	GMT +3
Morocco	MA	MEA	Arabic	.ma	GMT
Mozambique	MZ	MEA	Portuguese	.mz	GMT +2
Namibia	NA	MEA	English	.na	GMT +1
Niger	NE	MEA	French	.ne	GMT +1
Nigeria	NG	MEA	English, Hausa, Igbo,	.ng	GMT +1
Oman	OM	MEA	Arabic	.om	GMT +4
Pakistan	PK	MEA	English, Urdu	.pk	GMT +5
Qatar	QA	MEA	Arabic	.qa	GMT +3
Réunion	RE	MEA	French	.re	GMT +4
Rwanda	RW	MEA	French, English	.rw	GMT +2
Saint Helena	SH	MEA	English	.sh	GMT
Sao Tome and Principe	ST	MEA	Portuguese	.st	GMT
Saudi Arabia	SA	MEA	Arabic	.sa	GMT +3
Senegal	SN	MEA	Frensh	.sn	GMT
Seychelles	SC	MEA	English, Seychellois Creole	.sc	GMT +4
Sierra Leone	SL	MEA	English	.sl	GMT
Somalia	SO	MEA	Somali, Arabic	.so	GMT +3
South Africa	ZA	MEA	English	.za	GMT +2
South Georgia and the South Sandwich Islands	GS	MEA	English	.gs	GMT –2

TABLE 1.4   Emerging Markets in the MEA Region

Country	ISO Code	Region	Language	Domain	Time Zone
Sudan	SD	MEA	Arabic, English	.sd	GMT +3
Swaziland	SZ	MEA	English, Swati	.sz	GMT +2
Syrian Arab Republic	SY	MEA	Arabic	.sy	GMT +2
Tanzania, United Republic of	TZ	MEA	Swahili, English	.tz	GMT +3
Togo	TG	MEA	French	.tg	GMT
Tunisia	TN	MEA	Arabic	.tn	GMT +1
Uganda	UG	MEA	English, Swahili	.ug	GMT +3
United Arab Emirates	AE	MEA	Arabic	.ae	GMT +4
Western Sahara	EH	MEA	Arabic, Spanish	.eh	GMT
Yemen	YE	MEA	Arabic	.ye	GMT +3
Zambia	ZM	MEA	English	.zm	GMT +2
Zimbabwe	ZW	MEA	English	.zw	GMT +2

Russia and the Commonwealth of Independent States

Russia is the largest country in the world (geographically speaking), covering more than one-ninth of the earth's land mass. With 142 million people, Russia is the ninth largest by population.[8] It extends across the whole of northern Asia and 40% of Europe, spans 11 time zones, and incorporates a great range of environments and topography.

Russia has the world's greatest known reserves of mineral, precious stones, metals, and energy resources and is considered an energy superpower. Russia can be divided into several broad geographic regions.

Twelve countries in this region are referred to as the Commonwealth of Independent States (CIS). Our research for this book focused mostly on Russia, where we concentrated the bulk of our marketing effort because it is the largest country in the region and is home to the majority of businesses (which are, for the most part, clustered in and around Moscow). Many people in smaller states that were formerly part of the Russian Federation (the former Soviet Union) understand the Russian language (see Table 1.5), but you still want to test your campaigns with different languages.

TABLE 1.5   Emerging Markets in the Russia and CIS Region

Country	ISO Code	Region	Language	Domain	Time Zone
Armenia	AM	Russia & CIS	Armenian	.am	GMT +4
Azerbaijan	AZ	Russia & CIS	Azerbaijani	.az	GMT +4
Belarus	BY	Russia & CIS	Belarusian, Russian	.by	GMT +2
Georgia	GE	Russia & CIS	Georgian	.ge	GMT +4
Kazakhstan	KZ	Russia & CIS	Kazakh, Russian	.kz	GMT +5/6
Kyrgyzstan	KG	Russia & CIS	Kyrgyz, Russian	.kg	GMT +6
Moldova	MD	Russia & CIS	Moldovan (Romanian)	.md	GMT +2
Russia	RU	Russia & CIS	Russian	.ru	GMT +2 to +12
Tajikistan	TJ	Russia & CIS	Tajik	.tj	GMT +5
Turkmenistan	TM	Russia & CIS	Turkmen	.tm	GMT +5
Ukraine	UA	Russia & CIS	Ukranian	.ua	GMT +2
Uzbekistan	UZ	Russia & CIS	Uzbek	.uz	GMT +5

Why These Markets Are Significant

One defining factor of an EM is that it is experiencing strong economic growth. This was certainly the case of the nations mentioned so far in this chapter, at least until the current global recession. These markets are even more significant now, however, because of the economic slowdown in *developed* markets.

Many of these markets have historically been considered high risk. Some have even had sanctions applied against them, including embargos and otherwise restricted trade. A number of megashifts in the global economy have caused these markets to become more stable and open to trade. As corporations reengineered their operations through global outsourcing and new market development, they also imported into "client" EM nations advanced expertise in finance and business processes. Global intermediaries such as the International Monetary Fund (IMF) became more sophisticated in advising EM nations on economic management. As China and India drove economic supergrowth during this time, they also generated secondary waves of demand and market activity for less-developed nations.

Although the less-developed world has been impacted by the global recession, "there is no doubt that there is still huge growth potential in emerging markets," said Paul Mountford, president of Cisco emerging markets in 2009, "to the point where we probably will not be able to call some of them *emerging* anymore in a few years' time."[9]

The Internet has removed travel and time boundaries by allowing trade among markets in real time. The global reach of the Internet may be the most significant transformative development since the industrial age. As infrastructure and telephony bring Internet penetration to billions more of the world's people over the next few years, the EM phenomenon will be exponential. The Internet will become the major platform that allows the free flow of business activity, leveraged by applications and tools such as websites, video applications, and databases. Therefore, EMs will only become easier to access and to do business with.

EMs are also able to leapfrog developed economies in terms of Internet technology because they do not have legacy infrastructure. Service providers, such as mobile companies, are investing in powerful devices and high-speed mobile networks such as 3G, and faster connected mobile broadband led by consumer demand.

The West and Outsourcing

As mentioned previously, EMs received massive economic stimulus through foreign direct investment as Western corporations outsourced processes and operations. The role of India and its technology services industries as the major example of outsourcing economics is well known. Egypt is also fast becoming a hotspot for outsourcing.

The past ten years have been exciting times for Egypt. The list of multinationals outsourcing to Egypt has been growing at an unprecedented rate (e.g., Microsoft, IBM, Vodafone, Oracle, and Hewlett-Packard). The government has been wooing industry investment for years and has made outsourcing a key foreign investment attracter, while leveraging key advantages such as languages and proximity to Europe and North America.

Turkey also has high-skilled, low-cost labor and a well-educated pool (as have many countries in the CEE region). China is renowned for manufacturing outsourcing. Outsourcing has stimulated local markets in EMs by creating jobs, wealth, and making these countries part of the global economy.

Future Superpowers

Investment in these countries has huge potential for high returns and high reward. The initial hype about EMs has subsided during the global recession, but that has allowed us to instead focus on their long and steady growth. These economies are resource rich. Resources include gold, petroleum, diamonds, and other natural resources. A lot of these EMs have enormous populations and a growing middle class. Some EM nations are predicted to become future superpowers, powerful enough to influence the global economy and other sociopolitical realities.

According to the *Financial Times,* "China overtook Germany to become the world's third-largest economy in 2007 after the Chinese authorities revised upward the figures for growth during that year." China surpassed Germany in terms of gross domestic product (GDP), just behind Japan and the United States.[10] Goldman Sachs forecasts that the Chinese economy will overtake that of the United States by about 2040.

The ebocube can help your business reach all these markets at the click of a button, and can help you to develop your B2B relations in EM regions/nations.

Internet Penetration: Fundamental to the ebocube Model

Through the Internet, almost any business can reach their targets in these markets, directly and economically, no matter the size or location of the business. In terms of the ebocube model, reliable Internet access in a particular market is a prerequisite for launching successful integrated Internet campaigns. The Internet works as a response mechanism for customers and vendors and transfers data back into your company databases. Internet applications enable you to track and measure successful integrated campaigns. Therefore, reliable Internet access and service is a major consideration when deciding in which market to implement ebocube. Internet or web-based tools are also used for planning, executing, and reporting through ebocube. In addition, partners may execute campaigns on your behalf, and ebocube can be used by companies in those areas.

Over the past ten years, Internet penetration has grown rapidly in developing economies as a result of continued government and service provider investment and direct investment by technology companies. Technology is also improving, facilitating the implementation of the Internet. For example, from 2000 to 2009, the MEA region had the highest percentage increase in the number of Internet users (a world-leading 2,196% gain). This was followed by the LatAM region, which increased its web users by 883%. More mature Internet markets such as Asia are up 545%;[11] considering the size of the population, this still translates into millions of more users. Internet penetration rates and investment are set to increase in line with global demand as the Internet becomes more of a pivotal role in business and consumer lives.

The adoption of mobile broadband is also likely to continue in EMs. Global mobile operators with experience in developing markets are introducing their bundled data services into these regions.

Emerging on Emerging

Global competition is intensifying as EM countries build trade relationships with other less-developed markets and meet demand in their own domestic markets. For developed economies, the time window to get a business foothold in some of these markets may begin to close over the next decade. Internet marketing and ebocube can give you quick entry to market in terms of raising brand awareness, generating interest, and creating sales leads. As nations, including Russia and China, expand global market reach, competition will intensify in the near future.

These statistics relate to country Internet penetration rates as a whole, including the usage increase rates for consumers and businesses. In some markets, Internet penetration rates may be lower in rural areas. However, they are likely to be higher in business areas because the Internet is a prerequisite for many companies to compete globally.

Many EMs have also witnessed significant investment in mobile broadband telephony. Following on this trend will be an increase in web applications, communications innovations, and collaborative tools and ways of working.

In July 2009, the company SEACOM announced that its submarine fiber-optic cable system linking south and east Africa to global networks via India and Europe was up and running. That system creates unprecedented opportunities. After all, government, business leaders, and citizens can now use the network to compete globally, foster economic growth, and raise living standards across the continent.[12] The move heralds the advent of affordable, high-quality broadband capacity and experience in East African economies.

Mobile Phones

The ebocube model also shows you how to plan, execute, track, measure, and learn from mobile Internet, email, and SMS marketing. All of this marketing is measurable. The ebocube model shows marketers what to measure and how to measure it.

Currently, fast-growing opportunities to market via mobile phone include SMS marketing, multimedia messaging (MMS), push email, and mobile web. The general population in China has access to mobile web, and so you can leverage this in the way that you market in a B2B context, because consumer habits carry over to the workplace.

A profound influence in the mobile world and mobile web is the iPhone 3G and its large touchscreen and browsing capability. Not only can you download content, you can also create and use applications. The iPhone 3G is being sold in EMs, and now the iPad has been introduced and promises even more possibilities.

Internet usage via mobile phones will see a massive surge driven by growth in EMs. China's Internet penetration via mobile phone is set to grow. And some predict that India will have the fastest growing mobile Internet population, doubling by 2013. The number of mobile devices will increase accordingly.[13]

Internet-connected mobile phones are reshaping the way people go about their personal and business lives, offering new opportunities to marketers and a new way to reach prospective customer in EMs.

Smartphones

As mobile broadband infrastructure and coverage expands, smartphone adoption will also grow, allowing marketers new opportunities. Businesses in these areas are ramping up use of smartphones such as iPhones, BlackBerrys, and Nokias. Smartphones enable business users, as well as consumers, to be connected on the move to mobile web, with email delivered to their phones or to other web applications. The Apple iPad is also popular in emerging markets. The aggressive promotion of smartphones and wider portfolios is creating this growth. Many EM nations are younger demographically, and young people are more willing to adopt the latest technologies and think in wireless and digital terms. These also allow B2B marketers new opportunities.

Developed Markets: Maturity and Decline

Developed markets can be described as mature, which means for a lot of sectors growth in sales is slowing down or in decline. Demand is slowing down, and competition is intense. Customers are more sophisticated in their needs. A slowdown in growth is also compounded by the recession in developed markets. Naturally, in a mature market, smaller and less-dominant firms are squeezed out of the market. In this current recession, however, we have also seen large global companies collapse.

Traditionally, strategies for selling in mature markets, depending on the service or product, rely on the following:

- Cost cutting
- Producing innovation in the market (line extensions)
- Repeat purchases from existing customers

As competition continues to intensify, companies need to innovate with new value propositions, price promotions, and sophisticated marketing to grab attention and sell. The years 2010, 2011, and beyond are the time to market and to sell to EMs. While the developed economies experience a historically devastating recession during this period, emerging economies are leading indicators of recovery. Figure 1.1 shows the life cycle of emerging and developed markets seen through classic market-cycle theory.

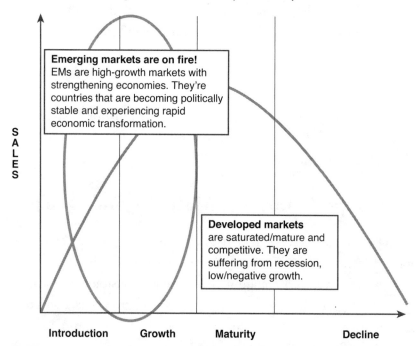

Figure 1.1   Emerging market's life cycle

EM Strategies

EMs promise growth, but businesses may face challenges in terms of education and adoption of products/services. For instance, local businesses might know nothing of your products/services/ brands. There is also a risk that your products/services will not be adopted. Your strategy in these markets must, therefore, differ from your strategy in developed markets. The ebocube offers a well-tested sales and marketing strategy.

The next chapter discusses analysis and strategy in more detail and examines how to use the Internet in a B2B context and reach these new markets.

Endnotes

[1] Wikipedia, "BRIC," http://en.wikipedia.org/wiki/BRIC.

[2] The World Fact Book, "South Asia India, Economy—Overview," https://www.cia.gov/library/publications/the-world-factbook/geos/in.html.

[3] Wikipedia, "Central and Eastern Europe," http://en.wikipedia.org/wiki/Central_and_Eastern_Europe.

[4] Wikipedia, "Member State of European Union," http://en.wikipedia.org/wiki/Member_state_of_the_European_Union.

[5] The World Factbook, "CIA Field Listing—Religions," https://www.cia.gov/library/publications/the-world-factbook/fields/2122.html.

[6] Wikipedia, "Middle East," http://en.wikipedia.org/wiki/Middle_East.

[7] South African Consulate General, "South Africa Open for Business," http://www.southafrica-newyork.net/consulate/openforbusiness.htm.

[8] Wikipedia, "Russia," http://en.wikipedia.org/wiki/Russia.

[9] Cisco Newsroom, "Cisco Tailors its Strategy to Meet the Specific Requirements of Economies in Emerging Markets," http://newsroom.cisco.com/dlls/2009/ts_020909c.html.

[10] Geoff Dyer, "China Becomes Third Largest Economy," January 14, 2009, http://www.ft.com/cms/s/0/8d9337be-e245-11dd-b1dd-0000779fd2ac.html.

[11] Internet World Stats Usage and Population Statistics, "INTERNET USAGE STATISTICS: The Internet Big Picture World Internet Users and Population Stats," http://www.internetworldstats.com/stats.htm.

[12] Seacom news update, "SEACOM GOES LIVE—23 Jul 2009," http://www.seacom.mu/news/news_details.asp?iID=100.

[13] Jennifer Scott, "Emerging Markets to Push Mobile Internet Users Past Billion Mark," http://www.itpro.co.uk/618631/emerging-markets-to-push-mobile-internet-users-past-billion-mark.

2

Business Strategy

Upon completion of this chapter, you should be able to

- Explain how your business strategy relates to the ebocube model
- Identify the components of SWOT analysis
- Use the EM attractiveness template to segment and target emerging markets
- Discuss the advantages/disadvantages of direct or indirect partner/channel marketing and distribution
- Collaborate virtually with business stakeholders, both local and international
- Specify branding policies to help your company compete in emerging markets
- Understand the risks and benefits of co-branding

The main impetus for entering emerging markets (EMs) is to grow sales and increase profit. After all, potential demand is huge when compared to developed, saturated markets. However, it is important to assess each identified country before entering that market with an Internet strategy. We offer various tools to help you make this assessment.

As you survey, you may identify countries that are high growth, but your company might not have the resources required to penetrate them. The ebocube model represents an efficient, green, low-cost way to analyze and learn from the market and to raise your company's profile (via marketing) and profits (via lead generation).

While EMs offer huge sales potential, they also pose significant risk, complexity, and uncertainty. Therefore, choosing the right market is critical for success. Entering a new market is similar to any start-up situation where there is an absence of sales, marketing, or infrastructure and little or no knowledge of the market.[1]

Many articles have been written about multinationals and organizations of various sizes that have entered these markets and then had to exit because they underestimated the challenges or made incorrect assumptions. You can avoid making similar mistakes by, as part of your research, analyzing and evaluating organizations that have failed and organizations that have succeeded in a particular market.

Do not enter EMs based on assumptions! Do your research, test the marketing, and analyze results using the ebocube.

Business Strategy and the ebocube Model

First, define your business strategy, including the countries that you plan to target. Even before you implement the ebocube model, your organization needs to have top-level business analysis and planned business objectives. Once your company starts marketing and selling to companies, you can deploy the phase one of the ebocube: the dashboard and the datacube. When you implement the ebocube for data analysis, the dashboard will feed your strategy with results and metrics and help you to iteratively strengthen market penetration.

The ebocube business model has three linked phases. It essentially reflects how an organization can set up marketing and customer relationship management (CRM) functions, departments, or resources. It demonstrates what each function or area should focus on. Or, if implemented by a small company, the model may encompass all the elements of one person's marketing job—that is, reporting through the dashboard and datacube (phase one); planning effective localized campaigns based on CRM, segmenting data, budgeting, creating a proposition and offer (phase two); and finally testing campaigns and setting them up in campaign management tools for tracking and executing through in-house campaign management tools or an agency, with the capabilities to execute integrated online campaigns (phase three). The marketer would instruct the agency, for example, on the results they would like to see in the dashboard. For example, in phase one, the results may feature the company or agency reporting tools dashboard.

The dashboards (phase one) should feed and direct business marketing strategy through marketing and sales results—for example, by demonstrating which countries are generating the best marketing and sales results, the dashboards can help management decide where to invest more.

The datacube should be another reporting partition of the dashboard, providing visibility in the form of reports on the data a company has for firms it's targeting in EMs. If data quality is low for a specific focus country, management might decide to invest in data acquisition as part of its strategy.

The first phase of the ebocube process is implementing and using a dashboard to represent marketing and sales results. Your dashboard will always track and provide data views from your CRM database; we call this the *datacube.*

There are marketing and business tools that can help you analyze microfactors and therefore specific factors both in your business sector and in the EMs. Microfactors are either internal or close to the company and directly impact the company's strategy, profitability, or survival, especially as it pertains to customer prospects. We explain the importance of these momentarily.

Dashboard Analysis

The first phase of the ebocube process is implementing and using a dashboard to represent marketing and sales results. These results can be fully tracked through CRM applications and Internet marketing. Dashboard reports can be presented in graphs or tables, and can be used to develop analysis on marketing performance and lead generation, which should feed strategy in terms of market penetration and the products and solutions sold in EMs. Your dashboard will always track and provide data views from your CRM database; we call this the *datacube*.

The datacube reveals gaps in your organization's data and contact database that you can then use to identify leads and other marketing potential. It can also indicate whether you need to purchase data or acquire data through alternative means, such as external data lists. External data coverage analysis can be used as part of your planning stage. For example, you might want to enter Nigeria but realize that no company or customer data for this market exists within your organization and so you may need to obtain it through external sources.

Localization

Your company can learn from potential markets by running test campaigns on existing data. For example, your company may have run webcasts in developed markets that contacts in EMs have registered to view. For example, a webcast registration may be hosted on your website and allow anyone to register globally. Such a scenario means that you can collect, store, and analyze data using the ebocube dashboard and datacube.

Social media (i.e., blogs, forums, and social networks) is also an effective way to understand customer needs and to gain insight into customers in any EM. These tools shouldn't be used as definitive sources of information alone. Your company should use them alongside quantitative reports on the market.

Social media metrics provide information, news, and commentary about an EM in real time. Remember, however, you cannot just create a blog, forum, or Facebook page targeting a market and expect people to use it. Any forum or account you create must be relevant and localized specifically to the market. Your company may learn from third-party blogs or social networks in local markets, but to learn from these, your company will need someone (local or in-house) who can read and understand the local language (if used), meanings, and culture.

Sales Management

Before entering an emerging market, ensure that your employees support the strategy (including online marketers and anyone else who represents your organization). Your company will also need a sales force to follow up leads generated in local markets. You must consider whether the sales force will be based locally in the EM or in your own market and whether you'll use an in-house team or use external partners or a local (in the EM) agency. You also want to determine whether you need to employ staff with language skills or whether you'll outsource translation tasks. (You might start by conducting an audit of languages spoken within your company by just asking employees to update a spreadsheet hosted on a web space.)

Company Culture

Each new market is unique, with business practices that differ from companies in developed markets. For example, time zones will impact working hours. Is your company open to new ideas? How bureaucratic is your company? To implement the ebocube in a new market may require change management, organizational restructures, recruitment, and training. Senior managers should have international experience and knowledge (perhaps having worked or lived in an EM or worked directly with an EM). This is a core skill for future leadership in today's global economy. Cultural sensitivity and awareness is also critical to successful global business prosperity; lack of sensitivity and understanding can be hugely damaging to relationships and therefore the bottom line.

Many companies tailor their strategy to meet specific requirements of economies and cultures in an EM. For example, Cisco Systems, Inc., has split its company into distinct profit and loss centers (P&Ls): One focuses entirely on EMs in terms of revenue, profit, and dedicated resources; the other P&L focuses on developed economies.

Before entering any new market, you need to consider whether you go it alone or work with or though partners or channels; the latter may be a way to lower investment and risk. If you do decide to use a local distributor, partner, or agency for marketing, you can still use the ebocube model to learn through them via Internet marketing results and reports.

Media and Sponsorship

Public relations is an important tool in EM nations. It can help you to introduce your firm and build a reputation. It's important to understand how the media works in an EM and to build relationships with the media or with media buyers. If your company can also afford media sponsorship (i.e., to sponsor a program), this can also be an effective way to establish your brand.

The ebocube model promotes micromarketing (targeted marketing) rather than mass marketing (although sponsorship can be used to raise brand awareness). We recommend that you track success by using online calls to action, friendly tracked web URLs, and inbound phone numbers that encourage contacts to get in touch. Friendly URLs are web addresses that are memorable for users. They are short, and a promotion may be indicated in the URL name. They may mask and redirect users to longer, less-memorable URLs. For example, instead of having www.ebocube.com/events/webcast/BT?2010_3474765_eventtalk, you might use www.ebocube.com/webcast; typing or clicking this URL redirects users to the original long URL but the friendly URL can still be tracked for clicks. Responses should be recorded in your marketing database with unique ebocodes.

SWOT Analysis

To exploit the potential of EMs, you must be able to analyze strengths, weaknesses, opportunities, and threats (SWOT), both internal (microfactors) and external (macrofactors) to the business (see Figure 2.1). Macrofactors are external factors in an EM (e.g., political, economic, social, technological, legal, and environmental [PESTLE]). They are usually beyond a company's control but still impact its planning and performance. The SWOT framework was created by Edmund P. Learned, C. Roland Christiansen, Kenneth Andrews, and William D. Guth in *Business Policy, Text and Cases* (Irwin, 1969).

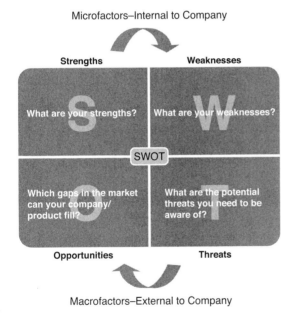

Figure 2.1 A SWOT analysis considers microfactors as well as macro-factors. These factors can either pose a threat or an opportunity, and you will classify them as such in your SWOT[2] analysis.

Strengths and weaknesses are internal to your company. For example, a weakness might be that your company has little experience in EM markets. A strength might be a relationship with a local partner.

Even a fully web-based company still needs to consider these factors. For instance, you might need to consider whether broadband penetration is high enough to penetrate a market with an online shop. Your company needs to consider whether the product you offer is legal and socially acceptable in the EM. Do not use a SWOT chart to plan your marketing entry per country. Instead, use one to establish the criteria for success.

A strategic planning exercise such as a SWOT analysis creates opportunities for staff to challenge their assumptions, acquire new knowledge, generate insights, and eliminate mistakes. This is an opportunity for your team to debate and discuss the SWOT factors and incorporate external knowledge of your target market via a forum or an online polling system to gain local insight. A SWOT process will help you make better decisions and investments.

The exercise will also illuminate how to use strengths to overcome weaknesses and how to turn threats into opportunities by proactive planning. If a threat is likely to occur in a year's time, it's good to start planning ahead and consider how you can turn the threat into an opportunity. An EM SWOT analysis must be culturally sensitive, and reporting and recommendations should reflect this. For example, in the MEA region, a *deadline* may be interpreted as a "suggested date," so you might want to adjust your expectations accordingly.

EM Attractiveness Template

An EM attractiveness template is used to segment and decide which EM region or nation your company should target, or should be thinking of targeting in the future. The market attractiveness tool is critical to your growth models and strategy. The tool helps define the most attractive market based on overall attractiveness compared to your company's strength in terms of the competition, based on defined variables. (We've adapted this model from the McKinsey

Matrix, which is used to analyze a business portfolio of products or services.)

Unless your company has a huge pool of capital, or is already a multinational, your business should focus on targeting one country as a starting point. Each EM is structured differently, making it challenging to compete. You need to consider all the costs involved, including translation, maintaining websites, logistics, staff, and agency fees (among others). Even though online marketing is significantly cheaper than traditional offline marketing, there are still costs incurred and resources required that should not be underestimated.

Segmenting and Targeting Markets

The EM attractiveness template we have created is divided into nine cells to highlight EM attractiveness and company capabilities (see Figure 2.2). Therefore, the starting point is to define your company's business, marketing, and sales objectives.

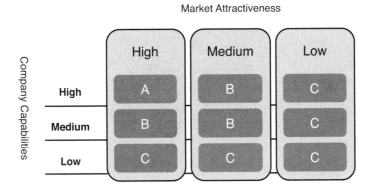

Figure 2.2   Market attractiveness versus company capabilities selecting A, B, and C countries

The template allows you to segment these markets in numerous ways (e.g., country, cities, or industries), but we advise beginning your analysis by country. You can then use the same structure to segment markets based on cities or industries after you've defined your top-level markets. You can target your selected segments by using company/contact data that you own, or you can obtain it from outside sources or acquire the data in-house.

Market attractiveness may be defined by the following:

- Sales growth
- Gross domestic product (GDP)
- Competitor presence
- Industry profitability
- Languages
- PESTLE concerns (including Internet penetration, which is fundamental to your ebocube strategy)
- Results in the dashboard after you start to penetrate the EM and collect marketing and sales results reports and data

Can Doesn't Mean Should

Just because a market is attractive, that doesn't mean you should enter it. You should consider whether you have the right products versus the competitors' solutions, whether your brand will be accepted, and whether you have the sales force to follow up leads. As Jack Welch (Former CEO and Chairman of General Electric GE) said, "If you don't have a competitive advantage, don't compete." The ebocube can help generate high-quality sales leads and raise your profile in the market, but you still need a differentiating advantage (e.g., an innovative product, low-cost offer, good relationship, or strong brand).

If a market is highly attractive and you have the capabilities to compete, this becomes your A country, with B countries being the second most attractive (see Figures 2.3 and 2.4). You will need to consider whether to invest in a C country or avoid it during the current planning period (see Figure 2.5).

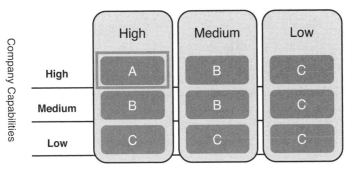

Figure 2.3 **Segment A: The countries in this segment offer the best opportunity for growth. You can cluster your A countries for reference in the table above after you have scored each country, which should be done individually because each are so diverse. If the country is attractive and the company has the capabilities to grow or penetrate these markets, it should allocate resources to this market and focus on growing the business and increasing market share through Internet marketing based on the ebocube methodology and through sales.**

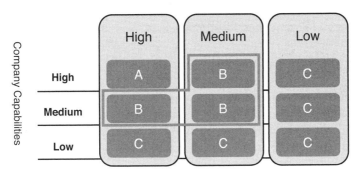

Figure 2.4 **Segment B: Your company either has strong capabilities but the EM is not as attractive as an A country or the market is attractive but your business is not as strong. If your business is not as strong, decision makers should decide how to further improve the company to penetrate the market. If the company's capabilities are wanting, management needs to consider if making improvements is realistic and acceptable to stakeholders such as shareholders and employees. If the country itself is not as attractive, but your company does have the capabilities, (for example, sales are not as high in Brazil as they are in China), and your product is unique and in demand, you need to weigh investing less in country B and becoming more aggressive in country A.**

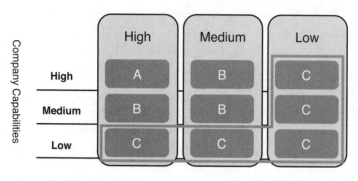

Figure 2.5   Segment C: This is the least attractive in terms of opportunity, although it may be more attractive in the future. Business capabilities in this segment are weak or the market is not attractive or both. If the case is that the company is not strong enough but the market is attractive, you'll need to decide whether to invest or divest. If the market is unattractive and company capabilities are weak, we do not advise that you focus your resources on this segment at the current time. The benefit of Internet marketing is that your company can market to many countries, including C countries, with little cost. For example, an email can be sent to multiple countries (as long as it's suitable to the culture) at minimal cost. Therefore, you can still learn from C countries and raise your profile without investing too much in resources, although any sales leads will require follow up and time, which is an expense.

Scoring Variables

To determine whether a country fits into the A/B/C segment, you need to score the country's attractiveness and your company's capabilities (see Table 2.1). This should be done per country. Although you can start at a regional level, it's recommended that you score each country on its own. EMs are diverse, and the economic situation in a country may differ completely from its neighboring country even in the same region. For example, Dubai's economy differs greatly from Abu Dhabi's economy in the Emirates, similar to how many E.U. countries differ economically (e.g., Greece versus Germany).

TABLE 2.1 Scoring Attractiveness and Capabilities

Market Attractiveness	Score	Company Capabilities	Score
Internet penetration	1 to 10	Online marketing skills	1 to 10
Political	1 to 10	Data	1 to 10
Economic	1 to 10	Suppliers	1 to 10
Social	1 to 10	Logistics	1 to 10
Technological	1 to 10	Language skills	1 to 10
Legal	1 to 10	Sales teams	1 to 10
Economic growth rates	1 to 10	Products	1 to 10
Reports in ebocube dashboard	1 to 10	Partnerships in EM	1 to 10
Competition	1 to 10	Brand	1 to 10
Company/contact data availability	1 to 10	Company culture	1 to 10
Total	x/100	Total	x/100

SWOT Analysis of Attractiveness and Capabilities

A SWOT analysis will incorporate a range of microfactors (those that are internal to or have a direct impact on the company's strategy) along with macrofactors (those that are external and are beyond its control, such as socio-economic, but still impact your company's planning and performance; e.g., legal and technological change). Both should be used to assess your company's overall capabilities and market attractiveness.

You can also add or remove variables; the aim is to get an overall score for market attractiveness and company capabilities. The maximum total should be the same for each country to ensure subjectivity. Remember to make the tools work for you, instead of forcing the tool to give you anticipated (or desired) results.

Scores Ranges and Variable Analysis

Scoring should be based on data and not personal or subjective opinions.

A markets: 90–100

B markets: 50–89

C markets: 0–49

Scoring should be based on qualitative and quantitative (macro and micro) data along with discussions among your management team. For example, with regard to online penetration, you want to research quantitative Internet statistics. For political stability, research election and public policy history of the past five years. There are many factors to consider as you review each variable. Take brand, for example. It may be scored based on brand acceptability or awareness in a specific market.

Direct or Indirect Partner/Channel Marketing and Distribution

Your company will need to decide whether to market directly to an EM or through partners. The challenges and risks associated with partnerships must be evaluated but are beyond the scope of this book.

Joint marketing with or through partners can be planned, tracked, and measured through the ebocube model; the partner will need to be trained and buy in to the benefits of using the ebocube methodology. Partners can also provide you their databases to market directly. Just remember that contacts need to opt in for third-party emails, because legal considerations apply here in terms of privacy.

Tracking and measurement through ebocube for partner marketing needs to be considered from an operational setup, and needs to be planned for and discussed prior to the campaigns beginning with partners.

Distribution

With regard to distribution, you might question the need for using reseller or partners because the Internet does enable disintermediation (selling directly to customers/prospects without third-party intervention). However, some of your products or services may not warrant you selling directly over the Internet to businesses in an EM. It all depends on your company's products or services. For example, if you're selling hardware, you might need resellers or partners. If you're selling software, you might use the model of disintermediation. Penetrating markets from scratch without any infrastructure will remain risky. You might be able to minimize risk by using partners, distributors, or local agencies for distribution. You want to consider how much of a risk the product is to the customer (in terms of cost, implementation, or complexity) when deciding on distribution and customer service.

Collaboration Across Borders

Digital collaboration tools can transform the way you work with partners or local offices and introduce new ways to work virtually globally. They can also help partners to service customers in local markets. Web collaboration tools should be part of your operational strategy. Their benefits include working across borders and reducing costs, travel, and environmental damage. Many new and emerging web-based collaboration tools allow you to interact in real time, or almost instantly.

Web applications can be used to help companies within markets to collaborate with partners/suppliers/distributors/extended teams for knowledge sharing among countries, while accelerating productivity and improving communications. Online tools can be used for training and communications, as well. Sales representatives or partners in local markets can get trained faster, lead generation improves, and products get to market quicker. All of this can be achieved without traveling.

The main consideration is language. If you create a blog or use social media, you and all the parties involved need to understand what is being posted. Many EM countries/regions work in English, such as India and countries in the MEA region; however, many do not, so this needs to be considered when interacting with some of these tools.

Partner portals can be used to link partners to general information and updates from a range of sources. One portal can be used to target all partners in local countries; you can control access levels so that some content is available only to certain partners. A portal should be a hub for all other links to resources. Portals can also be used to provide local marketing collateral for agencies and partners that can be set up for tracking.

Instant messaging (IM) can be used to communicate with partners and extended teams in real time to aid problem solving at low cost. Using IM on wireless or PDA devices is an excellent way to provide quick responses to questions to virtual teams on the move. The benefits of IM include the following:

- Real-time communication between people in different locations, saving time and money (no long-distance call charges) by enabling you to resolve questions or problems immediately while using natural conversation.
- Reducing the number of emails sent and received through the day. Many people want an answer to a simple question quickly. IM facilitates quick and easy communication.[3]
- Ability to determine who is online and ready for a message. Presence indicators are a standard feature of IM applications. You can easily see whether a partner is available to chat with you. This is a great feature when working across different time zones.[4]

Voice over Internet Protocol (VoIP) enables you to make calls over the Internet at reduced costs when calling partners in different countries. VoIP can help reduce communication and infrastructure costs. Web conferencing tools can facilitate virtual meetings with partners so that you can share documents, presentations, and other content. Conferencing tools also include group voice/video call facilities over the Internet. The following are a few examples of web/videoconferencing tools that facilitate virtual meetings:

• WebEx
• Microsoft Live Meeting
• Adobe Acrobat Connect
• GoToMeeting

Discussion forums, web blogging, and wikis are great for idea sharing/building between your company and your partner company or local office. Teams and partners can interact via comments on blogs or engage in full discussion in forums.

Content-sharing web servers can be used to upload large files that may be difficult to send by email. This works similarly to your standard company shared drive, but you use specific content management web-based tools. Content-sharing servers can be used to store documents, such as team event photos, videos, and files that need to be accessed or updated/edited by partners. Content management tools offer functionalities such as calendar functions, discussion forums, bulletin boards, polls, and email feeds. Some tools also offer real time pop-up updates informing all when a partner/colleague has updated a file, informing other users of a group that they can now participate with or a file they can work on. Partners can log in globally in real time to edit and share files. Content managers can invite partners to various groups "spaces" to access servers.

Marketing Email

HTML or plain text email can be used to update partners with news (e.g., latest product releases, problems, promotions, discounts, and offers). Benefits of email include that it's quick, cheap, and measurable. You can also link emails to video demos, forums/discussions, and to product landing pages (all powerful ways to communicate new ideas).

Day-to-Day Email

On a day-to-day basis, email can be used to share information and attached documents with partners, coordinate events/meetings, and to discuss work.

Calendar Function

Calendar functionality enables you to coordinate meeting and schedule events. For example, Microsoft Outlook 2007 displays time zones in different countries, which allows you to schedule meeting at times that are appropriate for the people in different time zones. Outlook 2007 can also update calendar invites if there are changes in the clock due to daylight saving hours.

Calendar invites also show you the day of the month. This is helpful because the weekend in some countries differs from the weekend in other countries. For example, in some countries in the MEA region, the weekend consists of Thursday and Friday (Saudi Arabia) or Friday and Saturday (Egypt), and these are not workdays.

Email Groups

Your company can also set up a shared email alias for groups of people. Email groups offer a convenient way to communicate with others who share the same interests and ideas or are in the same functions/areas and need to be kept in the loop or updated.

Conferencing Tools

Conferencing tool applications can be added to email clients so that when a user sends a meeting request or calendar invite, the group web/voice conferencing details are automatically included.

Branding Policies

In China, the color red symbolizes luck. In India, the same color symbolizes purity. In many Western countries, however, red symbolizes danger. In some countries, green is either a symbol of prosperity or of nature. Nothing with regard to brand acceptance is simply black and white.

Each online and offline experience reinforces a brand message and promise to your target audience: Branding is a critical success factor to your entry and development. You will need to consider the implications of the colors, fonts, style, and tone of your brand. Most important, you must consider whether to use your own brand and take a standardized approach or use a local brand developed specifically for a market or region. Therefore, you need to develop a branding policy.

Strong brands establish the firm's identity in the marketplace and can help develop a solid customer franchise (Aaker 1996, Keller 1998, Kapferer 1997). In international markets, an important issue for a firm is whether to use the same brand name in different country markets, leveraging the brand's strength across boundaries, or whether to maintain local brands that respond to local business preferences.[5] With global name recognition, multinational companies such as Coca Cola, Cisco, Barclays, McDonalds, Google, and Microsoft have successfully penetrated EMs with one brand. However, these prestigious firms have localized products, marketing campaigns, and communications (including localized websites).

There are two branding approaches: consumer and business. Consumer brands tend to have an emotional connection with consumers, and so consumers need to connect with the brand before making their purchasing decision. Business brands tend to emphasize company benefits, and buyers tend to take a more practical analytical approach to those purchases. There tends to be more than one person involved in the decision-making process with different levels of influence.

Using your established brand may costs less because you get economies of scale, but localized brands may prove more effective. You need to research the best approach. In either case, you can use local agencies to research your brand acceptance and to ensure your branding isn't offensive or negative. Ask your local partners for their thoughts. Use a web analytics tool to look at your website statistics to see if you're receiving international traffic, or carry out research with local businesses via online communications, perhaps capturing research on a localized survey on your local website, or through an email blast with a survey link asking businesses what they think of your brand.

Co-Branding

The ebocube model enables you to fully track closed-loop campaigns executed directly by your company or indirectly by your partner; tracking and measurement should be discussed upfront and in advance of the campaign, whether selling directly to the end user or through your partners (retailers or distributors).

Consider co-branding when using indirect channels. This can be done with online or offline campaigns. A local partner may already be recognized and established, and joint marketing can be an effective way to quickly raise awareness of your brand and build trust at a low cost.

If the partner's brand is new or unrecognized, but is designed with local cultural understanding and insight, it may also benefit your brand, making it stronger and more trusted by local businesses. When partnering with localized new brands in an EM, it's riskier than partnering with local, well-recognized, established partner brands.

It's important to ensure the co-branding will strengthen your brand values and what your company stands for. Be careful which partners you choose and associate your brand with to ensure that they adhere to your brand guidelines. It's an extremely good idea to approve any collateral that they may create and provide them with brand guidelines. Ensure they have a trusted brand, or are a trusted company, so that you don't damage your own company's reputation.

It's important to invest time training partners to track the success of your co-branded campaigns through the ebocube methodology. Case studies showing the benefits of the ebocube methodology through great results captured in the dashboard will help demonstrate the overall processes and how to plan, execute, and capture metrics in the form of results through the stages and processes of the ebocube model.

Endnotes

[1] David Arnold, "Strategies for Entering and Developing International Markets," *FT Press Financial Times* (October 17, 2003), http://www.ftpress.com/articles/article.aspx?p=101588.

[2] Wikipedia, "SWOT," http://en.wikipedia.org/wiki/SWOT_analysis.

[3] Enterprise Instant Messaging and Live Help Software, "Benefits of Instant Messaging," http://www.instantmessagingsystem.com/benefits.asp.

[4] Enterprise Instant Messaging and Live Help Software, "Benefits of Instant Messaging," http://www.instantmessagingsystem.com/benefits.asp.

[5] Susan P. Douglas, C. Samuel Craig, and Edwin J. Nijssen, "International Brand Architecture: Development, Drivers and Design," August 1999, http://pages.stern.nyu.edu/~sdouglas/rpubs/intbrand.html.

3

The ebocube and Business Models

Upon completion of this chapter, you should be able to

- Explain why business models are vital to successful businesses
- Describe the ebocube model
- Utilize the dashboard in phase one of the ebocube model
- Accomplish campaign and data planning in phase two of the ebocube model
- Understand how marketing operations, phase three, follows phase two of the ebocube model while also feeding phase one data-gathering objectives

To help organizations leverage the Internet, we developed the three-phase ebocube model. This will save your business time and money, help you avoid mistakes, and enable you to create meaningful marketing and sales results and metrics that impact the bottom line, profits. The ebocube will also show where and how to invest resources (e.g., in employees, systems, applications, and office buildings). Most important, it will help you identify when things have gone wrong or where the process has broken down.

Business Models

Business models are created and designed for particular needs of businesses (e.g., enhanced production of particular goods or services, cost reduction, enhanced customer services, and for distribution).

Models may evolve with growth and experience as a company becomes more established.

Over the years, business models has evolved and become more sophisticated in their usage.[1] The first business model, and perhaps the best known, is the shopkeeper model. For centuries, this model has helped businesses set up stores in specific locales and attract local customers via product/service displays. In the 1950s, McDonalds came out with its business model, followed by Toyota a few decades later. In the 1980s, technology businesses such as Intel, Blockbuster, and Dell developed their own unique models.[2] In the 1990s, Internet-based models such as eBay, Amazon.com, and Alibaba.com became international phenomena.

To create a competitive advantage, businesses need sound strategies for product development, service development, branding, and investing. Michael Porter of the Harvard Business School defines a competitive advantage as a way to sustain profit exceeding the average for the industry.[3] The advantage can be in terms of low cost or differentiation, and the ebocube model can help most companies in both aspects.

Your company should invest in a business model that will allow it to be innovative in your industry regardless of whether the model is based on logistics, marketing, manufacturing, or human resources. Just as effective models may help you to grow your business, badly designed, inefficient models may cost your business. For example, bookstore retailers and music retailers have lost out because they have not taken advantage of the Internet or electronic downloads that correspond to the new devices customers are purchasing to read with. Online purchases are also lower cost and e-books can be downloaded instantly.

All major corporations depend on efficient and effective business models, and they are integrated into business operations seamlessly. Amazon has revolutionized e-commerce by offering customers the option of getting a book delivered to their door within two days of placing their order, or within seconds for an electronic version downloaded on Kindle, their own hardware for e-books.

Business may also patent their business models to prevent other companies from using them (or at least to allow them to collect licensing fees for approved use). For example, Netflix, a seller of online videos and DVDs, patented their digital, Internet-driven renting system. Soon after they were granted the patent, they sued Blockbuster for running their Internet business under the same model and won.

Business models do not have to be complicated. Your company may have a single process, such as using online commercial transactions or ticket purchases. For example, online airfare and hotel providers can eliminate costs of call center or travel agents. Business models may be also built on a platform of many processes or functions. For example, company product implementation may involve suppliers, partners, and after-sales services as well as technical consultants to manage implementation, sales, and distributing and implementation of the product.

Businesses can use the Internet in many ways to generate revenue. For example, some companies (e.g., Facebook and Google) generate revenue by providing free services and selling online advertising space to companies. Others sell a product/service directly to online customers. Well-defined Internet business models are e-commerce and online auctions as well as Google's paid search model and Alibaba.com, the biggest B2B online marketplace.

Value

Creating value is fundamental to the existence of any successful business model. When we use the term *business model,* we're referring to the way a company or organization creates, delivers, and captures value[4] for the customer or for itself. This value can be economical, social, or any another aspect the customer or organization deems valuable to them.

Business intelligence contributes value to the company by providing data that informs decisions. This includes increasing sales and revenue through marketing leads and virtualization of marketing by using the Internet, and thus reducing risk, carbon footprint, and cost of travel and direct mail. Customer relationship building no longer depends on face-to-face transactions. Instead, companies can implement an electronic customer relationship strategy, which helps to generate profits by establishing and defining profitable segments in EMs.

The ebocube provides value to the market through globally accessible information at the right time. Business decision makers can browse through many sites or read emails and blogs about services/products around the globe. By so doing, they can identify numerous potential suppliers and thus leverage their purchasing power to their advantage.

Process

A business model can be implemented only through "good" (i.e., logically sequential and necessary to effect the ultimate goal) processes. For example, the Amazon online retail model is based on removing the "middleman" retailer and selling directly to the customer. A business model encompasses a host of activities that are executed through processes, such as a linked set of activities to reach a final goal. The process is the series of activities, actions, or tasks logically structured and required to carry out certain goals. These processes typically can be plotted out on a flow chart. For example, on Amazon.com, the customer logs in to the website, searches for a product, places an order, completes a credit card transaction, and then delivery of the product follows, whether that's a postal delivery or download.

Any multibillion-dollar project may turn into a disaster without well-tested, efficient processes. Each business and each product differs, so you can't operate based on mere assumptions. Instead, each business process must work in the unique circumstance for which it is

Terminal Five Is Working

Picture yourself arriving at London Heathrow, Terminal Five, from Beijing, as scheduled. You deplane, weave your way through the chaotic terminal, and arrive 45 minutes later at the baggage claim area. But your luggage isn't there! You stand in the customer service line, and once it's your turn, an exhausted customer services assistant hands you a complaint form for lost luggage; there are four assistants and thousands of angry customers.

You walk over to McDonalds to order some food. Your burger, fries, and drink arrive 46 seconds after you place your order and taste exactly the same as what you'd get back home in San Francisco. You wonder why your airline couldn't deliver your luggage on time and why you were kept on the plane for 45 minutes after you landed.

What is the root cause for these different events: landing on time, receiving your fast food so quickly, being kept on a plane after landing for 45 minutes, and losing your luggage? Does it boil down to advanced IT systems, service with a smile, or good management? All these aspects matter, but the key to overall success boils down to rigorously tested, robust processes.

The plane arrived on time because professionals at each link in the airline's staffing chain excel at "flight take-off procedure" and followed it, from ensuring customers were provided with boarding passes two hours before takeoff, to checking in customers at a specific gate, to monitoring that the flight was in a queue ready to take off at a scheduled time. Appropriate staff were allocated to each task, appropriate resources were allocated at the right time, safety procedures were followed on the plane, and a planned route was scheduled (with a backup route if required), and touchdown was on time as scheduled.

At McDonalds, the cashier knew to take your order and place it into a queue in an automated system. She completed the cash transaction as part two of the process. Then, the job was carried to the kitchen operator, and the kitchen operator expected the turnaround to take 30 seconds. Then the job was sent back to the cashier, as planned, and the cashier inspected the order as part of the process. The order was given to the customer, and the satisfied customer moved to a table with a hot meal. This McDonalds process can be mapped out onto a flow chart and implemented successfully throughout franchises globally. It's well thought out and easy to implement.

At baggage claim, the airline had not established a tested business process. The links at each step from customer complaint to investigation to remedy were loose and inconsistent at each terminal. Training (and therefore competency) was also inconsistent. Therefore, the airline workers could not achieve their goals in a timely and organized manner. You cannot blame them for the delay and loss of luggage; they have multiple tasks and processes that they followed in the same way as McDonalds employees did. You cannot blame any IT system or application or logistics. You can blame the process, which contains all these elements above (and even more) collaborating in one operational model, which probably didn't work from the day it was launched.

designed. Review your processes even if you have run very similar businesses and make necessary adaptations.

As you launch a new product/service, you want to focus on the following three factors:

- The overall process
- The tasks and activities involved in successfully creating the service/product
- Taking the product/service to market on time, in good quality and within budget

Some business executives may be nervous about entering EMs because they do not know what to expect. The ebocube business model helps ensure your Internet marketing strategy is planned and well thought out and that all processes are considered. It's a well-tested model, with proven processes, and so when you enter a market, you'll know how to plan, adapt, and execute your strategy successfully and cost-effectively. You will, however, need to measure whether it is working and make adjustments accordingly.

(The Heathrow airport model is complex, and the processes used in T5 contribute to the overall success or failure of the airport model. The process breakdown in T5 meant that the overall model wasn't executed successfully. The robust processes in McDonalds ensured that the fast food model could work.)

The ebocube Model

It makes perfect sense for a huge airline, handling millions of passengers, transactions, and planes, to have a business model and proven processes. The same applies for online bookstores. The same applies to franchised coffee shops (to ensure that the coffee tastes the same in New York City, Dubai, and Sydney, thus creating value for customers and the business). The same is true for your business and marketing campaigns. You need a plan to run events, to manage marketing communications, to blast emails, and to organize virtual events and other activities.

We designed the ebocube model as a low-cost, sustainable framework designed to help you use industry best communication practices to run your marketing activities effectively and efficiently and to generate value (marketing leads and sales) for your global marketing operations. You can administer your customer relationship management (CRM) with a full understanding of your data (thanks to the dashboards, with particular focus on the datacube). This can help you make sound business decisions, learn from your integrated online campaigns, and measure return on marketing investment. The ebocube model is a tested, replicable business model that can be applied to any company, anywhere in the world.

Real value derives from using or creating a sustainable business model, one that will survive even after the current management has left. Like McDonalds and other multinational corporations, a business model should be able to succeed or evolve to meet the macro- and microeconomic factors that impact any business. The ebocube is sustainable because it can leverage new technology, like the Internet, and thus reduce travel, mail/shipping, and other costs, which makes it sustainable and likely to last even if, for example, companies must comply with new environmental laws. It can also help you to decide which markets to enter and where to dedicate resources.

Model Functions

The ebocube model impacts a number of business functions, primarily strategy, marketing, sales, IT, and finance:

- **Strategy:**   The dashboard delivers business intelligence that will impact the market segments your company decides to continue to enter and the new markets to pursue. It can also inform new product development strategies (if you notice a peak in sales in specific products in the dashboards, for example).
- **Marketing:**   The ebocube will impact marketing operations, including resource allocation, contact management, and tracking. Because company data is fundamental to ebocube, in large companies the communications teams will need to work closer with customer relationship and data analyst teams. In small companies, there are process considerations for the person who may be managing both.
- **Sales:**   The sales and marketing departments will need to collaborate to plan campaigns upfront and to follow up on marketing-generated leads. After all, without sales buy-in as well as follow-up, revenue cannot be generated. They need to set the criteria as to what an acceptable sales lead is (e.g., who they need to speak to, what sort of project they would expect). Sales will also provide information on sales results, contact, and company data in CRM tools which will feed the dashboard with further results, like deals related to marketing leads. Without collaborating with sales, marketing might end up generating leads that are rejected by sales in their CRM tools.
- **IT:**   The IT folks must help implement the applications to make the model work; support the applications, packages, and systems; and enhance the IT process for ebocube and other Internet communication platforms. IT also needs to monitor Internet security, and understand the best campaign management

tools to implement and be comfortable supporting them, whether they use off-the-shelf packages or systems designed specifically for the company.

• **Finance:**   Reports provided by the dashboard help finance allocate the budget appropriately based on marketing results and return on investment, and to stop spending money on markets, campaigns, or activities that do not provide return on marketing investment (ROMI) and sales revenue. Traditionally finance has perceived marketing as a cost rather than an investment because established processes for showing results did not exist with traditional media. This has all changed with the use of the Internet and new ways of tracking offline media.

Marketing Campaigns

The ebocube model (see Figure 3.1) defines an end-to-end measurable marketing and sales process for EMs. It's a model that processes what has been tried and tested across EMs. The ebocube model is based on dashboard reports (metrics), company and contact data reporting (datacube), and the Internet. The ebocube was developed for B2B marketing in EMs. It can be adapted for planning, executing, tracking, and measuring marketing campaigns.

We face many challenges when managing complex campaigns, especially when marketing to unknown markets. Campaigns are devised of many elements, such as email, webcasts, and marketing collateral (whitepapers), all of which must be designed, targeted, tracked, and integrated with the core messages of the effort. They cannot be designed on-the-fly.

A campaign is a specific activity designed with clear, simple, measurable, achievable, realistic, timed objectives and run over a specific period, with a set budget, using a host of communication methods to deliver the message and to achieve the objectives. For example, a presidential campaign may run for months, if not years, with the overall aim of getting elected. A number of communication methods are used synergistically to raise awareness, increase consideration, and finally elicit a vote; this is what can be considered a campaign or integrated campaign. Barack Obama used YouTube and Twitter successfully to connect with followers to communicate change.

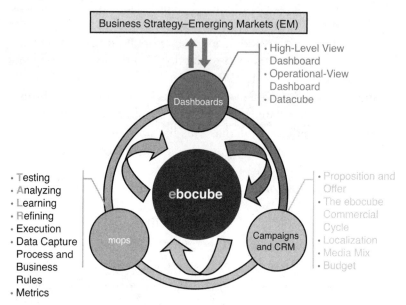

Figure 3.1   The ebocube model

Integrated campaigns can have many elements and can be complex to manage. For example, you might have many creative and communications channels, with different copy and events to manage. Managers, therefore, often divide campaigns into small parts to manage them efficiently and to ensure that they are executed on time, on budget, and for desired results. The ebocube model helps you manage different elements of integrated campaigns in the most efficient way through the methodical communications planning campaign management tools and best practices and processes in leveraging data, the Internet, and reporting.

The ebocube model enables you to review campaign results through reporting and analysis. Marketers manage campaigns in many different ways, aiming to find the best way to plan, execute, and report in an easy and manageable way, and to find these reports in one place.

Marketers use many different approaches for campaign execution, tracking, reporting, and analyzing. Some are very effective, whereas others are less effective and result in inconsistent reporting, without any replicable campaign engagement and execution process. Ineffectiveness increases costs and time, as mistakes are repeated, and waste is created. In such scenarios, customers may receive inconsistent messaging.

There is no need to reinvent campaign fundamentals each time you are due to launch a campaign in a new EM. Even as you are creative and customer focused in your themes and messages, the ebocube model means that your campaign planning, execution, tracking, and reporting will be planned, efficient, and effective. During business cycle downturns, ebocube ensures that you can prove ROMI and keep your budget or increase it so that you can grow your business in EMs.

The ebocube works in a cycle of three phases, and each phase is naturally the consequent of the previous one. For example, if you set up your campaign execution correctly, tracking and measuring results, you will be able to feed numbers and data into the dashboard. However, if you skip a phase or do not follow the processes within the phases, your dashboard will not reflect accurate results, even if your campaign is extremely successful beyond industry benchmark metrics!

The ebocube Commercial Cycle

The ebocube dashboard is fundamental to phase one. It presents metrics for your campaigns along with the datacube, which is a view of the marketing data for your company and contact data stored in your data warehouse and available to target in the EM.

No one wants to drown in metrics, so the ebocube commercial cycle helps you to define metrics for your ebocube dashboard that count, and to define metrics that will result in financial results. Table 3.1 describes metrics that can form your ebocube commercial cycle objectives.

TABLE 3.1 Possible ebocube Commercial Cycle Objectives

	Email	Webcast	Site/Parent/ Campaign Landing Page	External Web Banners and Social Network	Offline Events	Direct Mail	Telemarketing	Print/TV/Outdoor
All Phases of ebocube Commercial Cycle	Opt-out rate/ unsub-scribe	Registrations	Data submission		Attendees	Bounce rate	Invalid phone numbers	
	Soft bounce	Attendee	Downstream traffic		Registration source	Data submission	Number of lead candidates sent to call center for further qualification	
	Number targeted	Evaluation (postevent report)	Upstream traffic			Response call/text back/email/ click through to site		
	Actual sent	Lead candi-dates	Exit survey, customer satisfaction survey				Lead candidates rejected	
	Hard bounce rate		Information from forums of blogs					
	Data sub-mission		Most popular pages (time spent and unique visitors)					

TABLE 3.1 Possible ebocube Commercial Cycle Objectives

	Email	Webcast	Site/Parent/Campaign Landing Page	External Web Banners and Social Network	Offline Events	Direct Mail	Telemarketing	Print/TV/Outdoor
	Open rate	Registrations	Unique visitors/page	Number of impressions on external site	Attendees	Response call/text back/email/click through to site	Inbound calls to call center from trackable source	Response call/text back/email/click through to site
	Click-through links	Attendee	New visitors/page	Number of clicks	Total registrations from all sources	Data submission		
	Email forwards	Evaluation (postevent report)	Data submission	Data submission on banner or landing page				
	Data submission		Bounce rate	Bounce rate on landing page		Bounce rate		
	Number of new contacts in Customer Insights (CI)		Subscribe to newsletter/RSS	Follow up on landing page CTA (download/data submission)				
Awareness/ Acquisition			Click to chat					
			Click on CTA or download (podcast/vod/whitepaper/case study/webcast link)	Unique visitors to campaign landing page (new/returning)				

TABLE 3.1 Possible ebocube Commercial Cycle Objectives

	Email	Webcast	Site/Parent/Campaign Landing Page	External Web Banners and Social Network	Offline Events	Direct Mail	Telemarketing	Print/TV/Outdoor
	Data submission	Registrations	Click on CTA or download (podcast/vod/whitepaper/case study/webcast link)	Click on CTA or download (podcast/vod/whitepaper/case study/webcast link)	Registrations	Number of lead candidates from response channels	Number of outbound calls	Number of lead candidates from response channels
		Attendee	Click to chat	Click to chat	Attendees		Number of leads generated	
	Open rate	Data submission, with budget, authority, need, timeframe (BANT) considered	Return visitors based on cookies	Data submission		Data submission	Number of inbound calls to center	
Consideration/ Nurture and Develop	Click-through links	Evaluation (postevent report)	Data submission	Lead candidates/leads			Lead candidates sent to call center	
	Registrations	Registrations	Lead candidates/leads	Number of impressions on external site			Lead candidates closed	
			Bounce rate	Unique visitors/page				
			Data submission	New visitors/page			Total leads	
			Unique visitors/page	Data submission			Number of open lead candidates	
			New visitors/page	Bounce rate				

TABLE 3.1 Possible ebocube Commercial Cycle Objectives

	Email	Webcast	Site/Parent/ Campaign Landing Page	External Web Banners and Social Network	Offline Events	Direct Mail	Telemarketing	Print/TV/Outdoor
	Data submission	Data submission, with BANT	Sales, e-commerce	Sales	Sales	Sales captured from response channels	Conversion of lead candidates to sales	Sales captured from response channels
	Lead candidates	Lead candidates	Data submission	Lead candidates collected through banner or site converted into sales	Lead conversions	Lead conversions from response channels		Lead conversions from response channels
Purchase/ Develop	Open rate	Lead candidates						
		Registrations		Registrations				
		Attendee		Attendees				
	Click-through links	Evaluation (postevent report)						

TABLE 3.1   Possible ebocube Commercial Cycle Objectives

	Email	Webcast	Site/Parent/Campaign Landing Page	External Web Banners and Social Network	Offline Events	Direct Mail	Telemarketing	Print/TV/Outdoor
	Click-through special offers	Registrations	Customer portal login usage	Click through for customer offers plus follow up	Customer registrations		Number of up-sell/cross-sell	Log in to customer portal/calls to account managers or call center
	Entering loyalty codes	Attendees	Return customers to site		Customer attendees			
Loyalty/ Retention		Evaluation (postevent report)	Unique visitors/page					
	Open rates	Lead candidates	New visitors/page		Up-sell/cross-sell			
			Data submission					

We designed the ebocube commercial cycle for the ultimate goal of lead generation. The model is geared toward sales and generating marketing leads. This is a good approach to take in EM because they are fast-growth markets and opportunities for new customer acquisition exist. In developed economies, companies may be a little more skeptical of some marketing campaigns, and harder to win over, because they may be locked into other suppliers and have established relationships. They are constantly bombarded with online and offline marketing and may not be receptive at first.

Two in One

As an electronic CRM model, the ebocube model integrates the buying cycle of business contacts and the contact data life cycle. The buying cycle represents the readiness of the prospect or existing customer to buy from your company. The contact will typically migrate from being aware of your company, brand, product, or service to considering it, and then finally purchasing it (or becoming a loyal customer). Each phase of an integrated marketing campaign is aimed at encouraging customers to advance through the phases of the buying cycle. The business objectives are ultimately to sell to the prospects and existing customers or to retain existing loyal customers and to up-sell or cross-sell.

The contact data life cycle represents the data objectives for the campaign for each phase of the buying cycle and the data that should be contacted and used for each phase of the buying cycle. The buying cycle defines what to say, and the data life cycle defines who to say it to. The phases of the buying cycle can be combined with the phases of the data cycle. For example, if the initial phase of your campaign is to raise awareness, you are likely to target newly acquired data.

Marketing operations (mops) is concerned with tracking and executing integrated campaigns for EMs. The ebocube commercial cycle objectives planned in phase two should be documented in an online brief in phase three and tracked through execution to measure these objectives. The results of the ebocube commercial cycle objectives can be measured and assessed in reports in the dashboard and dat-acube, phase one.

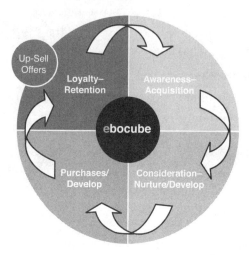

Figure 3.2   The ebocube commercial cycle

The ebocube commercial cycle is deployed in phase two to deter-mine communications objectives and to decide on the best media mix to achieve these objectives and data planning in unison. The cycle combines data and communication objectives that are inextricably linked when campaigning. This is fundamental to the success of a campaign; good communications poorly targeted provide poor results.

In the high-level view of the dashboard, you'll be measuring the number of leads and ROMI. To create leads and sales, you'll target the loyal segment of your customers contact base and develop prospects so that they become leads. You'll use your database to do this. Preceding the phases of purchase and loyalty, you'll aim to raise awareness among the contacts, acquiring data to target or building data on existing contacts.

Phase One: The Dashboard

The dashboard gathers marketing and sales reporting for campaigns executed through ebocube and can be used to measure the results of the ebocube commercial cycle objectives. You should set objectives based on the ebocube commercial cycle.

The dashboard reports on all of your metrics for all of your marketing and sales results for your campaigns. The metrics in the dashboard can be split into an operational and high-level view. Ideally you have one dashboard with three partitions—one to show operational metrics, one to show the high level, and one to show the datacube (data results). The operational view represents granular metrics of your campaigns, which impact the day-to-day operations of marketing (e.g., click-through rates, open rates, and site views). The high-level view of the dashboard shows the financial results of your marketing, ROMI, which can be measured through marketing leads generated, closed deals, and estimated opportunity pipeline (an approximation of the deal size multiplied by the number of deals for the company in EMs).

The datacube provides reports and views of information contained in your database for companies and marketable contacts. It can be illustrated graphically or in tabular format. The report is a snapshot of your company and contact data contained in your company database for the time it has been extracted. Your database should be continuously updated from various systems feeding it, whether from sales systems, finance systems, or marketing tools like your website. The report should be extracted as close to the time of campaign planning and execution as possible to show the most accurate picture of your data.

The report is just a snapshot for the period of time it has been extracted. It can be used to identify where your data gaps lie in your database or if you're missing company or contact information (otherwise known as your data completeness). Data analysts can use this data to identify opportunities for further marketing and sales and to inform the data-acquisition or data-enhancement plan.

Phase one, the ebocube dashboard (see Figure 3.3), shows meaningful marketing and sales metrics generated by integrated campaigns (planned in phase II) targeting EMs. Metrics include operational metrics that impact everyday execution and high-level metrics that impact the bottom line and revenue. The datacube is the partition of the dashboard that represents your contact and company data for your selected EMs, highlighting opportunities, gaps, updates, and trends—your database being a key asset for e-CRM. Results are tracked and captured through phase III mops.

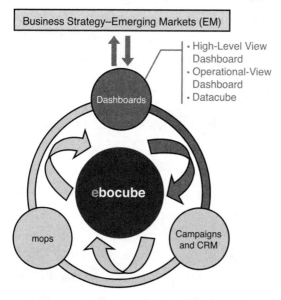

Figure 3.3   The ebocube model, phase one: the dashboard

Phase one is the point where you start to plan your campaigns, based on a number of meaningful metrics gained from your dashboard, which can be accessed by user-friendly web application interfaces. Therefore, results are used to plan rather than instincts and assumptions. The dashboard will guide your overall marketing and sales results, and provide powerful analytic tools for understanding your contact and company database. Your primary data tool will be the datacube. The loop on the model comes full circle through marketing campaigns' reports and results. The results are the end of your efforts, but also the beginning of your campaign planning in phase two.

The dashboard is also used for post-campaign analysis. Results can be viewed iteratively throughout campaigns for granular metrics (e.g., open rates, click rates) to ensure your campaign is on track or used to access longer-term campaign results such as financial metrics at the end of the quarter in terms of marketing leads, sales. The dashboard helps you and your business understand and learn from past activities. You will discover what worked in a particular EM and what didn't. You can also evaluate your top-performing countries and campaigns in terms of sales and marketing results. These results should feed your planning and business strategy.

You can learn a lot from the dashboards. You can analyze ROMI, lead conversion, and the number of marketing leads converted into sales or rejected. You can also track granular, operational-level information such as the month the open rates for your monthly newsletter were the highest. This may be used as part of a nurture/development activity (a stage of the ebocube commercial cycle).

The datacube should be a starting point of planning your campaigns. It is your living reference of the data you have, and can also be used to measure results for the end of your campaigns. Quickly and simply, you can determine whether you have available data for the campaign you are planning to launch. Before you start creating collateral or localizing your campaigns, you should ensure that you have contacts in your database whom you can reach with your campaign. After all, you need a target audience. The datacube will give you insight and understanding of the gaps in the database and inform you of the data quality and numbers of contactable records so that you know what you can expect in terms of campaign results (or even whether you can launch a direct marketing campaign). Overall, it allows you to communicate directly with contacts.

Suppose, for instance, that you've been tasked to generate 500 leads (i.e., contacts who are ready to speak to sales) in Mexico for your next campaign. The audience for this campaigns is very specific: only C-level executives from the manufacturing industry. Your datacube shows that you only have 359 contacts, which you can contact. Following this data-segmentation criteria, you instantly know that you will not be able to achieve the objective of 500 leads because there is not enough data. Therefore, you either need to rethink your campaign objectives or acquire the data to make your target realistic.

All too often, marketers are reengineering their campaigns to meet data needs, turning the wheel in the opposite direction. They create collateral and then they try to work backward and find the data to use for the costly campaign. However, that simply doesn't work, especially not in EMs where you have little understanding of your audience.

The creative art work/concept stage of marketing is attractive to marketers because it's the fun part of the campaign, where they may work on the collateral, design, localize campaigns, and engage with creative agencies, either in-house or externally. Data collection is overlooked. Then when the data criteria for the campaign is finally created and submitted, the data team may come back with the results that the number of contacts records is in single digits, which means poor results and wasted money.

We've seen experienced marketers blaming the data teams, arguing that the data teams can't manage data properly, and even escalating lack of good data in their data warehouse to top management. This is an act of desperation, because they've invested budget in localization, campaign execution setup, and so forth. They have gathered whichever contact may be available to email blast and send their campaign out to them. Does it make sense to contact any contact just to have a higher target audience number? *No!*

In this instance, marketing is contacting anybody, throwing out anything. Their message is irrelevant, so marketing results can be received negatively in the EM and email opt-out or unsubscription rates may be high, which means you lose the opportunity to communicate via email to these contacts again. High-quality data in EMs is still scarce, so you don't want to lose opt-ins for data you have worked hard to gather. If you contact randomly with nothing specific to say, your response rate will be low. You are wasting resources and creating a negative ROMI. Would you appreciate receiving email with dog food offers when you are a cat owner? The same applies in any business.

To avoid this situation, only one solution exists: reviewing and analyzing your datacube before you even think about launching your campaign. You might even decide that you cannot launch a campaign because you have no data, no budget, or no resources to acquire contacts. Data is the very first step to make your campaign successful in EMs. No matter how creative your content is, no matter how great the proposition or incentive is, no matter how great the tracking, measurement, campaign execution, or agency you use is, this is all going to be wasted if you contact irrelevant people with the direct marketing element of your campaign, which is fundamental to driving results. Not only will you want to see the number of contacts you have for a specific segment in your database, via the datacube, you may also want to look at the history of marketing contacts (i.e., when they last upgraded their products or last purchased products). You may also wish to see the contacts that responded positively to a previous related campaign.

Phase Two: Campaign Management and CRM

Phase two (see Figure 3.4) of ebocube demonstrates campaign and data planning using the ebocube commercial cycle. It demonstrates the use of a proposition, incentive, localization, and the use of an integrated media mix (online and offline communications). At this stage, you should also plan your budget requirements. You should be aware of how much your media mix and incentives will cost, and you should estimate the expected ROMI (e.g., number of leads to be produced, sales). Even if you're starting out with an awareness/acquisition campaign, eventually this campaign should result in lead generation.

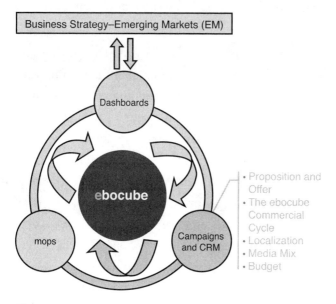

Figure 3.4   The ebocube model, phase two: Campaigns and CRM

When phase one is complete, after you've analyzed your dashboard, including the datacube, and you're aware of the "counts" or numbers for your target audience, you should move on to setting up SMART (simple, measurable, achievable, realistic, timed) campaign objectives. Objectives may differ but are quantifiable, whereas aims are more like statements. At this stage, you should define the customer proposition suitable for the local markets needs. Analyze how the overall customer benefits from your company's products/services or how your various products/services are an overall solution for emerging markets. You should plan whether you will utilize online offers or incentives. Your marketing collateral should be created and prepared at this stage. This includes localizing your marketing communications. The entire campaign and execution should be localized per country or region where applicable.

Campaign objectives may differ from one country to the other. In some countries, awareness of your product or brand is much stronger than in others. If your product is well known, you might spend less time and effort on the awareness stage of your campaign and focus more on the consideration and purchase stage (ebocube commercial cycle stages). In a country where your products, solutions, or services are not really known, you might want to build strong awareness and acquire new data, to move contacts in that country to the next step of the ebocube commercial cycle, moving the contact into the consideration and purchase phase.

In phase two, you want to test and demonstrate online communication methods and channels. The following pages will help you decide which online or trackable offline channels to use for each of the phases in the ebocube commercial cycle. You will learn why localization is such a critical aspect of your campaign in EMs and how it helps you increase your response rate, lead conversion, and general brand acceptance. You'll see why poor localized campaigns can reduce your campaign results and how wrong assumptions can damage your brand.

Although online customer relationships are the core strategy for ebocube, online strategies need to be integrated with offline elements. Phase two will help you understand how to use and integrate these channels:

Online and Digital

✓ Email
✓ Webcasts
✓ Websites
✓ Microsites (landing pages)
✓ Social media
✓ Web banners
✓ Mobile marketing

Offline

✓ Events

✓ Direct mail

✓ Telemarketing

✓ Above the line (print, television, billboards)

Your strategy will allow you to achieve ebocube commercial cycle goals, ultimately high-quality leads, with the various media and will identify which metrics to look for in the dashboard.

Phase Three: Marketing Operations

This phase (see Figure 3.5) demonstrates how to budget, execute, track, and measure campaigns using web application tools to feed the dashboard with the ebocube commercial cycle objectives to create meaningful metrics and show ROMI, and to feed your database with high-quality company and contact data for an EM as reflected by the datacube.

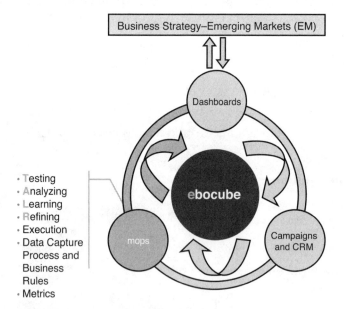

Figure 3.5   The ebocube model, phase three: mops

Although this is the most technical phase of ebocube, it is not necessary to get into the technical elements. You'll learn what you need by examining the process, and will thus understand how you can execute, track, and measure your campaigns. Your company can implement any number of solutions (off the shelf or bespoke) for this phase. Research what will work best for your organization based on the information provided below.

mops is a new discipline that has been adopted by many big enterprises (and even small businesses). These companies have recognized and realized its benefits in managing and analyzing data reports and automating marketing execution.

It's all about tracking. The beauty of the Internet is that everything that is digital, online, or sent over the Internet can be tracked and measured. When we refer to *tracking*, we mean that marketing communications can be "located individually" and measured. For example, you can now see whether your emails have been opened and which individual specific form of communication generated the best metrics. You can compare the web banner on x website or the web banner or y website to determine which communication channel can be assessed individually or if either one has resulted in the intended objective.

There can be times when there are too many metrics, too many reports, tables, and numbers to analyze. The dashboard is for marketers, not analysts, and that's why it is important to focus on metrics that are meaningful to your organization. How can you determine which marketing metrics are helpful to you? That depends on your marketing objectives, which, through ebocube, should be based on the ebocube commercial cycle aims. You might find yourself sinking in numbers in tables and reports, but you might not be able to determine anything meaningful for your business if you don't do this initial planning. You must define what is helpful and what information is important and significant for you as marketer and for your business. Phase three of ebocube helps you to take advantage of the digital era in the most effective way and to set up campaigns to deliver meaningful results. At this stage, you need to define how you should track and measure, based on planning in phase two, and what metrics or data should feed your dashboard to create meaningful business intelligence.

mops allows you to determine whether all your hard work in phase two will pay off and whether you can gather business intelligence and data for phase one. This stage helps you decide how to gather all the information required for your dashboard. Phase one is the visual representation of results, whereas mops feeds reports with meaningful metrics to enable results. In this implementation and execution stage, you can track, measure, and feed it back into the dashboards in a meaningful way to close the loop on marketing and sales in targeted EMs.

mops is an emerging function in organizations and will continue to be important in accounting for marketing, measurement, intelligence, and representing how marketing impacts the top (sales) and bottom line (profit) in an increasingly complex world, especially in a global context. Having and using the appropriate research and measurement tools will help your business succeed in EMs (and any other markets, for that matter).

Endnotes

[1] Wikipedia, "Business model," http://en.wikipedia.org/wiki/Business_model.

[2] Ibid.

[3] "Quick MBA, Knowledge to Power Your Business Competitive Advantage," http://www.quickmba.com/strategy/competitive-advantage.

[4] Wikipedia, "Business Model," http://en.wikipedia.org/wiki/Business_model.

4

Marketing by the Dashboard Light

Upon completion of this chapter, you should be able to

- Identify your key metrics and performance indicators and how to measure them
- Understand the significance and uses of the dashboard
- Understand how business intelligence can be gained from the dashboard and help your businesses make marketing decisions and plan
- Demonstrate the financial worth of marketing expenditures through return on marketing investment (ROMI) metrics
- Identify which online and marketing metrics are meaningful aided by ebocube commercial cycle
- Understand the significance of the three different views of the dashboard: high-level view, marketing operational view, and datacube
- Know how to think about starting to scope your dashboard
- Understand the significance of your data as an asset in emerging markets and use the datacube to view firmographic and contact level information and to plan your campaigns
- Understand how to review your data inventory and data health

A pilot flies on the basis of the information that appears on the screen in front of him (that is, his dashboard). The dashboard is a visual element fed by many operational elements of the plane. For example, the pilot knows whether there's enough fuel to fly. In the same way, marketers know that a campaign has been successful, because they can see marketing leads in the dashboard, captured by operational tools, and can review investment areas through budgeting, tracking, and reporting tools. Without the tools to track and measure fuel usage, airspeed, weather conditions, and other indicators, the pilot would not be able to make vital decisions. Likewise in business, you need marketing indicators to move your organization forward.

No airline would allow a pilot to fly without the operational information about the plane. Therefore, the pilot receives only meaningful reports that are tracked and measured through operational tools. Without these views, pilots wouldn't know where they were flying to or how long the trip should take. Now imagine that your company shareholders are the passengers, and they're flying on your first-ever flight into emerging markets (EMs). They rely on you for good results. You rely on well-defined metrics for meaningful results—results that can be captured through tracking and measurement through marketing operations (mops).

What Can Be Measured and How?

It's important for you to understand what to measure so that you don't end up swimming in metrics, and so that you know when you've achieved a good result. It's also important to know how to measure each specific communication channel. Time and technology have changed, and so has marketing; it is now possible to track results in real time—therefore, as they happen.

Individual tools can generate a great many reports for you, including web analytics reports, email tracking, database reports, registration systems, and many more. However, you must define objectives, what you want to see in your dashboard, and how you want to tell the story. This information is fed through multiple reports or sources. You want to demonstrate to your stakeholders how campaign results flowed from campaign execution, based on clear objectives and what's been achieved. You and only you as a campaign manager should define and brief your team, either in-house or through an external agency, with the metrics that you want to see tracked.

You need to set up defined simple, measurable, achievable, realistic, timed objectives (SMART) before execution takes place to make sure that you don't miss out on vital elements when tracking communications for measurement and reporting. Although it doesn't hurt to track all elements of your communication (after all, you might learn new things which were unplanned), your reports should report on your defined objectives so that you know whether you have achieved what you planned. As with any presentation, your metrics should be defined with a specific audience in mind. Use the metrics to present your case to stakeholders; don't be led by them. You can complement the metrics with qualitative information, campaign images, or animated metrics, data, and results.

However, don't go to the other extreme and track only the minimum of each communication channel. Define how you want to divide the information to learn as much as possible about various markets. You need to understand your objectives and what you want to achieve.

A department or a client may request tracking in a region based on an email blast. If you send it out only in English to countries in the Middle East and Africa, the response rate may be different than if you take into account the multiple languages spoken in the region. You could set up the system to generate reports based on emails sent out in two languages (e.g., Arabic and English) to see which variant generates the best result. This criteria needs to be defined clearly and set up in the campaign management tool because it isn't possible to identify open rates per individual segment of data with different language emails in the dashboard after the fact.

As a marketing professional, you don't need to be an IT expert, but you need to be aware of tracking methods. In small organizations, you might be responsible for defining mops. The results for each and every communication targeting each segment needs to be tracked. This is integral to your campaign. Make the dashboard deliver what you've requested. Create a definition of success (see Figure 4.1).

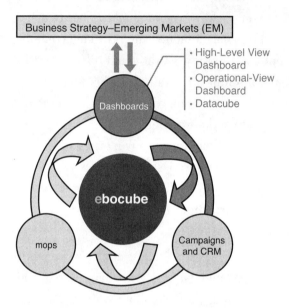

Figure 4.1   The ebocube model (phase one: the dashboard)

The Dashboard

Your dashboard should be an interface, typically on a web application, that organizes and presents information on marketing, sales, and company/contact data. The results are presented in a way that is easy to read and can be extracted from the application.

The dashboard integrates information from multiple data sources into a unified display. For example, the results may be drawn from sales account management tools, email execution tools, web analytic tools, call center tools, and customer databases. As CRM technology develops and new communication tools, such as social media, emerge, sources feeding the dashboard may grow.

Dashboards may be customized in a multitude of ways. In ebocube, we refer to the high-level view of the dashboard that shows strategic marketing and sales results that can also be translated into financial results. The operational view shows day-to-day marketing results, which contribute to sales results. The datacube provides a view on company and contact data, including inventory in local areas. All views are from one dashboard, but represent different metrics.

Information can be displayed graphically; it should be laid out in a logical structure and should be intuitive for the user. Data displays should be customized to meet the needs of specific users whether chief marketing officers (CMOs) or executives.

Business Intelligence

Based on our research, chief marketing officers (CMOs) would like to see marketing and sales dashboards to feed their strategies in EMs, and to show accountability and return on investment for marketing. Business intelligence can be gained from the dashboard and help businesses make decisions about future strategy and marketing. This may include pursuing a certain region or country more aggressively and spending more budget or understanding what is not working and reducing costs. It may also impact how resources, such as employees, are allocated to markets. Lastly, it may identify problems—for example, that salespeople are not following up on leads or that they are rejecting many marketing leads.

The dashboard can be accessed globally through a web application and fed by multiple data sources. Imagine starting a new job in a new company or changing your role (for example, moving to a different product department, or expanding the region you are looking after). Your first questions may be, "Where are we now? Where do I start?" Wouldn't it be great if you could just pull a report informing you of past results of campaigns in your new markets, before having to ask anyone?

Imagine having a view of data in the company you've just joined, informing you of the condition of the data in the company for contacts. You could instantly analyze the data gaps, quality of the data, and issues that indicate what you should focus on initially. For example, if an SMB (small to medium-sized business) segment is performing great in a new region you've just been assigned to, you want to keep this trend going.

Based on the reports and analysis from the dashboard, you can plan the next phase of your campaign. That phase can include awareness and acquisition of data; consideration and developing a contact; purchase and further development of contacts, or loyalty and retention of a customer. These campaign aims define the ebocube commercial cycle. These campaigns aims should also be combined with your overall business strategy—for example, your product or service focus for growth and investment.

Financial Results

Another issue facing marketing organizations today is proving the financial worth of marketing expenditures. To exist in EMs, you need dedicated investment in marketing to build your brand and to generate leads. This should not be an add-on to your existing marketing but a focused approach to penetrate new markets. Although the ebocube model is a low-cost business model, this doesn't mean that there are no costs. There are still the usual expenses involved with campaign creation, copywriting, localization, events, and employees.

Senior management can place huge pressure on marketing to justify expenditures as financially viable, relative to other ways the organization could spend its money. Marketing needs to show its worth, as do other departments, when fighting for budget consideration.

The dashboard helps you translate marketing results into a financial return. In marketing, we use metrics such as click-through rates, bounce rates, open rates, and leads, but the dashboard also provides financial information. Marketers may use terms such as *awareness* to justify results, but this simply doesn't mean much to others unless it can be quantified, which the dashboard helps to do.

Meaningful Metrics

Marketers are under increasing pressure to prove return on marketing investment for their budgets, especially during tough economic times and particularly in EMs, but they should avoid becoming overwhelmed in data and use SMART objectives to know what they need to achieve. Metrics are essential in proving to the sales teams

Specifying the Time Period for When Reports Should Be Pulled

A time lag occurs between marketing and sales results (of course), as contacts may need to pass through each individual phase of the ebocube commercial cycle. In addition, closing the deal by sales requires time, which means results won't be visible in the dashboard instantly. However, the ebocube model will deliver metrics to show the results of the customer journey from awareness to purchase or loyalty, so that marketers can still present meaningful results and build trust with other stakeholders in the company.

You should review the dashboard and overall marketing responses and sales for the month, quarter, or year. How often you review the dashboard depends on your campaign setup, which is defined by your campaign objectives in phase two. For example, if your campaign delivers results in the first quarter, you should conduct quarterly business reviews (QBRs) on your dashboard in each subsequent quarter.

Creating marketing dashboard reports manually (e.g., via Excel spreadsheet) can be time-consuming and error-prone, but it's not impossible. However, the best practice is to automate this process and to have an electronic database organize this for you and send you automated predefined reports.

and executives what can be done, with the ultimate aim of growth in sales and revenue.

Too many metrics can leave you confused and unclear about what you're trying to prove and what you need to communicate to the sales teams and the executive board. They need to see the value of your marketing through meaningful metrics. Before you set up your campaigns, create your communications strategy and communications collateral; you should have SMART objectives and metrics documented in an online brief and be absolutely clear about what your communications should achieve. This ensures that from the outset that your campaign has clearly defined documented objectives that can be measured in the dashboard.

Marketers are sometimes unsure what to measure and why, which is why we use the ebocube commercial cycle to clearly define objectives and metrics. The ebocube commercial cycle gives your metrics context and meaning and helps you take action.

The metrics in the dashboard and datacube will show whether you have achieved your ebocube commercial cycle objectives, achieved return on investment, or whether a campaign should be pulled. Don't be led by metrics, let metrics support your case. So before you access any form of marketing report, know exactly what you're aiming to prove and which metrics matter.

Three Views of the Dashboard

The ultimate aspiration with the ebocube model is to have one dashboard that can be accessed globally, by web application, providing meaningful metrics for sales, marketing, and contacts and company data. The dashboard is fed by multiple systems constantly and updated in real time and can be used, with a high-level of accuracy, before executing and planning a campaign.

The ebocube model for a dashboard can be sliced and diced to present many different views, showing data from many points of view, depending on who is viewing the dashboard and what is requested. You might have your own reporting tools or methodology to create your own meaningful dashboards. However, it can become frustrating when it comes to the end of the quarter and you have to present results to senior management, your colleagues, and even external vendors.

They may all request different views or reports on your campaigns. Senior management may request leads reports, or sales, marketing stakeholders may ask about data improvement or open rates. You need to have a plan.

Over the years, through creating and compiling manual or automated reports, we came to the conclusion that a standardized approach for efficient and valuable reporting was required. We developed three main views, which deliver results for different groups: the high-level view, the operational view, and the datacube.

The high-level dashboard view is what is expected by C-level management. Execution teams, campaign management teams, agencies, and data teams use the operational-level view and the datacube regularly. The operational metrics help these teams to create leads. If you imagine these views in the form of a hierarchy, the operational results are the basis for generating leads or sales presented in the high-level view.

We split the views so that people aren't confused by too many metrics and so that they get to see metrics relevant to their roles and needs. Some users just want the financial picture, whereas others need the detail. The different views provide users the metrics they need without crowding too much information on any single view of the ebocube dashboard.

The operational view enables you to review operational metrics and should be used by campaign managers and staff responsible for executing campaigns.

The marketing opportunity and sales view (high-level metrics) can be used to show executives how marketing is contributing to sales and the revenue and profitability of the company. Both views will help you to determine which county/region/activity/campaign in EM is performing the best in terms of marketing and sales results, which is defined through the dashboard setup and execution through mops.

The high-level view does not show the granular detail. For example, open rates, click-through rates, and bounce rates are details that executives don't want to review; they are interested in sales and revenue, opportunity, and the big picture. However, team members who do want to see these granular results should be able to drill down in the dashboard. The granular level is important for marketers and helps them to drive campaigns to generate leads/sales. For example, if a contact opens an awareness email, a marketer may target that contact with a second email inviting them to a webcast for further consideration, developing the contact relationship in accordance to the ebocube commercial cycle.

The operational dashboard and datacube help campaign managers to understand and learn from campaign results, which helps to achieve higher results (such as sales) and can inform decisions (such as whether to purchase data).

Operational metrics and learning is covered in more detail in Chapter 9, "Marketing Operations (mops)." In that chapter, we also discuss how, through mops, you can test, analyze, learn, and refine campaigns launched in EMs.

High-Level View

This is the report or the view expected by execs, new business development, and sales managers. It's basically about the bottom line, and people who are responsible for making money, or finance, in EM will be concerned with this view, and they may use it for their key performance indicators (KPIs). When designing the high-level view of the ebocube dashboard, you can work with these stakeholders to identify and further develop the obtainable metrics they require.

The high-level report consists of marketing and sales results; these are the results that can be translated easily into financial metrics and mainly link to the purchase/develop and loyalty/retention aims of the ebocube commercial cycle. This report links to purchase and driving loyalty with campaigns.

Figure 4.2 shows the ebocube commercial cycle, illustrating the combined data and campaign goals for campaign phases. It should be used for planning data segmentation and communication messages. The following high-level metrics represent results for the last two quadrants of the cycle—the purchase campaign and developing responses—which should result in financial metrics in the form of sales leads as well as a campaign focused on loyalty, targeting the contacts you want to retain in your company (i.e., the loyal segment).

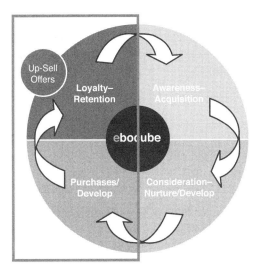

Figure 4.2 The ebocube commercial cycle, loyalty and purchases segments

Marketing tracking tools can generate a lot of data. The following are some marketing metric examples split between high-level results and operational results:

- **Country targeted/region:** This should be the name of the county or the region targeted for a campaign. This field will also help to determine which EM is generating the best results.

- **Campaign name:** This should be a unique campaign name, following a naming convention; one consistent name should flow across all operational systems, starting from online briefing tools, to budgeting tools, execution tools, and to reporting.

- **Allocated budget:** Funds allocated to this campaign.

- **The ebocube commercial cycle aim:** Awareness/acquisition, consideration/development, purchase/development, loyalty/retention.

- **Number of contacts targeted:** This is the total number of targeted contacts with this campaign. This useful metric helps to identify the response rate in term of leads. For example, if you have two leads and you have targeted two thousand contacts, the results in terms of leads could be considered poor.

- **Return on marketing investment (ROMI):** This can be measured by two methods. The first is estimated return on budget (based on estimated sales lead value, sales versus marketing investment). The second is actual return on marketing investment based on actual sales, closed deal value as a ratio against marketing investment.

- **Launch date:** The date the campaign is launched, DD/MM/YYYY.

- **End date:** The date the campaign ends, DD/MM/YYYY. This will help to determine the duration of the campaign and let you know whether it has just launched or whether it has been in progress for a while. This will also help to determine how well the campaign is progressing over time and whether it's time to end the campaign!

- **Quarter:** This includes the fiscal quarter (Q1, Q2, Q3, Q4), and this is the division of your fiscal year (i.e., the period of 12 months without regard to the calendar year).

Sales metrics include the following:

- **Lead candidates:** Lead candidates are contacts that directly respond to your campaign, following a call to action on a form of communication, and by submitting their data in a form, through an inbound number answered by a call centre, or, if offline, at a trade event (for example).

They are potentially worth talking to for a sale but may require further follow up by a call center agent or salesperson to be qualified as a lead.

CI's (customer insight) business rules are applied to the contact for initial cleansing, removing response contacts who cannot be sold to—for example, students, competitors, partners. They are blocked and excluded for further lead qualification and will not be sent to a call center, account manager, or partner for further qualification to determine whether they are a valid marketing leads. This stops all responses being sent to sales and should improve lead quality (because they have been screened).

- **Lead conversion rate:** This is the rate of lead candidates converted into qualified leads (actual real sales opportunities). Lead qualification can be carried out and managed by a call center, internal sales force, external partner, or online form (email survey) requesting further information from a lead candidate. If the lead candidates are not real sales leads, they will be closed, which will show in reporting.

- **Number of account-managed leads generated:** This is the number of account-managed leads generated as a result of a marketing campaign.

- **Number of leads passed to partners:** This is the number of call center qualified leads, nonaccount-managed leads passed to partners.

- **Total leads regardless of source:** A qualified lead will respond positively to BANT questions—BANT refers to budget, authority, need (i.e., project), and time (i.e., project will commence in a specific frame time [e.g., 0–3 months, 3–12 months, 12+ months]). To ensure marketing leads are satisfactory for sales, you should agree to lead qualification questions or a scoring system with sales and answers within the sales teams so that sales teams will accept and follow up on high-quality leads. BANT is industry standard and fundamental for qualification, but can be developed by your company specifically for EMs.

- **Opportunity pipeline:** This is the estimated value of leads. The formula is number of leads * lead value for deal size = estimated value.

- **Closed deals:** This is the actual sales value that is fed by sales systems or financial transactions that feed the database and ebocube dashboard.

- **Closed deals partners or closed opportunities:** This is revenue reported by regional/county partners or an internal regional sales force. This is applied in cases where you use partners as your sales force (e.g., local channels).

- **Waiting leads:** These are leads not followed up by partners or by the internal sales force.

- **Rejected marketing leads:** These are leads rejected either by an internal sale force or by an external partner. (This will inform you of the quality of your qualified marketing leads.)

Marketing Operational Dashboard

This segment, highlighted in Figure 4.3, reports on the stages of the ebocube commercial cycle preceding purchase and loyalty and may include awareness and acquisition of data and consideration development of the contact. The operational segment represents results for the first two quadrants of the cycle—an awareness/acquisition phase of a campaign may result in email address submission as well as high open rates. These do not translate into financial high-level reports, however. Instead, the intention is to further nurture responses with consideration campaigns, the second quadrant in the ebocube commercial cycle; to do this, you might use a webcast. Results will include the number of attendees, for example—again illustrated in the operational view of your dashboard.

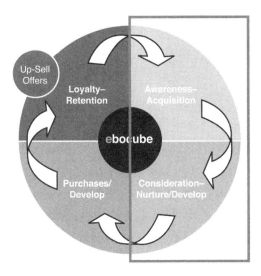

Figure 4.3   The ebocube commercial cycle, awareness and considera-tion segments

Operational View

The operational view helps assess the communications channels that have generated results in an EM, and is also used to determine whether contacts can be marketed to for the following stages of the ebocube commercial cycle. Unlike the high-level view, which is purely concerned with results that can be translated into financial results, the operational view allows you to "drill down" to as much detail as you like.

Here you can check the results of both precampaign testing and executed-campaign results. This will help you to develop future e-marketing campaigns, even though some elements may also be offline. Your results will determine the success of your campaign. Through the results, you can determine whether your campaign objectives have been met and improve future campaigns. The ebocube commercial cycle should be used to plan campaign phases. These are necessary steps in your campaign to develop contacts to go through to the purchase stage.

With all of your communications, you should aim to capture respondent data by providing an online data-capture form or inbound phone number as a call to action, or, if you do use offline events, you should set up sophisticated data capture, too. You can migrate the customer through the ebocube commercial cycle only when you capture his or her data. If you cannot do this, your efforts to make sales will not be achieved, nor will the next stages of the ebocube commercial cycle be effective. For example, web hits and visitors are appropriate if your campaign is aimed at raising awareness. At the next step, you want customers to move to a landing page with a data-capture form to move them into the consideration stage with further communications. It may interest you as a marketer to know how many people have come to your site; but to create opportunities, you need to capture contact information that you can use to further communicate to and understand profiles of your prospects.

Testing, Analyzing, Learning, and Refining

Metrics in the operational view of the dashboard can be used to refine and test campaigns. For example, you can run A/B testing, using 10% of your data, splitting it into two segments and sending two email variants to the segments to see which variant elicits the best response. You can measure this in the operational view. Because this is a test effort, you should include *test* in the campaign name and make sure it will not be tracked in the high-level view of the dashboard, unless it generates legitimate leads and contacts to feed your database. With the operational-level view, you can see all the details or results and fields that aren't visible in the high-level dashboard.

Operational View Metrics to Capture

- **Country targeted/region:** This should be the name of the county or the region name; the user may look at the campaign results for a particular region or country.

- **Campaign name:**   This should be a unique campaign name convention that will identify the campaign you're monitoring.
- **ebocube commercial cycle aim:**   Awareness/acquisition, consideration/development, purchase/development, loyalty/retention.
- **Incentive:**   Your incentive to end users should be monitored here.
- **Communication channel:**   Any email, SMS, webcast, website, social network, landing page, microsite, web banners, events, direct mail, telemarketing, print, TV, or outdoor advertising used in the campaign.
- **Segment name:**   A specific segment of data connected to contacts in your target audience from your database in your data segmentation campaign tools, indicating clearly who you're talking to. You may have multiple segment labels for a one communication and target audience. The segment can be named after the data segment characteristics—for example, you could split your target audience between decision-makers and nondecision-makers. In the operational report, you can then analyze which segment of data from your target audience was the most responsive. For example, you could review which segment generated the highest open rate for email. You could also create segment names per vertical or company size. It all depends on what you want to see reported about your audience.
- **Launch date:**   This is the date the campaign is launched, DD/MM/YYYY.
- **End date:**   The date the campaign ends, DD/MM/YYYY.
- **Data source:**   You might use various sources of data for your campaign including CI (customer insight—your internal marketing database), partner database data, sales and account manager (AM) lists, or newly acquired lists. You want to specify that in your campaign brief, execution tools, and therefore dashboard via reports. This enables you to see and compare results for various lists. For example, in comparing the existing database (CI) versus a newly acquired list, you might discover an acquired list is not as good as your in-house database in terms of results— for example, you might notice a high rate of undelivered emails.

- **Response channel:** Shows how a contact has responded. Data can be captured through online forms on various web pages (including social networks) or via email, call centers, or offline events.

- **Call center follow up inbound versus outbound:** Where contacts (responders) should be routed by CRM system. Inbound calls may be routed to sales. Email responders or lead candidates may be routed to outbound call center or account management for follow up.

- **Number of targeted contacts, or total impressions:** The total number of targeted contacts for campaign or individual communication. This useful metric helps identify the response rate in term of leads.

- **Actual targeted contacts:** Number of targeted contacts minus email bounces (soft/hard) and invalid phone numbers rejected by the call center.

- **Unique responses:** Number of responses to call to action (CTA) either to a call center free phone number/AM or data-capture form. Respondents should be counted only once no matter how many times they have respond to your campaign, including survey responses, event registrations, and marketing responses

- **Open rates:** Number of email open rate. (Note this metric does not show responders who have only read email through the preview reading pane on email clients like Outlook.)

- **Click-through rates:** Number of clicks per link. Links can be tracked and measured individually. These metrics are good for a newsletter, email, or site. If you use a data-capture form and lots of respondents click but do not fill in the data form, review the form for length, creativity, and so on to increase data submission in future campaigns.

- **Responses rate:** Percentage of unique respondents versus number actually targeted. This rate measures when customers have called the call center, completed a data form, or responded to any tracked CTA.

- **New contacts in your marketing database:** Where responders are identified as new contacts in CI.

- **Number of opt ins:** Contacts that have opted in to communications from your company; for example, they may have done this through a website.
- **Number of opt outs:** Contacts that have opted out from any or specific communication method.
- **Lead candidates:** Lead candidates are generated through communications and consideration or purchase phases of the campaign.
- **Lead candidate rejects:** The number of leads rejected requires further lead qualification and could be identified as belonging to a competitor when run through your marketing database.
- **First-tier leads:** The most valuable leads that have budgeted and projected that in zero to three months they will need your solution. The contact considers the need for products/services and has the authority as the budget holder or decision maker.
- **Second-tier leads:** The leads that have been budgeted, have a project due in three to nine months, have a need for product or services, and have the authority to purchase; i.e., has a decision-maker as the budget holder. (This can be identified based on job title questions or simply asking if the responded makes purchasing decisions.) Due to the budget and project timeframe (three to nine months), the lead can't be sent directly to the salesforce or partner to work on so close the deal.
- **Total leads:** A qualified lead will respond positively to BANT questions—budget, authority, need (i.e., project), and time (i.e., project will commence in a specific frame time [e.g., zero to three months, three to twelve months, twelve plus months]). To ensure marketing leads are satisfactory for sales, you should agree to lead qualification criteria or questions or a scoring system with sales and answers within the sales teams so that the teams will accept and follow up on high-quality leads. BANT is an industry standard and fundamental for qualification, but it can be developed by your company specifically for EMs. This metric shows the total amount of leads created for the entire campaign.

As you can see, some metrics in the operational view flow to the high-level view. These metrics may also overlap. It's important for campaign managers to see the high-level view, and so it isn't problematic if these metrics feed the operational view. However, senior managers or finance people using the high-level view do not want to be bombarded with granular metrics that do not help them to see the overall picture. These are considerations for when you design the dashboard.

Designing the Dashboard

We've described what the operational dashboard may look like. Realistically, this dashboard may have several more columns showing results for various communication channels and will evolve as communications mediums continue to develop. The view may be fed by web analytics reports, email reports, customer database, sales tool, or field reports. The aim of both views of the dashboard are to show metrics that relate to the ebocube commercial cycle and that will lead to sales and financial results being measured.

We've listed a number of metrics that can be tracked in the ebocube dashboard per communication channel for every stage of the ebocube commercial cycle. This chart can be used to create your dashboard and to define the fields. It can be used to define the fields that should appear in both the high-level and operational views. It comes down to you how you decide to structure both views and over time to define your own meaningful dashboard.

The metrics described in Table 4.1 can also be used as objectives in the ebocube commercial cycle planning stage, phase two. The metrics will help you design the high-level and operational view of metrics and to define sources from which to gather the data, specifically if you're building a bespoke tool, some off-the-shelf campaign tools will have inbuilt reporting as a first step. Our previous description of the dashboard may help you design and develop your own ebocube dashboard.

TABLE 4.1 The ebocube Commercial Cycle Metrics Matrix

Stage in ebocube commercial cycle	Email	Webcast	Site/Parent/Campaign Landing Page	External Web Banners and Social Network	Offline Events	Direct Mail	Telemarketing	Print/TV/Outdoor
	Opt-out rate/unsubscribe	Registrations	Data submission		Attendees	Bounce rate	Invalid phone numbers	
						Data submission		
	Soft bounce	Attendees	Downstream traffic			Response call/text back/email/click through to site	Number of lead candidates sent to call center for further qualification	
All phases of ebocube commercial cycle	Number targeted	Evaluation (postevent report)	Upstream traffic		Registration source			
			Exit survey, customer satisfaction survey				Lead candidates rejected	
	Actual sent	Lead candidates						
			Information from forums of blogs					
	Hard-bounce rate							
	Data submission		Most popular pages (time spent and unique visitor)					

TABLE 4.1   The ebocube Commercial Cycle Metrics Matrix

Stage in ebocube commercial cycle	Email	Webcast	Site/Parent/Campaign Landing Page	External Web Banners and Social Network	Offline Events	Direct Mail	Telemarketing	Print/TV/Outdoor
Awareness/Acquisition	Open rate Click-through links Email forwards Data submission Number of new contacts in CI	Registrations Attendees Evaluation (postevent report)	Unique visitors/page New visitors/page Data submission Bounce rate Subscribe to newsletter/RSS Click on CTA or download (podcast/vod/whitepaper/case study/webcast link)	Number of impressions on external site Number of clicks Data submission on banner or landing page Bounce rate on landing page Follow up on landing page CTA (download/data submission) Unique visitors to campaign landing page (new/returning)	Attendees Total registrations from all sources	Response call/text back/email/click through to site Data submission Bounce rate	Inbound calls to call center from trackable source	Response call/text back/email/click through to site

TABLE 4.1　The ebocube Commercial Cycle Metrics Matrix

Stage in ebocube commercial cycle	Email	Webcast	Site/Parent/Campaign Landing Page	External Web Banners and Social Network	Offline Events	Direct Mail	Telemarketing	Print/TV/Outdoor
	Data submission	Registrations	Click on CTA or download (podcast/vod/whitepaper/case study/webcast link)	Click on CTA or download (podcast/vod/whitepaper/case study/webcast link)	Registrations	Number of lead candidates from response channels	Number of outbound calls	Number of lead candidates from response channels
		Attendees	Click to chat	Click to chat	Attendees	Data submission	Number of leads generated	
	Open rate	Data submission, with BANT	Return visitors based on cookies	Data submission			Number of inbound calls to center	
		Evaluation (postevent report)	Data submission	Lead candidates/leads			Lead candidates sent to call center	
Consideration/ Nurture and Develop	Click-through links	Registrations	Lead candidates/leads	Number of impressions on external site			Lead candidates closed	
			Bounce rate	Unique visitors/page			Total leads	
			Data submission	New visitors/page			Number of open lead candidates	
			Unique visitors/page	Data submission				
			New visitors/page	Bounce rate				

TABLE 4.1 The ebocube Commercial Cycle Metrics Matrix

Stage in ebocube commercial cycle	Email	Webcast	Site/Parent/Campaign Landing Page	External Web Banners and Social Network	Offline Events	Direct Mail	Telemarketing	Print/TV/Outdoor
Purchase/Develop	Data submission Lead candidates °Leads/Sales Open rate Click-through links	Data submission, with BANT Leads Lead candidates Registrations Evaluation (postevent report)	Sale, e-commerce Data submission	Sales Lead candidates collected through banner or site converted into sales	Sale Lead conversions Registrations Attendees	Sales captured from response channels Lead conversions from response channels	Conversion of lead candidates to sales	Sales captured from response channels Lead conversions from response channels
Loyalty/Retention	Click-through special offers Entering loyalty codes Open rates °Leads/cross-sell, up-sell	Registrations Attendees Evaluation (postevent report) Lead candidates °Leads/cross-sell, up-sell	Customer portal login usage Return customers to site Unique visitors/page New visitors/page Data submission	Click through for customer offers plus follow up	Customer registrations Customer attendees Up-sell/cross-sell		Number of up-sell/cross-sell	Log in to customer portal/calls to account managers or call center

° Leads can be generated by emails or webcasts (or targeted purchase/development/loyalty communications using data-capture forms with BANT questions or call to action to contact sales), capturing BANT through a data-capture form or providing a call to action to call a sales/account manager. Leads can be converted into sales by your sales force. Some mar-

Because fundamental decisions about EM are informed through the dashboard reports, it is essential to determine, before starting dashboard design, the sources of data that will feed it, and the ownership and quality of the data to be used. Make sure they are reliable and updated regularly to get the most up-to-date and reliable picture.

The design should be user friendly and intuitive. The ebocube dashboard should function for the user in the same way that a pilot's dashboard functions. You want data that is quick, easy to read, and of course, meaningful.

Table 4.1 shows units to be measured in an ebocube dashboard. Designing your ebocube dashboard will take time, as you think of the reliable sources to feed it, the fields you want to see, the process to feed it. The latter is a project alone and requires planning. This is why we have linked it to the ebocube commercial cycle. Taking time to do this upfront will ensure that you're campaigns can be continuously improved as your strategy grows in an EM. It will enable you to cut costs over time and invest in the best options and define your mops processes and planning in phase two.

Over time, you will develop internal global benchmarks that will allow you to compare results for various communications and campaigns and with competitors and industry benchmarks available from whitepapers and external sources, these results should help you to create case study material! Your dashboard is also likely to evolve with time as you become clearer on what you need or want to see, present internally, in the form of metrics and as you leverage new communication media.

The Datacube

The datacube is one view of the ebocube dashboard providing information on your contact and company database, which will inform marketers on data availability during campaign planning. It doesn't do any good to assume you have data and invest in a campaign, only to find out you do not. You might design for data coverage of how many contacts or company records you have for the amount of available companies in a market, as well as marketing history or the transactional information for your customer. This can help you to define your most profitable segments, loyal segment (based on RFM [recency, frequency, monetary] scoring), or companies in EMs.

The datacube enables you to "see" your data for EMs, whether contactable or not. It is a representation of the state of your data. To improve your data in EMs, you should have some understanding of your data warehouse and some of the processes running in the background, because ebocube is based on electronic customer relation management. We explain more about your data warehouse in the next chapter.

The datacube is typically presented in a tabular format or graphs and can be split by many variables, such as countries, region, or company size, industry you should be able to filter your report. Because the ebocube is developed for business-to-business (B2B) marketing, your datacube report will need to cover company, site information, and contact data. Although you might target and sell products to companies, you need to consider how you will communicate to contacts in those companies. Therefore, you need to analyze two views or levels in your datacube. First, you need to start with the higher-level view at the company level (firmographics), and then filter or "drill down" to the contact level. This will help you to determine how many contacts are available for your target market. Company data should be linked to contact data. Contact numbers in selected companies will help determine if you can communicate to targeted companies using direct marketing communications. The fact that you have some contacts or companies in your database doesn't mean that you can communicate. For example, you may have HSBC Bank as a company in your database (CI), but you may have zero contactable contacts within this company, either because emails are invalid (i.e., wrong format), phone numbers are missing digits, or you don't have permission to contact them (opt-in) and therefore they are uncontactable. The datacube should highlight these issues. Rules for validating contactability information should be defined.

Not all contacts in your database will link to a company. This could be because a contact reports wrong data, and you cannot match it to an existing company in your database. You should try to enrich the contact data, perhaps by emailing them and asking for further information, or by updating a profile page (known as a subscription center), when contact update information on themselves and permissions.

With the datacube, as with any other dashboard, you shouldn't be overwhelmed with metrics, so this report should be based on marketer needs, and primary metrics should be around data inventory numbers for your target audience. The datacube may also show metrics that represent the health of your database CI, which should be reviewed periodically. Health metrics may include the increase in the number of company records, number of contacts linked to companies, number of phonable/emailable contacts, number of new contact records, and so on.

Firmographics

You're probably familiar with the consumer term *demographics*; it applies to our private lives and to the consumer segment. Demographics present numbers and information about customers and the consumer's home. This information may include the number of children and pets, people living in the home and people working outside the home, their annual income, and annual spending. It can be as detailed as to the number of cars, computers, and soap purchases. This helps consumer marketers target various segments with offers relevant to the household throughout the family life cycle. For example, a bank may sell home insurance to newlyweds, life insurance to parents, and pension packages to retired couples.

The same principle is applied to firmographic data, but instead of consumer information we gather information about business (e.g., the number of employees, annual income, industry expenditures, number of office/branches, size of car fleet, number of credit cards, and mobile phones per company).

The company-level datacube should present attributes about companies that you are aiming to target with your campaigns. Depending on your proposition, the firmographic will differ. You might need to know what the company size is, or you might want to see industry firmographics only. It depends on the product and proposition, but typically you would like to see the split between headquarters and site level, which are subsidiaries that roll up to headquarters. You could also enquire about account-managed companies and prospects. Account-managed companies are businesses that have a relationship with an account manager in your company. A site is a standalone office and can be part of a bigger company, or an enterprise may have several sites, whereas a small business may have one office.

Your company-level datacube should show data completeness for companies in your database, identifying gaps and challenges. This may be represented in graphs or tables and may contain information such as the following:

- ZIP code/postal address and company location
- Number of employees, divided in standardized size as large enterprise (1,000 > employees), medium enterprise (500–999), midmarket (250–499), SMB (20–249 employees), and small office home office (1–19)
- Standard industry code (SIC) or the sector the company is in
- Specific sites or departments that operate in an area

For example, if you're targeting the financial and banking industry in Russia, you need to know whether you're targeting the head office, a call center site (customer support), an operational site, or a retail branch. This will help you to define which site you should target. Although online marketing costs significantly less and is more environmentally friendly than offline, you shouldn't waste your marketing effort or target sites anywhere that will generate poor responses.

In developed economies, data brokers such as Dun & Bradstreet will provide this information. However, it's still a challenge to get this information for EMs because these markets are so new and data-reporting methods may not exist or may have been very recently established. For example in the United Kingdom, companies are registered after they are established, but this may not be the case in EMs. The critical mass for this data has not typically existed in EMs due to economics or technology availability. The ebocube can help you acquire data through online media and offline by driving respondents to the web or other CTAs. However, organically growing your own database is a lengthier process as opposed to buying a bulk of existing data, although growing your own database can be better for customer relationship management. Emailing a contact from a newly acquired list may seem out of the blue for them, even if they have subscribed for "third-party email." However, if you have grown your database organically, contacts are likely to be more receptive to messaging. All this can be tested through ebocube.

It's important to analyze the data you hold on companies in these markets, because this will help you to assess which companies you can successfully consider marketing to. You need to target contacts, however, and so you must drill down to contact level to assess whom you can communicate with and who can make the purchasing decisions. Your datacube should have filters.

Contact Level

If you're a marketing communications manager, campaigns manager, or marketing professional, you will be managing countless communications going out on behalf of your company, and you will need to drill down to the view of the contact level in the datacube. This view will give you an instant and quick understanding of your available marketable audience. The contact-level datacube will become your best friend and is the first step to creating your campaign plan. Checking company records in your datacube is the prior level you need to look at the granular level of contact.

We underscore that the most important strategic focus in B2B is targeting. We have seen over and over again in our frontline experience that many campaigns had to be rebooted because the creative was developed before anyone had run data queries on the target customers. Every word and aspect of ad copy needs to be localized and implemented into the culture, and that means data-research requests need to be the first, not the last step in the campaign process. Can you imagine spending money on a campaign and then finding out that the data showed the target audience number was fewer than a 100 contacts? Spend time acquiring relevant contacts before you waste resource and budget.

Bear in mind that campaigns you use in developed markets might not be replicable in an EM, which means you will need to budget for new campaigns. To avoid wasting budget, refer to your datacube before taking other action on any campaign. Although there will be elements where you do not use your database (for example, placing web banners on sites), ultimately you must communicate directly to your contacts to move them along the ebocube commercial cycle.

Datacube Optimization

The datacube can be expanded to represent company-level data and contact-level data. However, if you do expand the datacube, you don't want to be overwhelmed with too many fields. Regardless, if you drill down to contact level or look at company level alone, you should keep your datacube layout clean and simple. Your query filters used to drill down on the datacube should be as simple as possible but at the same time give you a meaningful overview on your data availability, allowing you to "roll up" to firmographic/company information/industry/country or drill down to contact and communication channels. You should see every single metric at each of these levels; otherwise, it's inefficiently designed and usability is poor. It should aid decision-making, not hinder.

It's important that all stakeholders in the business understand the benefits of the operational tools and the ebocube dashboard. To achieve full buy-in from senior management as well as buy-in from sales, distribution, or service partners, every stakeholder should be briefed and sign on to ebocube reports and tracking. There is likely to be an element of change management, and you can even go so far as to tie reporting (as well as training and education) into compensation.

It is important to build the IT process to support the model and operations. Imagine trying to execute and report on global marketing and sales activities without the ebocube automated dashboards. It would be tough if not impossible to learn and show accountability for marketing and financial results for these new markets without it.

What Next?

Have your database analyst or vendor provide you with the following attributes for your datacube contact report for selected countries in an EM:

- Company name
- First name, last name
- Email address
- Job title
- Permissions opt in, opt out
- Communication preferences
- Communication channel completeness (e.g., have you captured their email, telephone, mail address?)
- Number of valid email addresses, phone numbers, postal addresses
- Communication language preference

You might have thousands of contact records, but perhaps only a small percentage have email addresses or phone numbers. At this point, you must determine whether your communication plan is realistic and whether you can execute the plan based on contactable records. Maybe you need to take some further action (like data cleansing or data acquisition) before achieving your specified aims in the ebocube commercial cycle.

5

Managing Customer Relationships Through the Buying Cycle

Upon completion of this chapter, you should be able to

- Describe the campaigns process (phase two of ebocube)
- Understand the contact journey through the data life cycle
- Explain how to acquire a contact in EM in the most effective and efficient way using online and offline media and identifying the benefits of both "homegrown" data and purchasing data in EM
- Identify your RFM segment, the high-value segment of your database, and understand how to develop opportunities that will increase further growth for your company
- Understand how to integrate communications to the contact journey and move contacts along the ebocube commercial cycle

Welcome to phase two of ebocube (see Figure 5.1). This phase is the next step in the model. After analyzing your dashboards, including the datacube, you will have the necessary information to start working on your winning campaigns and CRM in EM.

We are all familiar with the term *campaign*; campaigns are everywhere—in the media for political races, to raise money for charity, or to raise awareness for issues such as the environment or health. All businesses and organizations depend on marketing campaigns to make people aware of their products and services and to generate sales leads.

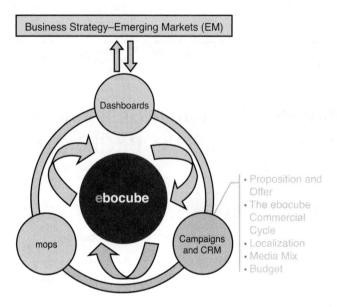

Figure 5.1   The ebocube model (phase two: campaigns and CRM)

While business and technology use campaigns extensively, the term itself derives from the military. Its comes from the Roman word for armies (*campania*), and originally meant a military operation intended to achieve a specific objective in a specific time frame.[1] The term became popular in American business in the early 1950s when advertisers developed marketing campaigns for television. Campaigns expanded into newspaper, radio, and outdoor venues such as roadside billboards. Now websites and Internet search engines rely on campaigns to inform global users.

Like a military campaign, a marketing campaign is composed of a sequence of integrated granular steps. These steps include analysis, planning, strategy, and operations. You need a clear strategy with well-defined measurable objectives and goals. You need to analyze your situation to ensure that your plan is realistic before you execute it. All campaigns need strategy. You have to be aggressive and willing to "attack" the marketplace more effectively than your enemy (i.e., competitor). Many factors will determine the success of your campaigns, and it's important to analyze them all carefully.

Planning a campaign requires focus. You cannot plan or create successful marketing campaigns in distracting environments in the office. Effective marketing campaigns need to be well researched, well thought out, and executed with precision. You start from the top to understand your position in the market and finish with the granular aspects of the campaign, such as copy for email blasts. The plan is your blueprint, and just like a house, your campaign has to be built on a strong foundation. Execution is as important as planning; a great strategy is of little value if it cannot be executed. Your campaign should be conducted in a friendly, creative, and focused environment free of interruptions.

The ebocube model, as with all tools, can work for you, but only if you plan, manage, and leverage its features. This is how productivity is improved and new business models created.

Marketers face challenges on a daily basis. Clients often ask us, "How can we design and create fantastic marketing campaigns and approach customers or prospects with better, more creative messages?" In this environment, reliable data is key for business-to-business (B2B) campaigns, where highly targeted, direct marketing is an effective medium to communicate. This should be the starting point for your campaigns. If you want to achieve high responses online and offline, it is imperative that you understand your data. As mentioned in the preceding chapter, the datacube will provide all the necessary visibility on information for you to establish a contact strategy and campaign plan for your strategy. First ask, "Whom should we contact in the emerging market (EM)?" The *how* comes later.

Contact and Campaign Planning

You might only be interested in one view of the datacube. For example, if you are launching a campaign to one targeted account or company, with many contacts, and you want to contact all contacts within that account, your datacube should represent the data for that segment.

If you are launching products or solutions that target a specific segment, such as financial managers, regardless of the company's size, location, headquarters, or branch site, you will choose the contact-level view. You should be able to drill down to this level as well as roll up to the company-level view to see which company the contact is associated to.

All campaigns should be data driven. You need to acquire contacts to convert into prospective customers. You also need to gain and retain loyalty from current customers and must customize your campaign for them. You cannot communicate to a loyal, long-standing customer the same way you would to a completely new contact and company. As explained in the following section, the data life cycle helps you to define data aims and to enhance the business relationship with customers and prospects.

The Data Life Cycle

The data life cycle will define communication goals targeting the customer or prospect. Marketers can sometimes create messages and creative materials, and then look for contacts to reach. We've seen this before and this rarely works. First, know how to microtarget contacts, with one-to-one communications, within their organizations. The ebocube commercial cycle helps you organize communications in line with a contact strategy.

Figure 5.2 represents the data stages a contact passes through in customer relationship management. Initially the contact is acquired in your database, whether that's through online or offline acquisition. An example of the former might be data submission on your website; the latter data submission at an offline event. The acquisition could be of a contact from a prospective customer or a contact for an existing company/account.

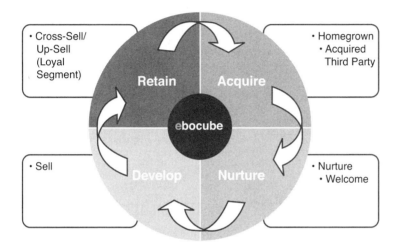

Figure 5.2   The ebocube data life cycle

Once contacts are acquired, they become a segment of data that needs to be nurtured/developed. After receiving consideration, they can be considered contacts who are in the "ready to purchase segment." At this stage, you may pass the contact to sales to communicate. There are advanced data analysis techniques to help you identify loyal customers. We discuss RFM modeling (recency, frequency, and monetary value). Contacts who are customers that buy regularly, have recently purchased, and whose sales are high in monetary value can be identified in your database. The communications you use for this segment will elicit up-sells and cross-sells—this is your loyal segment, those who already have a relationship with you, are loyal to you, and will provide you with more revenue, based on historical behavior.

Your contact strategy should be sequential. You should manage your relationships with the contact from acquisition through to the nurture, development, and retention. This flow helps define your communication plan, including any incentives and media. You communicate differently with a newly acquired contact than you do with your most profitable, loyal segment. The data life cycle helps you to define communication objectives around the contact.

In this chapter, we explain best practices for communication for all four steps of the data life cycle. We link the communication cycle to the data cycle. We show you how data objectives support your communications objectives, and guide you through this part of the communication cycle.

The datacube provides you with visibility on data you in your database. You don't need to extract the data yourself unless you're a small business. In some cases, your vendor or database analyst from your in-house team may provide your datacube with a simplified, standardized, and user-friendly format. Remember to "see" your marketing strategy from the customer's point of view!

How to Get Your Data in an Emerging Market

Acquisition is the process of obtaining contact and company data. Acquisition doesn't always mean that you need to purchase a list because you can capture data through campaigns or grow your own "homegrown" list. For example, you can run an integrated online campaign using web banners, press advertisements, and radio that directs people to a website where you can then capture data in an EM; or you can capture contact data through meeting and public events.

Through data acquisition, you can build customer records and gain new contacts in existing customer accounts. You are working to gain new customers or prospects to secure you a competitive advantage in an EM where high-quality data is still scarce. Depending on the type of campaign, even existing customers may be treated as a prospect. It's all about raising awareness. Whether you want to gain a greater foothold and increasing breadth in an account by penetrating new contacts or learning more about your customers by gathering information on them, it all starts with good data.

You might get a quicker return on your money if you purchase a permission-based contact list from any number of third-party vendors for EMs, instead of creating an integrated campaign to acquire "homegrown" data. If you have a large budget, it's good to do both. When we refer to "homegrown" data, we mean data that is organically captured by your company. This data can be captured through a point of contact through your website, attendee lists gathered through online or offline events, phone inquiries, and online social networks. Online capture can be a low-cost way to acquire data. When you capture the data yourself, it's also your own, not leased from another enterprise. Remember, you are not just collecting customer information; you are building lists of prospects.

To engage contacts and have them be more receptive to your communications, you should construct your data-collection method so that they can voluntarily opt in to your specific organization's communications, stating their preference (i.e., what they want to hear more about, whether that's specific product or service line and how—via email, webcasts, offline events, calls). Of course, collecting opt in to email is a legal and mandatory requirement. This is another benefit of homegrown data. Third-party lists may have contacts that have opted in to their communications and third-party emails, but these same contacts might not expect a message from your company. Therefore, temper your initial outreach with an explanation and offer an immediate opt out.

Always maintain and use the data you have, instead of rushing to purchase more contact data. Renting from a third-party is an efficient short-term strategy. It creates an immediate audience and serves as a supplement to your own contact database. Long term, it is important to build an in-house customer database, capturing contact data from sales meetings, events, and your own campaigns, to start to develop highly targeted campaigns based on marketing history. Also, even if you purchase a list for a new market, when you email the list, invite contacts to correct mistakes. When you purchase lists for an EM, you cannot assume that the quality is reliable. You might also need to find out more about your contact to enable your company to communicate more effectively.

After you have the data, you can use it to develop EM contacts. You'll need to scrub your lists. You're likely to find duplicates when purchasing from different data brokers, and the quality of lists might not be the same. Just because you've purchased a list doesn't mean you are done. You must analyze the data to verify what you have been given is reliable/valid. When gathering data through campaigns, you're also relying on self-reported data by contacts, which can result in poor-quality information. Your data capture should have validation rules. You might request that an email address, submitted by a data-capture form, be entered twice for accuracy, or send an automated email to recipients asking them to confirm their address. We have shown you how the *acquisition, awareness, and buying stages* are linked and sequential, and served by the ebocube commercial cycle (see Chapter 3, "The ebocube and Business Models"). An awareness campaign should focus its objective on being wide reaching and attention grabbing. This will allow you to obtain data from contacts who haven't heard of your company/products/services, update current customer data records with new information, and gather new contacts from a customer account. This approach will help you expand your market and sell your products.

Homegrown Data

As your business is operating, you will notice organic development of your own database through your marketing activities or because of the ongoing communication channels such as your website. As customer data is being uploaded to the system, this will form your homegrown database. Your ultimate goal is to get data into one location within your organization. Your aim is to obtain high-quality customer insight. It is possible to gather reliable data as long as you're maintaining your website, keeping the data-capture form turned on, and running integrated campaigns.

Growing your own database involves capturing contact information and company information. Some of the values are listed here. When you build your homegrown database, you need to start your data collection from scratch or build on your existing database. You might want to run an awareness campaign to do this. (Refer to the ebocube commercial cycle.)

Company information:

- ZIP code/postal address
- Number of employees/company size
- Standard industry code (SIC)/Industry
- Site departments
- Company shared email box (for example, consultant@ebocube.com)
- Contact level:

  First name, last name
  Email address
  Cell number
  Phone number
  Job title
  Permissions opt in, opt out
  Communication preferences

You can acquire data from EMs in several ways. We have divided all homegrown data-acquisition strategies into two categories: offline or online.

Online or Digital Methods of Data Capture

This involves all online activities that enable data capture of contact and company information; for example, website (including links posted on social/business network sites, directing users to data capture forms), online banners, webcasts (online events), and email responses to sur-vey/submission forms.

Offline Methods of Data Capture

Through offline activities, you can drive traffic back to the Inter-net or through data networks (e.g., mobile SMS responses to short codes). You can gather contact and company information via online data-capture forms, short codes, or manual uploads of data caught through events. RFID (radio-frequency identification) and bar-coding are other ways to capture data at event entry; these methods reduce manual work and improves data-capture efficiency and quality. Print media, radio, TV, billboards, and live-event sponsorship should be used for data capture, either by promoting URLs leading to landing pages with data-capture forms or through onsite data-capture tools. Attendees should be encouraged to register before the event online. Then ask attendees to bring their registration badges with barcodes, which event staff should be able to scan, allowing you to identify whether a registrant has attended. Both methods allow for accurate data capture.

Online Acquisition

You need to consider two factors for online data acquisition during an EM campaign: the data-capture form and the incentive. By "incen-tive," we mean an offer to persuade contacts to part with their infor-mation, whether that's a free gadget or educational whitepaper. (It's good to test which type of offer increases the data-submission rate.) Contacts always think, "What's in it for me?" and won't take time to submit their information if there is no value in it for them. The golden rule in media is to localize with an appealing offer or incentive, cap-ture the data, and then provide the offer (see Figure 5.3)! It's like fish-ing: If you use good tasty bait, you'll reel in the fish; just please don't confuse this with phishing!

Figure 5.3 The golden rule in media and data capture

Offer

The offer or incentive is what you give away free of charge and must offer value to the contact. Different types of offers include literature, whitepapers, trials, and registration for offline and online (webcast) events. Subscriptions work well, too (for example, subscriptions to newsletters). Some EM customers respond to gadgets such as mobile phones, cameras, or USB keys. Ensure your offer is localized, attractive, and doesn't offend the local culture. (For example, don't offer a bottle of wine in the MEA region.)

When you capture any data, preplan what you expect to do with that data, how you intend to follow up, and how to nurture a contact. This should follow the ebocube commercial cycle by taking the contact through to the awareness stage, further acquisition of data, nurture, and development, For example, if you capture data though a web banner campaign, you might use the data for an awareness follow-up email, and then the respondents may be pushed through to development nurture. Always keep in mind not only the contact journey but also the ultimate goal for your organization.

Data-Capture Form

Set up the data-capture form with standardized fields that match the fields you use for your data warehouse questions:

- Don't collect data that can't be stored or extracted and used for future campaigns.
- Remember this adage: Garbage in, garbage out! Don't collect data poorly; otherwise, what you extract from the database will be poor. This is key, particularly in EMs where good-quality

data is challenging to purchase. Anything you collect and store should be of high quality.

- You shouldn't bore the contact with a long data-capture form. However, if you do not request enough information, you might not be able to match the record to a company that may already exist in your system.

- Your form should collect opt-in permissions. (For example, to email contacts, they need to agree to receive your email.) It's also a good idea to capture preferences. For example, allow the contact to subscribe to certain communication on various products or topics. Remember, contacts should be clearly aware that they are opting in. It is important to watch your opt-in rate. If contacts feel deceived into opting in, they'll not only opt out, it can damage your reputation.

- Validate data before final submission. You don't need to validate all details, but contact data should be accurate. When a contact enters an email address twice, make sure the two entries match before saving it to your database. You can also validate data after submission, by sending an email to the contact's address before it reaches the database and asking the contact to confirm his or her details by clicking a link. You can choose from among several methods to validate data before it enters your data warehouse. We've also seen data forms requesting company website, and this can be one method of matching a contact to a company. Do not provide the offer before data is submitted (if the nature of the offer allows for immediate download, e.g. whitepaper). Remember: media $\Rightarrow$ data capture $\Rightarrow$ offer.

- Keep it simple. A survey that's too long and not localized is likely to drive users away. At an awareness stage, you ideally want to start with the minimal company and contact data. As you develop the contact, you will need to understand more and start to request lead questions. You can measure whether contacts click your link but don't leave data. Try to figure out why they are not responding—running a test communication will help you understand.

- Ideally, the data-capture form should feed your customer insight (CI) database automatically without manual intervention.

Websites, Microsites, and Campaign Landing Pages

To boost acquisition data via your website in EMs, you might use an offer on your site and a data-capture form. (For example, by giving something away, you can encourage end users to give you their personal information.)

You will ensure you attract viewers by offering engaging, creative, and localized content on your website, web page, or microsites. You also should give them an engaging incentive accessible only after the data-capture form has been submitted. Encourage every single unique visitor to submit a form. Web analytics tools will report on your web traffic, and should feed your ebocube dashboard. The data-cube shows only what you have in your database, but the view can be divided by source of contacts, such as live events versus a website. You can't really do anything with this great traffic coming to your web pages until you gather their contact information.

High traffic doesn't equal quantifiable value. Your efforts are largely wasted in the fast-growth EMs if you can't capture contacts. Don't use the old excuse, "We've generated awareness." This is true, but awareness should link to value, sales. Otherwise, marketing will not be respected as a discipline and your budget will get cut!

In other words, you might know that this month you had 10,000 unique visitors to your .com website. Can you follow up with any communications related to your offers and news if you don't have the visitors' email address or contact details? You know the country that they come from, the time they visited your web, the time they spent on your website, where they came from and where they went after, but that means little if you can't communicate with them, although the information will help you to optimize your site to improve the user journey and improve data submission. Make sure your website has a data-capture form with many links to it—i.e., on the top pages of your site so that you can gather significant information, contact information that enables you to push them further along the ebocube commercial cycle to nurture and development steps. As part of your campaigns, give the end user the option to subscribe to a localized whitepaper. You can also put an example of your newsletter on the site. An offer makes people want to register, give their contact details, and go through to the next step. After all, people in EM businesses are as eager to learn as you are.

Online Live Chat and Survey

We also recommend experimenting with live chat on your website, supported by call center agents or a sales force. This form of interaction will also allow you to collect data in real time. It's a "contact us" method. It can be set up so that visitors can talk live in real time, or visitors to your site can leave their details on a survey for a follow up call. If you use live chat and data capture, ensure that your team is responsive in real time or makes the follow-up call.

Online chat is a good way to speak to existing and new customers. It doesn't necessarily belong with your integrated campaign plan. It can serve as an ongoing tool you put on your site to capture data and leads. It can also be used for service purposes.

You can adopt behavioral targeting to understand business users' interests. By anonymously observing user behavior through "cookies" over a period of time, your company can gain a deeper understanding of a visitor's needs and online tendencies and therefore deliver relevant and timely content related to what they have searched. For example, user x returns to page y three times in one week. Your company makes reference to their search criteria and presents a pop-up online chat box (because you recognize they are a potential sales lead because they have demonstrated interest). At this point, the customer has accepted the request for live chat, and you should capture information. You might capture the most minimum data (e.g., first name, last name, and email address). That minimum data allows you to follow up with your prospects and to update your contact database. The result is that you take people from a search consideration into the next step of purchase.

You might also allow people to click on to an online chat option regardless of their search behavior so that they can instant message an agent or sales representative. Under this scenario, you should also capture data. The first scenario is based on monitoring behavior of people who are likely to buy based on previous behavior and may generate higher-quality leads rather than inquiries, which is probable for the latter.

Online Banners

You can also capture data through web banners on third-party sites or your own sites, also using data-capture forms, and again you need a good relevant offer to get information in return. If your banner then redirects to a landing page, optimize the page to retain traffic and to get the data. Before any data is captured, you need to plan follow-up communication.

Email Data

You might have a customer or prospect data in your database from which you need more information or further acquisition. You might send them an awareness email as part of a campaign and acquire more information about them through a data-capture form.

Live Event/Sponsorship Press/Radio/TV/Billboard

Because of its high cost and broad targeting, offline activities such as sponsorship, radio, and TV are secondary choices of communication in B2B marketing as a source of lead generation. Events can be slightly more targeted, and sometimes physical events are preferred in certain EM nations to virtual events, because people like one-to-one relationships. But you should only stage live events for data capture if you can justify return on investment, or if the event is integrated with other sources of communication with a specific objective in mind. Encourage end users to submit data at the event, perhaps through online registration or attendee registration. Regardless of the method, just make sure you acquire data. For other media (e.g., sponsorship, radio, TV, billboard), where you encourage an online/digital or telephone call to action, provide an incentive, perhaps a whitepaper on a website, which can be sent via email, which is also an opportunity to collect and verify email addresses.

For press, radio, TV, or billboard, you might provide a vanity URL to the website, landing page, or microsite, where contacts can get their incentive by leaving contact information. You should use individual vanity URLs per each media source, and track which form of media delivers the best, most valuable data.

Third-Party Data Acquisition

Homegrown database collection is cost-effective, but it's time-consuming to build. By acquiring third-party lists through a data broker or partners, you can get immediate results, growing your database quickly in a particular EM. In some specific circumstances, you will be under pressure to get an opted-in data list quicker than the time that it would take to build an organic homegrown list. Under these circumstances, you will need to rent or purchase a list to be able to launch your campaign.

It's more challenging to find good-quality lists in an EM nation than it is in developed economies. As of this writing, we have found that you will need more than one agency in an EM nation—but that trend is most likely changing. Do your research before contracting with any agency.

Talk to specialist data agencies you can learn about by visiting the region. Ask your partners or local agencies for recommendations or search online. Spend time researching good brokers. Remember, just because a list broker provides good data for Romania, they might not provide the best data for Poland.

Local list brokers sometimes provide better data than global or worldwide suppliers. These smaller agencies are usually based in the country or EM, and you will need to source them locally because they might not be known or promoted in developed markets. Try to negotiate for a sample, and test the value of the data. You can test a sample list by doing the following:

- Matching a sample list to your existing database to see whether their information duplicates what you have in your own database. If you notice too many duplicates, you might decide not to purchase the full list.
- Checking to see whether contacts are repeated in different lists from different brokers.
- Testing email samples for bounce-backs.
- Calling contact numbers to verify contact is valid.
- Researching the cost of local agencies and comparing price versus difficulty of managing the relationship, especially with regard to employing people who speak the language and understand the culture.

You shouldn't buy new contact lists for every campaign; you should review the marketing datacube to see what prospects or customer data you already have that can be modified or expanded and develop those relationships based on marketing and transactional history.

Quality of Acquired Data

The quality and cost of data will vary depending on the sources. Table 5.1 shows the relationship between quality versus price for acquiring data in EMs.

TABLE 5.1   Quality Versus Price: Data Acquisition in EMs

		Quality	
	High	**Medium**	**Low**
Price High	Call center, partner data, offline event, data gained through multinational relationships.	Trusted and well-recognized data broker in EM. Request data sample to match to home database and to test.	New unrecognized data broker in EM. No guarantee; no recognized industry standards, no customer case studies. Request data sample to match to home database and to test.
Low	Homegrown data captured through highly targeted online campaigns, or websites. Self-reported data - online; e.g., validation of the data.	Account managers/sales updating databases.	Publicly available data, government lists, public directories.

High-High

Phone numbers and email addresses acquired should be accurate, and valid, the contact recent, and all the information confirmed. However, keeping this information up-to-date and verified by a call center agent is more expensive to maintain. The time required to capture this information in-house and through your website should be compared to third-party costs.

Low-Low

Relying on self-reported data by contacts might not be as high quality or as thorough as information cleared by a call center, because end users might just fill in forms for the incentive or may give inaccurate information. You should aim to reduce this by targeting audiences with relevant content over time. For example, they might claim they work for a multinational company when in fact it is a mid-size or local enterprise. Try to make your questions as clear as possible and validate the information given as much as your resources allow. If the country requires, use data-capture forms in local language, to increase data submission and quality. (You need to be able to store in your marketing database any data captured in a local language.)

Medium Quality-Low Price

You might notice we put sales/account manager reported data in this field. Although you might expect this to be highly accurate, in our experience salespeople do not always understand how to maintain or use the tools to update their database, although this might be different for your organization.

Nurturing Prospects

Nurture is the next step in the ebocube data life cycle (see Figure 5.4). This step addresses how to identify and manage the potential customers, or existing customers ready for the nurture step of your campaigns. Contacts that you can migrate to the nurture stage include newly acquired contacts, or contacts new to your marketing or sales relationship, or respondents to a new campaign. Nurturing a contact includes the following:

- Making them feel welcome by building and maintaining a dialogue with the prospect to convert them into a future customer or repeat customer.
- Following up with prospective warm leads that may not have been quite ready to make a purchase, and were disqualified as sales leads previously. To nurture communications, make sure they have the latest news about your organization through localized e-newsletters and webcasts.
- Gathering more information about the contacts and their preferences.

This is linked to the consideration stage in the ebocube commercial cycle; the aim is to increase consideration of purchasing your service, goods, or products in the contact's mind and to ensure your brand is at the top of their minds.

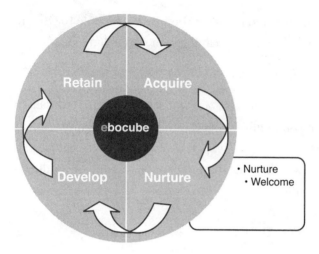

Figure 5.4   The ebocube data life cycle: nurture stage

Developing Customers and Prospects

Figure 5.5 shows this stage, which involves attempting to convert prospects into leads or up-selling and cross-selling to customers. The campaign should focus on eliciting a purchase. This data should solely focus on lead generation communications as part of your campaign. By now, contacts should already be prepared to receive and understand lead-generation communication. (Lead-generation campaigns shouldn't be communicated to new contacts who have not yet reached the nurture step.)

Retaining Customers

Figure 5.6 shows the final phase in the ebocube data life cycle, which is focused on retaining and building loyalty of existing customers. This phase is informed by a recency, frequency, and monetary (RFM) scoring model.

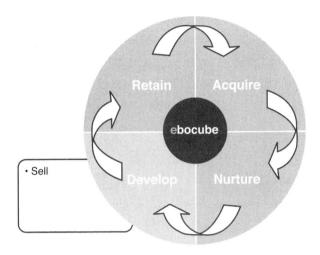

Figure 5.5 The ebocube data life cycle: develop stage

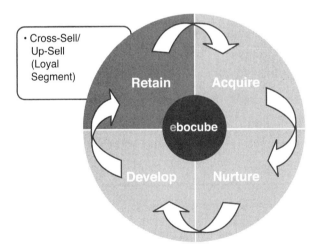

Figure 5.6 The ebocube data life cycle: retain stage

RFM Scoring

This data should be treated differently from other segments of data collected by your organization and should not be sent communications such as mass emails. Focus on the loyalty campaigns for this segment. You might damage your reputation if you contact a person about a product that he already knows about (and perhaps has already spent thousands of dollars on), and yet he still gets information about your campaign with a generic awareness message.

You should examine each element of RFM, as follows:

- **Recency:** The time between the date of the last database update and the date of a customer's last purchase
- **Frequency:** The average number of purchases per year made by a customer
- **Monetary:** The total amount associated with all the purchases made by a customer

The aim of RFM is to identify opportunities by looking at customers who are high value scored against recency of purchase, frequency, and monetary value (see Figure 5.7). RFM value scores are calculated for each customer based on the customer's entire purchase history.

Each customer is ranked from high to low for each of the three scores. Figure 5.7 shows the three variables and how a contact may be ranked per each—this enables you to create deciles, or rank customers into groups according to "loyalty" or value.

Once you have your RFM analyses from either an in-house database team or external vendor, you can segment your customers into four quartiles in the recency-monetary value grid (see Figure 5.8).

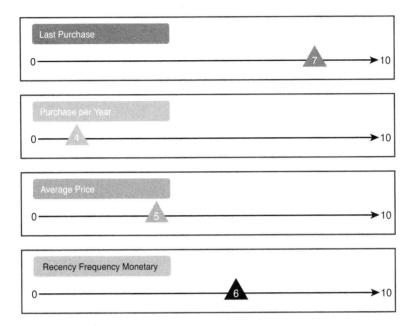

Figure 5.7   RFM deciles

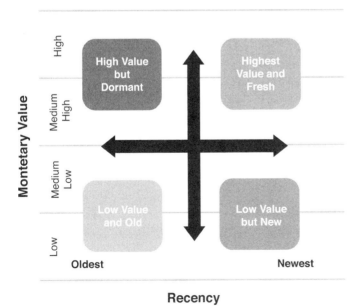

Figure 5.8   Recency-monetary value grid

Customer Calculations

The objective of RFM is to determine which segment will continue to generate high profits in terms of sales for your company and should be treated differently in terms of marketing efforts/communications/messages.

Customers who have purchased recently or who made more purchases than other customers and of higher value are worth maintaining strong relationships with through marketing and sales initiatives. Potentially losing these customers could significantly impact the bottom line for your company.

RFM analysis can also highlight new customers who need to be further developed to become loyal customers, who can be nurtured, or who simply need to be welcomed if they're completely new. This exercise can also identify customers who haven't upgraded for several years and may have "lapsed"—i.e., gone to the competitor—or customers whose purchases tend to be low value although frequent. There are different marketing strategies, communications, channels, and programs that can be used for each of the quartiles/segments:

- RFM value scores are calculated for each customer based on the customer's entire purchase history.
- Each customer is ranked from high to low for each of the three scores. Based on the ranking, customers are assigned to a quartile for each of the scores. The top 25% receive a score of 1, and the bottom 25% a score of 4. A score of 1 indicates the customer is ranked in the top quartile for that specific variable, and a score of 4 indicates the customer is ranked in the bottom quartile for that variable.
- Each customer is assigned a fourth, composite score, based on their RFM value quartiles. The highest composite score that a customer could receive is 1-1-1, and the lowest is 4-4-4.
- Finally, each quartile is subdivided into value ranges, depending on the actual distribution of the RFM scores. These subdivisions should be reevaluated periodically, preferably annually or semiannually.

The database field you use to create RFM scores should include the following:

- **Recency:**   The latest order date in database, which should be fed by invoice system or updated manually.
- **Frequency:**   The latest invoice date with revenue;
- **Monetary value:**   The annual monetary value to-date based on revenue per customer annually. (Your organization needs to establish how often to check these scores.)

Communicating with Loyal Customers to Increase Satisfaction

Campaigns should include highly targeted emails, one-to-one customer events, and high-value direct mail, plus rewards or incentives. Focus high-value direct mail and loyalty efforts on customers who generate revenue for your company, and direct high spending toward high-profit customers. Lower-value customers may be targeted with email or lower-value incentives.

Don't be confused by loyalty programs, such as frequent flyer programs, that enable businesses to track transactional behavior and award miles or points that can be exchanged for free flights, free calls, Christmas vouchers, and the like. The loyalty segment in your database is based on B2B marketing loyalty, which is slightly different from that which you experience as a consumer. Loyalty programs in B2B are targeted at high-value segments within EMs with the aim of increasing sales.

The biggest difference in the B2B world is that you as marketer define (based on your data base information) your loyal customer segment. Very often, this happens behind the scenes and without their involvement. To make sure your loyal segment of data is defined properly, work closely with your database team to analyze your own database, because the loyal segment might vary between specific campaigns. Campaigns are usually related to different products and solutions. Your loyal customer segment won't stay consistent with each campaign or proposition, unless you only have one product/service. Your committed customers should be predefined ahead of each loyalty campaign. You should have good contact details for them or a one-to-one relationship, so it's worth engaging with this group beyond just an email, although online methods are still effective, for example, highly targeted web conferences with video or TelePresence meetings, where perhaps your executives could meet theirs, virtually. The company may not have their own TelePresence suite; however, companies like Cisco are making public TelePresence rooms available to rent by the hour. Recently MTN Nigeria, part of the MTN Group, Africa's leading mobile telecommunications company,[2] launched public TelePresence rooms in Nigeria in three areas in collaboration with Cisco, which was a first for Nigeria! High-definition, virtual face-to-face meetings across the globe are no longer a future vision; they can exist today.

Buying Cycle

You collect data to plan how your campaign and communications will lead to a sale. Different phases in the purchase cycle move the customer to closing along the spectrum of prospect to purchase to repurchase. Figure 5.9 shows the readiness to buy model, which when merged with the data cycle forms the ebocube commercial cycle. These cycles will help you to plan phases of your localized campaign. Success can be measured through the datacube and the dashboard based on objectives that can be planned through the ebocube commercial cycle.

Awareness

For newly acquired contacts or for contacts who have had little exposure to your brand, products, or service, your first goal is to generate awareness (see Figure 5.10).

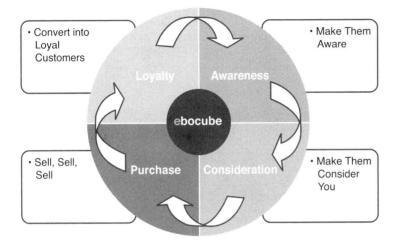

Figure 5.9   The ebocube buying cycle

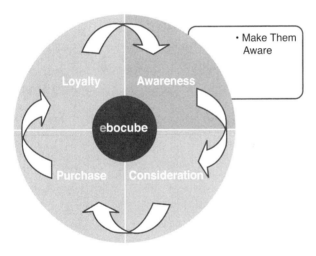

Figure 5.10   The ebocube buying cycle: awareness stage

If you are targeting contacts that have not had any experience with your company or brand, your first goal is to generate awareness. Your contacts may be newly acquired, or if you're launching a new or upgraded product/solution/service, this might also include existing customers. You might use this opportunity to acquire more data on the contact, or to acquire new contact records. Up-selling should target loyal, profitable segments identified through the data. With email, you can target a wider base if you have little or no marketing history on the contacts, which is likely to be the case with EMs. Awareness can be generated on various levels:

- Company level (e.g., your brand)
- Product/service level
- Event level
- News/PR/general company information

Consideration Stage

The consideration stage (see Figure 5.11) is linked to data nurture in the ebocube commercial cycle. Prospects/existing customers need to be convinced to move to the purchase stage. (We discuss the communication vehicles online and offline to achieve these goals in the next chapter.) These contacts have typically responded to a first-stage communication designed to make the individual aware of your campaign.

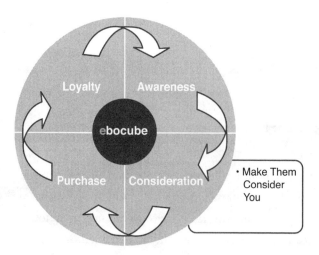

Figure 5.11 The ebocube buying cycle: consideration stage

Qualifying Lead Candidates

Potential sales leads, which we call lead candidates, can be qualified by the following:

- Online data-capture forms with lead-qualification questions
- Webcast registration forms with lead-qualification questions
- Call center agents qualifying contacts
- Sales teams following up and qualifying contacts
- Partners following up and qualifying contacts

Lead candidates are generated through your campaigns and are commonly referred to as respondents to your campaign and your call to action. They are generated through consideration campaigns, which target data. They need to be nurtured and developed when viewed in the ebocube commercial cycle.

Purchase

This is what business is all about: closing the loop and closing the sale (see Figure 5.12).

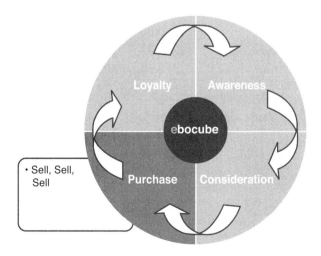

Figure 5.12   The ebocube buying cycle: purchase stage

Loyalty

Loyalty campaigns (see Figure 5.13) should target high-value customers, which we define though RFM modeling. Communicate to this segment in a different way from how you communicate to prospects or new/low value customers. These are the customers that, if lost, will significantly impact sales and profits. A loyalty campaign should encourage greater sales and also recognize customer loyalty.

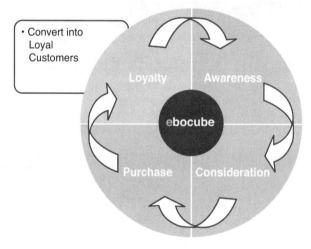

Figure 5.13   The ebocube buying cycle: loyalty stage

You should target your predefined segment based on the RFM indexing discussed previously. Loyalty should be approached with local cultural sensitivity. In the EMs we've researched, it's common to give customers gifts, but you need to check that the gifts do not offend the local culture or religion. If you have friends, local partners, agencies, or sales forces, it's definitely a good idea to check gift ideas with them. For example, in the MEA region, the main religion is Islam. It would not be advised to send alcoholic drinks or holiday hampers that may contain pork. Also in Saudi, high-quality value gifts are often exchanged. In Russia and some countries in Central Eastern Europe, the timing of Christmas differs from in Europe and the United States, and so it's important to have local insight, through an internal sales force or local partners. There is a lot to consider when giving gifts cross cultures. Understanding which gifts to give and how and when to give them can create good business relationships and vice versa! Gift giving in the Asian business culture—for example, in China and Japan—is extremely significant. If you are visiting a customer and you provide a gift that is not perceived to be acceptable, you may be left feeling slightly embarrassed, or, worse, you could do long-term damage to a business relationship.

Central Eastern European culture is closer to Western European cultures or developed economies. We advise you still check loyalty campaigns, gifts, and high-value direct mail with local partners, salespeople, or friends who understand the local culture and gift-giving etiquette.

Endnotes

[1] Wikipedia, "Military Campaign," http://en.wikipedia.org/wiki/Military_campaign.

[2] "About MTN Nigeria," http://www.mtnonline.com/index.php/about.html.

6

Campaign Optimization, "Glocalization," and the Power of Email

Upon completion of this chapter, you should be able to

- Explain how the integrate data and buying cycle form the ebocube commercial cycle, to achieve effective campaign results, through effective buying and data objectives
- Understand the effectiveness and benefits of localization of your campaigns and communication channels
- Understand the critical importance of defining SMART objectives upfront and defining what you are measuring
- Recognize the impact of email communications, its versatility, its immediacy, and how it can drive phenomenal response rates in relation to ebocube commercial cycle goals
- See how email enables you to reach and target the right audience at the right time
- Test, analyze, and learn from new markets with online communication metrics to refine what's working and eliminate what's not

Campaign Optimization

We developed the ebocube commercial cycle (see Figure 6.1) to simplify and optimize the phases of your campaign and communication, in a way that helps to define clear objectives and metrics to be

reviewed in the ebocube dashboard. This integration will allow you
to obtain the following:

- Contacts' awareness and acquisition of their data
- Consideration, nurture, and data development of contacts and
  potential leads
- Purchase and data development of leads
- Loyalty and retention of customers

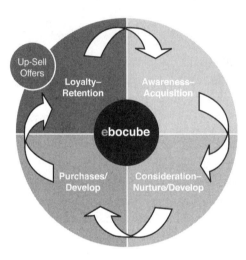

Figure 6.1　The ebocube commercial cycle

Last, but certainly not least, this will enable you to build business
relationships with contacts and achieve mutual business results, allowing you to target contacts with timely relevant offers, regardless of
their location.

Think Globally, Act Glocally

Being a global firm involves adapting to local country trends—
glocalizing. Localization is the process of adapting or creating a marketing campaign for a specific country or region. A successfully
localized campaign will appear to have been developed within the
local culture or with the local market in mind. Remember, localiza-

tion is not translation! The aim is not to deliver a literal interpretation of your message in the community, but to communicate it within the cultural awareness of the emerging market (EM) nation and culture.

When launching any marketing campaigns in EMs, you have to spend time on localization so your campaign will be understood by local customers and won't offend local culture. You must not only focus on what you want to communicate but also how it will be received in the marketplace. You will be required to invest part of your budget and time in localization because misunderstanding of local cultures can cause reputation damage and poor return on marketing investment (ROMI).

Your local sales force, partners, or local marketing agencies should review any written copy or artwork to ensure that it will be understood and that it won't offend the target audience. In many regions, such as the Middle East and Africa (MEA) region, one-to-one communication is preferred, and offline campaigns may be required to build loyalty. If your business does not have local partners, you might want to invest time in researching reputable marketing agencies with a target region that will have considerable understanding and knowledge of the local market. You might involve them when conceptualizing the proposition, incentive, and campaign. While translation technology now exists, it provides only literal conversion and does not take into consideration audience or culture sensibilities.

With ebocube, you can test and analyze variants of localization. For example, you can split content/email subject lines and send the two variants to two different lists (A/B tests). You can then check response rates to see which message generated the best results and impact before sending the message to your entire marketing list.

Business-to-business (B2B) case studies show that it's not necessary to change your business brand name (e.g., Cisco, Microsoft, IBM, HSBC, Boeing) to succeed in an EM. However, you might localize sub-brands, service names, products, and definitely marketing campaigns and communications. Various consumer marketers have localized exceptionally well over the years, and we advise you to learn from them and follow and adopt best practices. In some cases, global brands carry more prestige within an EM because some local markets consider imports to be better than locally produced products/services, and they benefit from the "country of origin" effect.

Failure to research local cultures can prove costly and may force a company to withdraw from a region. By using the ebocube model, you can reduce risk and costs. Even so, you still need to localize your communications to reflect the needs of your local target markets in terms of culture, language, and user requirements. This will also impact the message—the simplicity of it and complexity. Localization is the only way you can resonate with your audience and generate good results, especially against competitors in the same market space.

The tone of your message is as important as the message itself. It can be considered arrogant to communicate as if you are targeting developed economies or to flatten communication so that it doesn't have local flavor. Some countries need sophisticated messaging, whereas some require direct and simple messages. You must know the difference. For many markets, using the local language for content is paramount and is not only expected but will help you to compete with local companies and to build stronger contact relationships through communication.

Although regions might share cultural similarities, you must always consider each country's diversity. In the MEA region, Egypt and Saudi Arabia both use the Arabic language; however, the Saudi dress code differs significantly from the Egyptian dress code, and the dialects differ. Countries in Africa are very different from the nations of the Middle East, so they need to be considered differently. Latin American nations share cultural similarities, but different languages and time zones, and economic and technology advancement differ by country. In the Central and Eastern Europe (CEE) region, languages differ throughout the whole region.

Start by targeting EMs where you can offer relevant products and services for the region. You need to have a sales force and infrastructure to follow up in the area. Remember that localizing and building resources can be expensive and time-consuming, so focus on what you can manage and afford and where you can generate the best results. Although the ebocube is a low-cost business model and provides wide reach online, it still requires focus, investment, and sales follow up. Plan a budget that takes into account web and content developers, copywriters, translation agencies, and other in-house or outsourced professionals. Even tools like social media that might be free to use require time to update and monitor. You can use the ebocube with offline traditional marketing campaigns. You might use classified print advertisements in India; for example, you can tie print advertising to an online call to action (CTA). There is still a cost to consider for print, although you're marrying print to the power of the Internet for follow up and data capture.

Localization is the linchpin to your messaging, creative, and customer relationship management strategy. The benefits of localization include the following:

- **Generates revenue:** Fast-growth objectives are achieved through improved online engagement and response rates, while building a pipeline, leads, and revenue.
- **Builds a strong relationship with your local target audience:** Fast-moving consumer goods (FMCGs) and business-to-consumer (B2C) benefit, as exemplified by super brands such as Coca Cola or McDonalds (which has modified its product to meet local tastes). Coke actually tastes different in Egypt than it does in the UK!
- **Builds global brand recognition while catering to local market and needs:** For example, HSBC is becoming a globally recognized strong brand with the same consistent look and feel; at the same time, the brand connects with local markets because of localized campaigns.
- **Allows for reliable and trusted data capture:** If you ask contacts to submit information on a form they cannot understand,

you will compete poorly against local and established players who have already established an audience with their brands.

- **Ensures your audience understands the nature of your products/services and how to access information via your website or subscription to your e-newsletter:** Your audience will be able to understand your messages and follow your call to actions and understand how the benefits of a product or service address their needs.

- **Protects your brand's reputation:** Because people are more likely to remember mistakes created by companies rather than success stories, you must make sure your communication is accurate.

Translation and Interpretation

Use the local language in a meaningful way for the target audience. Some countries work in English for business transactions (such as India and countries in the MEA region), whereas others do not. The message should be simple enough for the region or country to comprehend. A local or domestic agency can translate a simple message from a developed economy. However, many times a literal translation will be "wrong," losing the intended meaning and translating into a different message. Always use experienced translators and not technology tools.

For example, the message "we will help to grow your business" is generic and might not give EM customers any insight into your company or what you can provide. While a small to medium-sized business in a developed economy may want to grow their revenue, a primary need for a small to medium-sized business in an EM may be to expand or secure their IT network. The business or government environment may require a local solution and not a generic offer. You must research local needs to create effective copy, propositions, and incentives. Do your research through surveys, blogs, other user-generated content, and B2B networks.

Time Zones, Weekends, and Work Schedules

In the MEA region, some countries' weekends start on Friday and end on Saturday; Sunday is the first day of the workweek. In Saudi Arabia, the weekend is Thursday and Friday. In some North African countries, weekends are Saturday and Sunday, and in the remainder of East, West, and South Africa, the weekend is on Saturday and Sunday.

In the CEE, Latin America (LatAM), Russia and Commonwealth of Independent States (CIS) regions, India, and China, weekends are the same as in Europe and America. This is an important consideration when executing campaigns because you might get a low response rate if you email someone on a weekend or organize an event on a weekend! You'll find that some people in the MEA region work on their weekends to accommodate the working week in developed economies.

If respondents use mobile email devices, you do not want to send them an email in the middle of the night, because they may use their mobile devices as alarm clocks. If you wake them with the sound of a message, you might have an adverse impact on your brand. Working with different time zones and weekends can affect your workweek, so you might want to work with local agencies and partners, although campaign management tools enable you to "schedule" campaigns to go out automatically. Therefore, you can set up a campaign to go out on your weekend or while you are asleep.

If you decide to launch a global webcast, consider the timing and dates. If you plan to broadcast a live webcast across different countries or regions, we recommend it be localized. This allows invitations and presentations to be prepared in the local language; however, you can test the response rate to one webcast in English across regions.

The time zone may change for summer or winter in America or Europe. But not all regions change their clocks at the same time. Automated campaign management tools exist so that you can schedule campaigns to go out across all time zones. If you don't take time zones into consideration, attendees could turn up for the event earlier or later than the presenters.

Campaign Considerations

As you can see, there are a number of considerations when managing localized campaigns in EM. There are general considerations you should make each time you launch a campaign, although of course you will learn each time. We've created a simplified and standardized check list for EMs based on our experience. You might keep this list in mind as your check list before considering, planning, or executing local campaigns and communications in EM:

- You must consider your drop date (e.g., the time and date an email arrives in a contact's inbox or direct mail lands on their desks). Dates for Christmas or other festive seasons, local new years, or bank and national holidays need to be known because they differ in different regions and the target may or may not be at work on those days. For example, the Chinese New Year, a major holiday, differs from the western calendar New Year, as does the lunar Islamic calendar year, although the latter isn't typically recognized with a long holiday.

- Strap lines or taglines for your business or brand are difficult to translate in EMs and can lose or change meaning in local cultures if literally translated.

- Look-and-feel images need to have a local look and feel. So that you don't offend local cultures, avoid images of people if you lack local insight. This includes all images used online and offline.

- Color has different meaning in different cultures. Red, orange, and gold are positive in Saudi Arabia. Red is also a popular color in China. In India, yellow and green are considered lucky. Make sure colors present well on desktop and mobile browsers/screens.

- Contacts may be local or expatriates. In the United Arab Emirates (UAE), particularly Dubai, there's a high percentage of expats. Only a small percentage of residents are from the local region. English is, therefore, a highly acceptable language to use in communication. However the message still needs to resonate with the local audience's business needs. Do **not** make assumptions.

- Numeric, date, and time formats differ by region. The U.S. format is MM/DD/YYYY; the European is DD/MM/YYYY. Know what is used where to avoid confusion. For example, if you're promoting an event, you want to ensure the event data is clear.

- Symbols, images, and icons can be reused in multiple campaigns. Start to build a "marketing library" in-house bank of images. This is cost-, resource-, and time-effective and helps to build consistency throughout messaging as recipients will begin to recognize consistently used images, but be careful not to overuse an image. You still want to use innovative imagery.

- Currency exchange rates can be expensive, and leads don't want to research conversion rates. Therefore, don't sell in dollars, pounds, or euros on a local website.

- Incentives are welcome but must be tested for responsiveness. For example, a free USB key in developed economies might not generate a response rate like in an EM. Offers don't need to be merchandise. They can be events, physical or virtual. Make sure the response isn't just for "free stuff." Your overall message is key.

- Toll-free numbers are not common in all regions. Know the exchange people are accustomed to calling to improve your response rate.

- A proposition is the overall products/service/solution that a company markets to the contacts to meet a problem they have. You should tailor your proposition for EMs and take into account the unique needs of the companys in the industry, market, and EM and in relation to the company size, the specifics, and firmographics (i.e., company characteristics will determine the need). Analyze how they are unique or differ from developed economies. Understanding local market needs should help you to create strong and relevant propositions.

Incentives

An incentive is the use of a freebie or giveaway. Examples include free information or the opportunity to attend an online or offline event. Freebies or marketing incentives work extremely well in EMs.

High-value incentives can be used, too, such as "win a free trial." Remember that the word **win** can trigger email spam filters, so try using a different word (e.g., **receive**) or not putting this in your subject line at all. Whitepapers (written in the local language) can also be used as an incentive; they allow prospects to learn about best practices in developed economies. Make sure the message is not too complex but use imagery to bring content to life and interest readers.

An offer or incentive can be used throughout the ebocube commercial cycle. Just make sure the offer entices the contact to click through, submit some data, or get in touch and move along toward the purchase stage to redeem the offer. If you request contacts to take the time to submit their data, they need to know that there's something in it for them. Just make sure they remember your message!

Test what works best and rewards you most generously on your ROMI. Try using controlled cells and emailing them using the offer to see whether the response rate increases. Measure whether there has been an uplift or increased response rate to the message with the offer to that specific controlled cell in relation to the data that wasn't targeted with an offer.

For your loyal, repeat customers, use high-value offers; this segment is likely to be the smaller percentage of your marketing database. Justify the extra cost based on previous transactions, RFM (regency, frequency, and monetary) value of purchase they are likely to buy, and future purchases. You may, for example, offer them breakfast with the executive board.

Communications Mix

You gain significant power for your message when you integrate online communication channels. As the online economy in EMs continues to grow, it's important that you know how to leverage key communication tools to continue to increase sales and ROMI.

Internet access and mobile phone use are growing at an extraordinary pace in EMs. Online marketing as a communications channel is becoming a huge industry in most regions of the world. Businesses are also researching the Web for business knowledge and information. They're going to websites and search engines all over the world to learn and to find out about the best products, services, and events. By tracking hits to your website, you can find out where the traffic comes from.

Online should form your main marketing strategy, supported through offline activity. Online forms the core of your ebocube strategy, while offline fills the gaps. Online used to be a support activity in developed markets, but with EMs this strategy is flipped. Online is more beneficial because it can override the infrastructure or logistical constraints in a region—for example, poor postal infrastructure or lack of transportation infrastructure to support post. Offline should also be used for more profitable accounts, or for customers in your RFM segment defined by your data to achieve maximum ROMI. Any data collected on customer offline should always be brought back in to your marketing database so that you can use the data for direct communications. You can also measure results in your datacube and the dashboard as part of an integrated campaign.

You can use online metrics to track offline campaigns and ROMI. For example, you can use a web CTA to measure and track responses to direct mail, TV, billboards, press, and radio. The more you execute, measure, and track through the online elements, the more knowledge you gain of your marketing and ROMI. Any responses that aren't captured online (e.g., responses from inbound calls or events) should be loaded manually into your database against ebocodes, which are tracking codes, that show the source of data capture, like the event/activity and date. Your sales team and channels should feed back on closed opportunities/sales generated through marketing campaigns into the ebocube dashboard. Examples include logging a customer interest or potential lead responding to a specific campaign or communication and any offer received.

Email

Email (electronic mail) alone is a powerful medium and can help you to achieve the majority of your ebocube commercial cycle goals. Combined with other communication channels, email is much more effective. Twenty years ago it might have been difficult, if not impossible, to buy a business marketing list for an EM with email addresses, but now this practice is common. EM businesses communicate daily via email.

Various formats of email exist. Plain text email messages contain no formatting. A Hypertext Markup Language (HTML) email message contains any type of formatting other than text. This may be as simple as programming that sets the text in a specific font (bold, italic). It also contains any graphic images, logos, colors, or rich text within the email or as an attachment.[1]

Standard graphic format such as JPEG and GIF are not considered rich media. Some popular formats commonly considered rich media are Macromedia Flash and Shockwave, along with various audio and video formats.

Email is a versatile, low-cost medium. Email allows the flexibility and responsiveness you need in dynamic EMs. Branded emails can be used to achieve various goals in the ebocube commercial cycle. Formats range from simple text, to HTML, to rich media. Combined with other elements of online marketing and offline, email can generate high response rates for your integrated campaigns. Email can build trust between your brand and your customers and prospects.

Unlike other online media, email is delivered to the contacts, whereas you have to rely on contacts to find your website (although you can make use of targeted online banner adverts; that is, you can advertise on websites you know your target audience uses regularly). Email is an outbound form of communication; a website is an inbound form of communication.

A starting point for any successful email campaign is planning. This includes your campaign and data objectives using the ebocube commercial cycle. Data is the crucial part of your campaign in an EM, and you need to continually update and validate your database and refresh it with new information, "firmographics," and new contacts and companies.

It is extremely important to keep the correct balance of time, effort, and resource invested in your direct marketing activates. All three aspects—creative, offer, and data—in the direct marketing activity are important. But you need to spend the right balance of time and effort on the split. We recommend (see Figure 6.2) the following rule: 40-40-20. If your direct marketing activity as a whole is 100%, you should spend 40% of your time and effort on data, 40% on the offer or proposition, and last (but not least) 20% on creative. There is no point using a nice creative targeting people who are not interested in what you are marketing or your proposition.

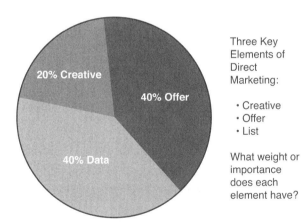

Figure 6.2 The ebocube direct marketing split

Because direct mail costs more to produce and distribute than email, you should use it only for the loyalty segment in the ebocube commercial cycle, or if contacts have opted out from all email communications and are still worth contacting, which can also be determined through RFM modeling. You may also have an address for a key contact in a prospective large company, but no email. You may then try to send them mail or get a salesperson to call them.

You need to retain loyal customers and make priority investments in those relationships. You should also have more accurate contact, marketing history, and transactional information on customers. Direct mail or brochures can be distributed by account managers on behalf of marketing to high-loyalty customers. Salespeople should either provide marketing with updated customer contact details or have a system that is integrated with marketing systems that they can update like an account management tool; a popular one for large organizations is Salesforce.com. Account managers can also provide Excel spreadsheets. (If you email contact details, you should password-protect/encrypt the Excel spreadsheets for security purposes.)

SMART Objectives

Email marketing is highly measurable, but you must know and clearly define what you want to measure in the form of objectives (i.e., quantifiable metrics). Some people say that social media doesn't work. However, the problem is that companies today may rush to use new communication channels without planning and defining what they want to achieve and measure...so how can they possibly determine what has or hasn't worked?

It is important to establish SMART (simple, measurable, achievable, realistic, timed) objectives from the start, and these should fit into your overall communication plan, which should be derived from your overall marketing plan or strategy. This is informed by previous year results from your ebocube dashboard and datacube. Campaign-level objectives should be based on the ebocube commercial cycle goals.

Managing Email

You can choose from a spectrum of user-friendly web-based or software applications that enable you to send email to your contacts. A lot of these packages have fallen in cost because the developers are targeting small to medium-sized businesses and home office entre-preneurs. Some applications are off-the-shelf. Others can be cus-tomized to your company needs and integrated with existing systems and IT infrastructure. These approaches can be used in-house as part of your marketing department and provide centralized control and cost savings (because you don't have to pay agencies or vendors).

Employees can access these web applications and the email cam-paigns you're working on, and your partners can also access the email tools and branded collateral. Email marketing is paper free, and no airmail or couriers are involved.

You can gain results for the ebocube commercial cycle in each stage via email. Email is a powerful tool to migrate contacts through the phases of the cycle. It can be used to nurture prospects and to keep them engaged and interested, and to retain valuable and loyal customers through e-newsletters or invitations to webcasts or other virtual events.

Metrics have been developed to measure email responses throughout the ebocube commercial cycle. Surveys can be used to enhance data capture with links to emails or registration forms or via webcasts or live events through email linking to event registration sites and landing pages.

Start with a name. When you purchase lists in EMs, you might have a name, and the email address is core, but you'll need to increase and build on a profile of your contact database to build "cus-tomer insight." Remember to use offers in email to entice contacts to give more information. Clearly define what data you need to capture to push the contact along the ebocube commercial cycle.

Table 6.1 shows the email metrics you should track and measure in relation to the ebocube commercial cycle stages and highlights email tactics through the four stages of the commercial cycle. You'll want to become familiar with and memorize these—you'll be engag-ing contacts regularly through the four-stage cycle. Let's review the goals of your outreach through these four stages.

TABLE 6.1   ebocube Commercial Cycle Metrics Matrix—Email

Stage in the ebocube Commercial Cycle	Email Primary response	Secondary metric response
All Phases of Ebocube Commercial Cycle	Opt-out rate/unsubscribe	
	Soft bounce	
	Number targeted	
	Actual sent	
	Hard-bounce rate	
	Data submission	
Awareness/Acquisition	Open rate	
	Click-through links	
	Email forwards	
	Data submission	
	Number of new contacts in CI	
Consideration/Nurture and Develop	Data submission	Open rate
		Click-through links
Purchase/Develop	Data submission	Open rate
	Lead candidates	Click-through links
	°Leads/sale	
Loyalty/Retention	Click-through special offers	Open rates
	Entering loyalty codes	
	Lead candidates/Leads/ up-sell, cross-sell	

°Leads can be generated by webcasts (or targeted purchase/development/loyalty communications using data-capture forms with BANT questions or call to action to contact sales), capturing BANT through the data-capture form or advising contacts to call their sales/account manager. Leads can be converted into sales by your sales force. Some marketers prefer to re-qualify data captured by registration forms, through a call center, to improve the quality of the lead and to provide more context/information on the marketing lead for sales. The quality of a webcast lead will depend on the data targeted; i.e., is the contact really ready to be developed, purchase, or is this newly acquired data? A sale can be attributed to the leads generated/influenced by the webcast; however, it may not show in the system until up two quarters later due to the sales cycle. Sales should update this information.

Stage One: Goals for Awareness

Awareness and acquisition are going to be the first stages of your marketing activities for most of your campaigns. This same principle applies to email as a communication channel. It's not advised to "jump" directly into consideration or purchase stage (with a lead-generation communication) of the ebocube commercial cycle with your marketing communication, without making the contact aware of your brand, product, or service. Why is awareness so important? Because it helps your business to do the following:

- Create awareness of your brand as you enter an EM region or country and raise its visibility to keep it top of mind when contacts consider purchasing a product or service in your industry.
- Stimulate new awareness of a product launch, new service that contacts were otherwise completely unaware of, or information on an upgrade. Apple has done this several times with their mobile phones.
- Spark awareness of marketing online and offline activities.

Stage Two: Goals for Consideration/Nurture

A lot of marketers say they are "nurturing" their prospects when in reality they are sending out nice brochures or marketing copy focused on product releases, company announcements, or things they want to sell. This stage is about sending contacts compelling communication they want to read. You might do this by sending them a newsletter (if they've opted in for such communication) that discusses topics that meet their preferences or information that targets to them based on a recent response to a communication or "conversation."

So how do you nurture prospects or existing customers with your marketing communications? There are a few key points to remember when successfully nurturing your contact so it benefits them as well as your business. You can do this by

- Sending your contacts emails or inviting contacts to a product webcast or online/offline event that they have indicated they are interested in. For example, they may have downloaded a whitepaper off your website previously related to a certain service/product—follow up and nuture them!

- Pushing your message to a target audience and encouraging them to respond instead of them discovering your website on their own.
- Targeting email messages followed up by telemarketing related to the message and campaign (lead qualification) can be a quick and easy way to generate qualified sales leads.
- Building permissions and preferences through a link on your email footer, which links to a website hosted on the Internet. This gives contacts the opportunity to sign up for content that they are interested in receiving and in the form of communication they opt in to (e.g., email, but no telemarketing).
- Seeking opt in from your contacts for all forms of direct marketing
- Seeking preferences to establish what your contact would like to receive (e.g., specific products, solutions, services, online/offline events, frequency of mailing, and email format [HTML or plain text]).

Stage Three: Goals for Purchase and Development

Purchase and development is the stage where the magic takes place, the stage which is the most important in your entire campaigning tactics. Here the communication should generate leads and pipelines for sales to make their follow-up calls to close deals and generate revenue for your business and the growth that EM promises. Of course, successful purchase and development stage is dependent on how successfully you have managed and executed previous stages or nurturing and even earlier in awareness and acquisition. Bear in mind that you may have only one chance to sell, to convince the contact to purchase your products or service, so don't waste that opportunity. Also, this stage builds a foundation for the last/next stage, keeping your customers loyal in the retained segment. To optimize this opportunity and increase those sales, do the following:

- Stimulate purchases with an email CTA that redirects the user to a website, call center, salesperson, or retailer if that channel is suitable.

- Follow up with an automated localized thank-you email instantly after a purchase.
- Welcome purchasers who made the transaction offline. For example, send your customers a "welcome e-pack/message" and congratulate their choice.
- Build a stronger profile of your customers. You can always use surveys to progressively profile or validate customer information, as well to gather permissions and preferences (e.g., allowing them to opt out of certain communications methods without opting out completely). You don't want to lose a contact in an EM, because clean data is scarce; however, you need to respect their preferences and permissions.

Goals for Stage Four: Loyalty and Retention

Last but by no means least is loyalty and retention. Once you do a great job and work successfully with sales teams to close the deal and convert prospects in to customers, you want to keep that customer loyal to your brand to keep buying or upgrading your product.

It's a huge loss if a valuable customer is going away to your competitors, if, after all the effort and money spent on your marketing, a business decides to not continue cooperation with you anymore.

Win-back campaigns are very expensive and time-consuming and require you to indentify in first place why businesses moved to competitors. Not all lost customers can be won back. To prevent their leaving, keep your customers retained and loyal to your product. You can do it in few simple and easy actions, such as the following:

- Keep customers up-to-date and informed through email newsletters, virtual events, and other timely, relevant communications
- Target special offers to high-value customers
- Offer promotional codes for discounts to an event or product that lower-value customers, accounts, or prospects would not receive

E-newsletters

E-newsletters effectively communicate news to target audiences throughout the ebocube commercial cycle and can be used to disseminate information to subscribers.

An email newsletter is content distributed to subscribers by email, on a regular schedule. Content is seen as valued editorial rather than primarily a commercial message with a sales offer, although it can be used to raise awareness, consideration, and purchase, or to gain loyalty; it can be used for acquisition, nurture, development, and loyalty segments.

You will need local insight to create relevant news for your local contacts. E-newsletters are a great way to achieve all the objectives in the ebocube commercial cycle, and a great way for account managers to keep their customers up-to-date on the market without being out and about in the field.

For loyal, profitable customers, e-newsletters should be highly tailored and appear to be sent through the account manager's email account (if applicable), with stories that may be relevant to only those accounts.

Testing and Learning (A/B Splits)

An A/B split refers to a test situation in which two randomized groups of users (from the same data segmentation) are sent different content to test performance of specific campaign elements. The A/B split method can be used to test only one variable at a time to test different assumptions on your audience. It is an effective way to look at different subject lines, design/format changes, time of day/day of week, copy style, offers, and use and style of graphics. Testing and actual results can help determine paths for future campaigns

To learn more about your prospective customers, it's imperative that you test email variables on a small sample of your target list (e.g., 20% of your target list for a county or region). The list needs to be small enough so as not to communicate to all, but large enough to be able to be statistically relevant. The aim is to understand which content or variable achieves the best results on the 20% sample data and to use the best variable for the remaining 80%.

By testing responses to email, you're testing contacts' responses to your outbound communications, testing contact lists from your market audiences, and providing customer insight. A simple test of a single element of your email will help improve your response rates. At worst, it will prove your current campaign works pretty well.

The testing sample or control cell allows you to split data into subsegments to (1) measure which segments (cells) are the most responsive to email variants (such as subject line, images, offers, messages, colors, call to actions, location of CTAs) and to (2) track the success of the variables. You can split and track control cells for emails by various categories.

Subject line/variables may generate a higher response rate in EMs, and with a degree of subjectivity you can make generalizations as to what works best and then test again. You can test subject lines in local languages versus subject lines in English by looking at open rate for the two variants.

Testing doesn't need to be complex; keep variables to a minimum. You should have an objective hypothesis in mind, and your test should aim to prove something. You should have an aim to learn, which will determine your variable.

Budget Benefits

Email is low cost in comparison to traditional direct mail, offline, and above-the-line media. In the age of new media, email has surpassed traditional direct mail in terms of capabilities and advantages. Advantages of email over direct mail include the following:

- **No print costs:** You can save thousands of pounds or dollars per year in the marketing budget in comparison to offline direct mail because you don't have printing or mailing fees.

- **Errors/print crunch:**   If you discover an error after printing **x** number of direct mail, you'll have to reprint, increasing costs; whereas email copy can be updated instantly. Have you ever had a senior manager ask for a change in a creative just before print deadline? With email, changes can be made a lot quicker without disrupting drop dates.

- **Testing:**   It's easier to test email. If you send direct mail to an EM list, it's difficult to test and to track, and you can't learn and lower your cost as a result.

- **No postal cost (mailing/wastage):**   It's difficult to get full valid addresses or postal codes in EMs, and it's expensive to mail hard copy direct mail (letter). If direct mail bounces back, it's hard to track and update data with invalid postal addresses, which would be a manual process. With email, you can quickly (and through a fully automated process) remove invalid addresses in your databases.

- **Get more for less:**   The cost of direct mail as a traditional marketing channel increases with the volume of units printed and posted. Also, call centers charge by the hour, or per contact called, and so the longer your target audience list is, the higher your costs. The cost of an email blast and setup can be fixed if you use internal tools and resources. Regardless of the number of contacts you email on your target list, the cost remains fixed. The cost per response is lower regardless of the number of contacts you target with the same email, and the fixed cost is split between the contacts. For example, the fixed cost of HTML and text plus setup = $1,000, if you have 1,000 contacts in your target audiences data cost per contacts = $1.00, but if the target is 10,000 contacts, the cost per contact = $0.10.

  This isn't the case with direct mail. The cost per direct mail increases as the number printed and posted increases. In Table 6.2, you can see costs for email versus direct mail per unit sent. As you can see, cost per direct mail stays the same because regardless how many mails you send, the post office charges you the same for each stamp. (Of course, you might be able to negotiate with private curriers, but they don't always operate in Ems.) Printing costs don't change either with the number or printed units (unless you can negotiate with your supplier).

TABLE 6.2 Price Comparison Table of Email vs. Direct Mail

Contacted Number of Records	Total Cost for Direct Mail	Cost per Contact Using Direct Mail	Total Cost for Email	Cost per Contact Using Email
100	$100	$1	$1000	$10,00
1000	$1000	$1	$1000	$01,00
10,000	$10,000	$1	$1000	$00,10
100,000	$100,000	$1	$1000	$00,01

°° Cost of printing and sending direct mail (per unit [letter]) $1 (cost of sending $0.50 + cost of printing $0.50)

° Fixed cost of email creative and set up = $1000

- **Cost of acquisition and development:** It costs less to email third party-data or homegrown data than to send direct mail or telephone contacts. Save these costs for when a prospect becomes a qualified lead or customer. Also, it's less risky than exhibiting or sponsoring at an event because you can test the market.

- **Template:** Reduce your costs by using email templates repeatedly and by only updating the text, which is quick, easy, and cheap through user-friendly software such as Dreamweaver. The template will already be designed to meet your brand guidelines and be localized for the region or country. The recipient will recognize the consistency in your communication and will be able to navigate an email that includes CTAs or redirections to your website.

  You can use the same template for email invites, reminders, and thank you notes; just tweak the copy or CTA as needed. With existing templates and campaign setup, you can target C segment countries that might not be as profitable as A countries; you just localize the header image (i.e., image above the fold or copy). For example, you can send an email to Ethiopia (which was originally used for Nigeria) with localized images and a localized message.

- **Remove hard-bounce emails (clean data):** Cleaning and maintaining lists is cheaper and easier with email than with direct mail. Small to medium-sized companies with smaller marketing budgets can still consider international market

development and new profit generation through email marketing and the ebocube. If you use third-party agencies that
charge by the number of contacts contacted, you can ask them
to remove hard bounces from the reminder email for events or
follow up. You can also choose not to email contacts who
haven't replied to any of your earlier emails.

Mass Media and Micromarketing

Email enables you to reach and target the right audience at the
right time. It allows you to send multiple variants of messages to different segments at the same time. For example, you could produce a
campaign on a new product or solution. You could raise awareness by
targeting multiple decision makers and influencers. You can use the
same creative but tailor the message to different job roles, for example one image but with technical copy for the IT manager and business benefits for the IT decision maker.

In developed economies with high-quality data or availability,
email marketing can be highly targeted to lots of discretely defined
segments. Although email data for EMs may be of lower quality at
first, your emails can still be targeted based on the firmographics or
contact details you have obtained.

It's more challenging to micromarket with direct mail. Monitoring mail houses can be challenging, particularly if they are not
based in your home market. If you're executing complex manual
data segmentation and the mailing house sends the incorrect message variant to the wrong segment, you might not know this. In this
scenario, you won't know why your campaign delivered poor
results.

Marketing response history for email can be used for targeting.
You might target people who responded to previous emails to follow
up, nurture, and develop them with consideration or purchase emails,
even targeting those who only opened and read your emails but did
not respond with data. This is impossible to track with direct mail,

unless you include an online or telemarketing CTA, which you'll rely on contacts to click or follow; you'll identify them by information they leave. As email marketing programs continue to mature, customers have come to expect more offers based on past purchases and interests. Therefore, email marketers have made great advances in the sophistication and targeting of their campaigns. Even if the original target data list is not clean, or segmented based on marketing history, you can test your segments to see whether they respond well to your new targeted message.

As your marketing database yields "customer insights," you can gather contact preferences. This is what they have specified they want to receive, which is collated by sales, account managers, or self-reported (data-capture forms) by the recipient and stored. Take time to analyze data before communicating.

Account management emails can appear to come from the client, and can be fully trackable and highly personalized. HTML-designed email content can be provided to account managers to send through account management tools, so basically marketing writes the message and provides the content/campaign, and then marketers can track open rates or click-through rates per contact through the tools account managers use to send the designed emails. Contact information can also be captured into your marketing database through surveys. Research tools enable account managers to have one-to-one or one-to-many conversations through email in a highly targeted measurable, cost-effective way.

You can build trust in the local market by co-branding your emails with trusted and recognized local companies. You should put the partner logo above the fold in the email so that the recipient sees it early. The logo image can be hyperlinked to the partner's site to improve trust. Or vice versa: Partners can use your logo on their email. Your logo or CTA should be hyperlinked to bring traffic to your site and tracked for unique clicks. As contacts are brought to your site, you can collect data through data-submission forms, again using a relevant incentive or offer.

To build trust, you can put the partner names in the subject line. Doing so might help to achieve higher open rates (e.g., re: ebocube and local company launch model). Remember to keep subject lines short and direct. In addition, localization of subject lines can help to achieve high open rates. You can use characters other than Latin characters in email subject lines, but test it in various email clients (like Google Mail, Yahoo!, MS Outlook, or Lotus) to ensure that local characters do not corrupt.

Timing Communications

Timely communications are important, an email allows you flexibility. You're working across multiple time zones in EM. However, with email setup tools, you can schedule emails to go out while you sleep or on your weekend. Email gives you control over when the recipient receives your message.

People are more receptive to messages that arrive at the right time, and you're more likely to get a response to an email sent during the day on a workday than one sent at night or on a weekend. If you have a webcast or live event scheduled, because of the risk of direct mail or the local postal service, you might not be able to ensure your mail arrives on time. Email provides the following options:

- **Inbox calendar invite:**   HTML or plain text email can be sent and used to send calendar invites and to drop calendar invites into recipient mailboxes.
- **Save the date:**   You can mail an invite prior to having all the event details to inform contacts that they need to book time in their diaries.
- **Reminders:**   Email reminders can be sent a day or even an hour before an online event or physical event.
- **Instant delivery:**   An email arrives soon after it's sent. Marketers can automatically trigger email messages to their contacts when they complete a specific action. These actions may include registration or an information request. (Automated email can be sent to end users after the data form is submitted.)

CHAPTER 6 • CAMPAIGN OPTIMIZATION

All these are vital opportunities to interact with customers and differentiate yourself from your competitors and move the contact from one stage in the ebocube commercial cycle to the next.

We once staged a huge annual physical event in an EM nation, and had already sent localized email invitations and gained thousands of registrations through a link to a localized online registration and data-capture event website. More than 2,000 registrations were received. Shortly afterward, the local government advised that we needed to move the location at the last minute. Luckily, with email, we were immediately able to advise registrants, captured through the online data-capture registration tool, that the location had changed. For those who hadn't opened the email, we were able to extract the list and call them if valid phone numbers had been provided. This would have been impossible to do with direct mail because of the restriction with timing. It may have been possible to do this all via the call center but would have been a costly and time-consuming exercise.

Mobile Email

Smartphones are very popular in many EM countries. Mobile phone producers are targeting EMs to increase sales, which means that people receive email on their mobile devices that are supported by wireless or 3G fast data connections. Instead of them referring to their desktop inboxes, their mobile devices are always switched on, and they can check email any time. Widely adopted standards for email marketing and tracking on mobile phones and devices are developing as the medium becomes more popular. Some old Black-Berrys and Treos, for example, strip out Cascading Style Sheets (CSS) code or convert HTML to text automatically, so the best solution for these devices may simply be to create a text version of the email and include a link that says something like, "Viewing this on a mobile device? Click here." This should then redirect the user to plain text; however, new smartphones will render HTML because it's so common now.

Companies that produce smartphones are targeting EMs aggressively for first-time buyers. Because mobile Internet penetration rates are set to soar in comparison to broadband, and because developed economies are now saturated, companies rely on replacement demand and upgrades to smartphones. Naturally, many mobile users in EMs are first-time buyers and EMs have large young populations who love gadgets.

In China, users are particularly savvy with mobile marketing because mobile Internet is more accessible than broadband, and these consumer habits are brought into the office. In countries such as Turkey, there is a huge population of young people, and they find these gadgets trendy and easy to access. Even if the wireless or data connection isn't great in some regions of the world—villages, deserts, or outskirts, as opposed to big business hubs, where coverage is much better—contacts still have the option to log on to their laptops and view email with a wired connection.

Devices such as BlackBerry and iPhone 3G and now the Ipad mean end users can receive HTML on high-resolution screens.

Unfortunately, it's difficult for recipients to fill in a data-capture form on a mobile, unless they're using some of the most current smartphones, such as the latest BlackBerry or iPhone or mobile devices like the iPad, with large screens and enabled for fast network connection speeds, but this will change rapidly based on trends.

If recipients open the email on their smartphone, unless they mark it as unread they are not likely to read this again on their desktop, which means that CTAs that are easier to action on a desktop might not be followed up. You might need to send the message out more than once. You can enhance the mobile email experience as follows:

- Create a simple page structure to keep it mobile friendly.
- Avoid using CSS.
- Keep the fixed width of emails narrow (600 pixels or less).
- Keep your message width short (no more than 60 to 65 characters).

- Consider adding a Mobile Version link at the top of your email that sends recipients to an XHTML landing page.
- Always have a text-based version of the email ready. It's not a good user experience to decipher an email message with HTML tags.

Tracking Recipient Behavior

As we have noted, the Internet's power to allow tracking and analytics is a gift that never stops giving. Instant tracking can check email blast responses minutes after emails have been sent, opened, or not opened and can check whether emails have bounced as hard bounces (invalid email addresses) or soft bounces (out of office, mailbox full). Recipient behavior or response to a newsletter allows you to check the most popular clicked links and find out which information is most relevant to your audience and how long they stayed on a particular page. They might log off right away. Your next e-newsletter should target the segment with the stories they were interested in, building on their specified preferences if defined. Behavioral reports enable marketers to ascertain what contacts are interested in and can be used for segmentation of future campaigns. You could segment them using a control cell, and compare the open rates in comparison to recipients who did not click the specific link. Other tracking techniques include the following:

- The CTA should be positioned "above the fold" and can be attractive buttons on HTML, with localized copy as hyperlinks, masking URLs created in Latin characters, encouraging recipients to follow up.
- Opt in and opt out should be offered, and both should be tracked. Do not waste ROMI on recipients who are not interested in your message.
- Bulk, localized email to prospects can still be personalized with the right tool that enables marketers to address recipients by first name, last name, or job title (e.g., Dear Marketing Manager). Personalization can help marketing raise awareness or consideration in a large audience. The ebocube commercial

cycle allows communication to be more timely and relevant, strengthening the relationship and opportunity to sell.

- Confidential information from your recipient should be directed to a secure site (SHTPP) so that recipients are not reluctant about providing it. In EMs, recipients are worried about phishing (people pretending to be companies fraudulently trying to capture sensitive information online), so you might want to provide a free phone number to ensure the recipient. You will strengthen your brand in EMs by being consistent and trustworthy.

- Shared email addresses in small companies and solo entrepreneurships are not that uncommon (info@company.com). You might want to create a more generic, less-targeted message for shared email accounts.

We would also share these seven big best practice ideas to keep in mind for email marketing, tracking, research, and communications:

- Capture the recipient's own email address if you're targeting a general shared mail alias, ideally a business address, via a data-capture form. The contacts should provide their details to get the offer, and their details should be captured and stored in your marketing database

- Do not allow the recipient to access an incentive (whitepaper, case study, prize USB key) unless they provide their information. Every customer should be prompted to fill in the data-capture form so that your marketing database has the most recent information.

- The data-capture form should be fully localized and should be able to capture local language characters (which your data warehouse should also be able to store).

- Use a free phone number as a CTA for more information. Your call center agent should collect contact details that should then be sent to your marketing database.

- The job title, department, or position (i.e., Hi/Dear Marketing Manager / Network Administrator, Finance) should be used when a contact name is not available. Know the proper greeting, and put emphasis on the employee's status in their organization. Knowing their position and gender will help you greet them properly. If someone is a doctor in an **EM**, it can be correct to address them by job title. A lot of EMs still have hierarchical business structures, whereas some Western countries' organizations can be less formal with senior staff and companies aiming to delayer organizations so that status isn't a barrier to innovation.

- Personalization can include adding the recipient's name in the subject line or message itself. Know when it is appropriate according to custom or culture to address them by their first name or last name. If you send the email with the incorrect name, it will undermine your relationship with the recipient and business. Do not personalize until your data is complete, verified, and up-to-date—quality of a large or small database will never be 100%.

- Consider localizing content and copy in EM nations that do not use English as a business language. Use vendors, partners, and local marketing teams to research job titles and department names in the local language.

Email Design and Engineering

- Alternative text tags (Alt tags) in HTML are tags used to provide alternative text that previews before an image downloads. The recipient usually has to click a button to display images, and Alt tags let the recipient know which images they should expect to see. Make sure your Alt tags are also in the local language. Always ensure your Alt tags are descriptive, meaningful, and memorable so that the recipient is enticed to download the pictures and follow up. For example, instead of the Alt tag reading "right-click to download image," update it so that it says "right-click to find out how to improve marketing return on investment."

- Images in email should be split up and not sent as one big image. Recipients won't see anything if the entire image downloads slowly, and if spam filters cannot read certain content, they will assume its spam and send the email to junk. If the HTML created by one big image does arrive, the recipient might have to wait a long time before seeing anything and might opt out, or just delete your emails, without reading it. In any case, text should not be typed into an image file. That way, the user can have all the important information of the email content even without seeing the images.

- Message size should be between 20K and 40K (or smaller). Never paste images into an email or attach files. Instead, always host them on an image server and link to them. Embedded video or sound files should not be part of your email because viruses are typically embedded into those types of files, and so antivirus programs will block them. Instead, link through to a landing page/microsite web page, video-sharing site such as YouTube, or other social media. Make sure your video is created to work for high-speed and low-speed connections and give the recipient the option to view the content at high or low speed. Content should be created based on standards that can be tested on different connection speeds and to satisfy the audience in the targeted EM.

Businesses within an EM use many different email applications, similar to how many people use different browsers. Several email client applications are available to download for free, which makes them especially useful for testing purposes. Not all businesses use Outlook or Lotus, although multinational enterprises tend to. Small and medium-sized businesses and small home offices, and quite often the public sector, use other accounts, including the following:

- Outlook 2000
- Outlook 2003
- Outlook 2007
- Outlook Express
- Entourage
- Apple Mail
- Lotus
- AOL 9
- Gmail
- Yahoo! Mail
- Hotmail
- Eudora

You need to consider that countries in EMs may also have their own local Internet service providers (ISPs) that provide email clients as one of their services.

Spam Filters and Unsolicited Emails

A message is spam only if it is both unsolicited and in bulk.[2] The recipient's personal identity and context are irrelevant because the message is equally applicable to many other potential recipients, who have not verifiably granted deliberate and explicit permission for it to be sent and are unlikely to be able to opt out.

In many EM nations, unsolicited email, spam, is common. This is because of the lack of privacy legislation. In many EM nations, people receive hundreds of irrelevant marketing emails per day, which often do not offer them the option to opt out from that communication and may clutter their inbox.

Don't get black listed. Spam filters are designed to stop email and to reduce unsolicited bulk email. ISPs invest significantly to create filters that block and restrict the amount of spam recipients receive through email clients.

Ensure that your emails end up in the intended inboxes and ensure that your email domain's name (i.e., what is after @ sign; e.g., x@ebocube.com) doesn't get black listed by ISPs. You can do this by registering with ISPs.

Ensure that your email contacts have opted in to receive email from your company or a third party. Work with your partners or local teams to locate the major ISPs for the local market and request that they register local/global domains with the ISPs so that the ISPs recognize that you're a legitimate business (e.g., marketing@ebocube.pl or consultant@ebocube.com).

Proper design and copy can keep your email from being considered spam if you

- Avoid using ALL CAPITALS in the subject line.
- Avoid exclamation marks in the subject line.
- Avoid using words such as *guarantee, savings, free, prizes, survey, win* in the subject line and any part of the body content.
- Avoid using exclamation marks in the Alt tags, <!— —>.
- Avoid using one big image as a HTML and always split your HTML into text and image. Try to use a balance of text and images in your HTML and keep words as text rather than images. If you must use a large image, cut up the image so that it's several small parts; however, this is not recommended and is bad practice.
- Keep the message size between 20K and 40K, or smaller.
- Do not send email too often. By developing an e-CRM strategy, which we define by the ebocube commercial cycle for lead generation, you should reduce the frequency of untargeted mail. Doing less is sometimes more!
- Request that recipients add your address to their "safe list" or contacts, and consequently keep the same email address. Adding your email address to his/her contact list is pointless if you're blasting email every time from a different email address.

Phishing

Phishing is an illegal online method used by fraudsters to gather personal information from email recipients, particularly financial information, and to identity information to be used illegally. They may use legitimate-looking emails designed to look like they've been sent from recognized companies (e.g., using the company template, branding, logo, or images). They may also use a display address that contains a recognized company name and might lead the recipient to a fake website.[3]

This is particularly a risk for e-commerce. Phishing occurs globally. In fact, it's a major problem for the United States as well as for EMs. As online business has grown at an explosive rate, unfortunately cybercriminals have emerged. Internet security companies have recognized these challenges, and have taken steps to police the Internet. In addition, some larger enterprises have recognized this problem and have invested in software to prevent phishing email from arriving in email clients and inboxes. Avoid being accused of phishing by doing the following:

- **Cybersurveillance 24/7:** Several cybersecurity companies partner with ISPs to reduce the risk of fraud and phishing. They monitor the Internet 24/7 in real time and can detect, report, and stop phishing globally. If your company's an e-commerce company, we highly recommend you research security products; this is your best insurance.

- **Credit cards:** If you trade via e-commerce or request cards details (e.g., payment for registration to attend an event), advise end users to pay via credit card so that they are covered for fraud.

- **HTTPS:** For any data capture of personal information, send the user to a site that uses HTTPS (Secure Hypertext Transfer Protocol). This provides security for document, contact information, and commercial transaction transfer over the Internet to ensure that their information cannot be stolen by a third party between the sender and the receiver. There are several trusted providers.

- **Brand and logo:** In the email design, ensure that your logo is in the upper-left corner. This is so that the recipient recognizes your brand immediately. You should use an image for HTML and text for the text version.

- **Subject line:** In the subject line, to increase trust and recognization start the subject line with your company name (e.g., Re: ebocube: صفحاتمنصر. This is an example in Arabic.

- **Footer:** It's a mandatory requirement in the United States and in the European Union to include an email footer that includes your company registration number, place of registration (e.g., Russia), and your registered office address.

- **Free number/local number:** In some EM countries, it's unheard of to provide a free inbound contact phone number. However, if you provide one when requesting personal information, and if the recipient is worried about submitting online information, they can call you. First, you provide reassurance and more information about your company, and then you can collect the information during the call and update your marketing database.

- **Build trust:** Raise awareness to gain trust, and localize your marketing to build strong relationships.

Achieving Maximum Impact

It's important to have email standards when you build or design an email. Be particular and protective over your brand consistency and identity. Use templates. Create style guides and make sure people stick to them. You might follow all following suggestions and still receive low response rates if your data targeting is poor, of if you send contacts untimely and irrelevant communications. Data targeting is key, as is continuing the conversation. Let's review our most critical practices:

- Avoid using CSS when you build your HTML. CSS is for web page design, not email. CSS gives website developers more control over how pages are displayed. However, CSS incurs rendering problems in email clients. Use inline HTML (no style defined). Every line of code has to be defined with font faces/attributes/sizes.
- Keep the subject line to 60 characters or fewer.
- Avoid spam triggers.
- Use Alt tags in the HTML code for each image used in the HTML design. Make sure Alt tags are localized, if you do decide to localize your email. Also make sure that they are exciting, not just descriptions, so that the recipient is enticed to download the images.
- Keep the message size between 20K and 40K, or lower.
- Always send multivariant emails through your campaign tools (i.e., text and HTML), so that if a user has disabled HTML in the email client, that user will still receive the text.
- "Above the fold" is a graphic design concept that refers to the location of an important news story or photograph on the upper half of the front page of a newspaper.[4] In online media, it refers to the portion of the message or web page you can see without

scrolling. The fold line should be between 300 x 600 pixels on email content. Don't waste precious space above the fold with HTML or plain text; use a call to action above the fold or think of the first thing you want your recipient to see.

- CTAs should be above the fold, and repeated in the body of the email.
- Clearly identify the CTA that you want the recipient to take. In an email with one specific CTA, do not distract reader attention by including lots of other links. We have seen this before, and the many links and response marketers were hoping for were not achieved. Keep things simple. The CTA may lead to a data-capture form (which should be consistently branded and hosted on a secure site) or it may lead to a branded localized website, landing page, or microsite that all should be consistently branded, easy to navigate, and lead to lead generation if intended to. You landing page should have a clear action.
- The upper-left corner of a HTML is the portion that shows in a preview window of clients such as Outlook and really deserves some extra thought. You have only two or three seconds to achieve recognition. Always make sure your brand is visible there.
- Set the maximum HTML email width to 620 pixels, unless you are specifically targeting mobile clients that render HTML; we'd say use half the width.
- Keep the design clean and simple.
- Use your design to move recipients toward the CTA.
- Use bullets to call attention to important details.
- Fully localize all online touchpoints.
- Only put key messages into content. For further information, link recipients through to website/landing pages or microsites, particularly for newsletters. You should use a link for all stories on your e-newsletter, so that if recipients want to read more about the fully localized news they can. You can also link to external sites.
- Use a signature graphic from senior members within your organization at the close of your emails, which can be effective.
- Regardless of the local language and special characters, use fonts that are universal on the Internet such as Arial, Verdana,

Tahoma, or Times New Roman. Any other fonts will resort to a default font if recipients don't have it installed on their computer and may corrupt the copy, which could be particularly problematic if the copy is already in local characters. Use the same font throughout your template and emails so that the emails are consistent.

- If you do not have localized images of people for the country you're targeting, use product images instead, location images, or graphics for services—as opposed to images of people who do not seem localized (in some countries this may be okay, others not).

- Include a redirect to the email content, hosted online, as a viewing workaround in case people can't view it when it arrived in their mailboax (e.g., "If you are having troubles viewing this email with images, click here"). Place this at the top of the email creative.

- Never use an image for your unsubscribe link.

- Include legal registration details in the email footer, plain text, and HTML.

- Add a link in the footer of the email that allows recipients to update preferences and permissions, so that you don't lose the contact all together if that contact decides to opt out of a specific message.

- Use one clear link to let recipients opt out. Also use one clear link to encourage recipients to update their permissions, preferences, contact information, and company information. A link to preference and permission should link to a profile page hosted on a site, which should feed and update your marketing database with up-to-date information.

- Don't send marketing emails with a from address of "do-not-reply@company.com" because such an address implies that no one is available in the company to follow up and it's not very personable.

- Avoid a statement at the top of your emails informing people not to respond (e.g., "Do not reply to this email as nobody will reply to it"). You should use a "from" address that can be responded to and has a valid person or people who will respond to incoming email. Email is a two-way communication channel.

Always make sure that you blast from a valid email address and give recipients options to reply to your communication. You can use an alias email address, though. In that case, if the recipient replies to it, that reply will be forwarded to the group of people behind the alias so that one of them can follow up with the customer or prospect request—or you could have a dedicated person to respond and route requests.

Any responses that can be picked up from marketing managers are good sources of local feedback. Recipients may reply with positive feedback, but are also likely to reply with criticisms, comments, and negative feedback, which should indicate what you need to avoid in the future and improve on. This is great market research, and it's free. You can get free opinions and feedback, the same way as you can through social networks.

Endnotes

[1] Wikipedia, "HTML," http://en.wikipedia.org/wiki/HTML.

[2] Spamhouse, "Definition of SPAM," http://www.spamhaus.org/definition.html.

[3] Wikipedia, "Phishing," http://en.wikipedia.org/wiki/Phishing.

[4] Wikipedia "above the fold," http://en.wikipedia.org/wiki/Above_the_fold.

7

Winning with Webcasts, Websites, and More

Upon completion of this chapter, you should be able to

- Describe the role that webcasts and video on demand can play in your marketing efforts in emerging markets
- Explain the importance of your website in your efforts in emerging markets and identify a number of ways to maximize its potential
- Identify the best practices that will keep your company's online efforts relevant in emerging markets

Webcasts and Video on Demand

A webcast is a form of real-time online media used to broadcast recorded or live events such as training, presentations, educational information, seminars, and product/service launches. End users can "telecommute" rather than physically attend. Viewers should register to watch the webcast or video on demand (VoD). The content is delivered through streamlined media over the Internet (i.e., the attendee can receive the content at the same time it's being broadcast). The content can be video, PowerPoint, or only audio.

A webcast can be delivered from a remote location (namely, the domestic country) and can be broadcast to thousands in the local country in the EM. Webcasts are an interactive medium between the broadcaster and the target audience, and you can ask the audience to participate in questions and answers or polling or communicate with them directly by private instant messaging, for example.

Events can be viewed after the broadcast by VoD (which can be accessed, over the Internet, at any time by a user or subscriber and can be placed on your website or the link can be posted to multiple locations).

A webcast is a great incentive/offer to encourage end users to provide information about themselves.

You can use also video-sharing websites to broadcast ideas for free, such as YouTube, although this site is currently restricted or blocked in some EM countries (e.g., China and Libya); if you want to reach countries where YouTube is restricted, you can upload your videos to other video servers. A disadvantage of YouTube is that you can't collect contact data before viewers watch your content if they arrive directly at YouTube, so you won't be able to move the contacts along the ebocube commercial cycle, unless you request their data by using a call to action (CTA) at the end of your video or before you redirect them to YouTube (for example, if you're redirecting them from an email).

You can also broadcast ideas via podcasts, audio and video, that can be downloaded from your website to MP3 players or devices such as the iPhone, iPad, or iPod Touch.

All the media previously mentioned are relatively new to emerging markets (EMs), and very popular. Therefore, results can be better than they are in developed economies, where the media's not so new, although EMs differ in terms of sophistication.

Webcast are broadcast in real time, and are an interactive medium. The medium means your audiences can interact with you. As well as being a great medium to deliver information, they're also a great medium to capture information. You can capture attendee behavior (e.g., what time they left, determining levels of interest in your content, and record the questions that they asked and who asked).

Webcasts are as equally measurable as physical events, but give you a little more insight on the level of interest in real time.

Metrics include the following:

- **Registrations:** You can determine prior to the webcast how many people have registered.

- **Attendees and attendee rates:** Once the webcast starts and is over, you can determine how many people have attended.

- **No shows:** Again, once the webcast has begun, you can determine how many people who have registered haven't attended, or "no shows."

- **Drop-off rate:** While the webcast is in progress, tools can monitor when people drop off the webcasts. Webcast tools can tell you at which part of the content an attendee dropped off, so you know if you lost them, and so on.

- **Cost per attendee:** You can determine how much the webcast cost you and hence split that per attendee to determine how much it has cost you to communicate to each attendee.

- **Number of questions asked or submitted and by whom:** You can look at reports after the webcast to determine contact questions and who asked them, you can also advise attendees to email you or the speaker if you are unable to answer all questions during the seminar.

- **The exact time a question was asked:** For example, questions may have increased during a specific section of the broadcast, and this may highlight specific areas of interest for you.

- **Voting/polling in real time:** You can invite people to vote on an opinion.

- **Attendee evaluation through a questionnaire at the end of the event:** Feedback is likely to be more honest because the attendees are not face to face with the presenter, and their opinions are not biased by a free lunch, likely to be available at a physical event.

- **Leads and lead conversions:** These are registrants who have answered lead-qualification questions while registering or requested to be contacted by sales in your evaluation questionnaire. These leads or potential leads can be loaded to your sales management tool to be contacted by sales or sent to a call center to be qualified further. Any leads or potential leads should be reported in your ebocube dashboard.

The process of updating your database and sales tool should be automated, as ideally your webcast registration interface should feed and update your customer insight database, account management, or call center tools with leads or potential leads. Ensure that, whichever process you chose, it's simple and as quick as possible. Leads get "colder" the longer they are left processing; contacts may find a new solution or may forget about your proposition, or another project may arise that they would rather spend their budget on.

- **Integration:** Your webcast registration tool should be integrated to your dashboard, and to your marketing database via any third-party provider you might use, even if you have to load and report the data by manually feeding your tools. However, tools should be provided by your webcast service provider. Ideally, you want a registration process and evaluation form that feeds the ebocube dashboard with leads and other meaningful metrics that you can use to determine whether or not you have achieved your aims and objectives.

- **Sales/closed opportunities for generated leads:** This shows you how many sales were generated from contacts that watched a webcast

- **New contact records in your database:** This is a key objective for you to build your CI database with contacts prospects and contacts for customers. You should monitor regularly how many new names you have gathered in your dashboard, particularly using the datacube.

You should aim to localize your email invite to the webcast, reminder, and thank-you email to the webcast, as well as the webcast registration page, webcast content (e.g., language, speaker's subject, case studies, and complexity of message). The more you localize, the higher the costs, but also the higher the likelihood of the return on marketing investment (ROMI) and high-quality marketing leads. Also, in comparison to a physical event, the cost and risks are much lower.

Webcast Applications

Numerous webcast web-based applications are on the market. Make sure that your webcast application choice will support your marketing and make webcast management easy and smooth. Subscription-based service providers for webcasts are also available. Make sure that you subscribe and pay for the service that you are actually going to use. Invest time in research. Doing so might help improve your ROMI. These providers can send you webcast reporting metrics (e.g., registration, attendee, and evaluation data or leads). The data fields received should match the minimum requirement fields in your marketing database and reporting dashboard. For example, minimum data required in your marketing database may include company name, company size, email address, opt-in permission, first name, and last name.

Also, if you want to localize the webcast and you want to provide a localized registration page and capture local characters to feed your marketing database (which is set up to receive local characters), you need to check whether the service provider can provide this. Otherwise, you might ask an agency to provide the registration page and just use the webcast service provider to broadcast your content—over time you will find an integrated solution to online communication that feeds your reports seamlessly or at least through a clear process. The trick is to start somewhere.

All stages in the ebocube commercial cycle can be achieved by webcast (see Table 7.1). Webcasts can move contacts along the ebocube commercial cycle. They can also be used to nurture prospects and keep them engaged and interested and can be used to retain valuable and loyal customers—content can be specialized by industry, company size, or company accounts; for example, content for a high-value account related to their specific needs. A webcast is particularly good at converting a lead candidate to a potential customer. Webcast registration forms can be used to capture new contact and company data, to enhance existing data.

TABLE 7.1   The ebocube Commercial Cycle Metrics Matrix—Webcast: Metric in Relation to the ebocube Commercial Cycle Stages/Goals

Stage in the ebocube Commercial Cycle	Webcast Primary response	Secondary metric response
All Phases of the ebocube Commercial Cycle	Registrations	
	Attendees	
	Evaluation (postevent report)	
	Lead candidates	
Awareness/Acquisition	Registrations	Evaluation (postevent report)
	Attendees	
Consideration/Nurture and Develop	Registrations	
	Attendee	
	Data submission, with BANT	
	Evaluation (postevent report)	
	Lead candidates	Attendees
Purchase/Develop	Registrations	
	Data submission, with BANT	Registrations
	Lead candidates	
	°Leads/sales	
	Evaluation (postevent report)	
Loyalty/Retention	Registrations	Evaluation (postevent report)
	Attendees	
	°Lead candidates	
	Leads/up-sell, cross-sell	

°Leads can be generated by webcasts (or targeted purchase/development/loyalty communications using data-capture forms with BANT questions or a call to action to contact sales), capturing BANT through a data-capture form or advising contacts to call a sales/account manager. Leads can be converted into sales by your sales force. Some marketers prefer to re-qualify data captured by registration forms, through a call center, to improve the quality of the lead and to provide more context/information on the marketing lead for sales. The quality of a webcast lead will depend on the data targeted; i.e., is the contact really ready to be developed, purchase, or is this newly acquired data? A sale can be attributed to the leads generated/influenced by the webcast; however, it may not show in the system until up two quarters later due to the sales cycle. Sales should update this information.

Data Capture

Webcasts can be promoted on your website, partner websites, third-party local websites, Facebook localized pages, LinkedIn local social media sites, third-party local banners, and in offline targeted press. The global audience crosses boundaries, so anyone can register to your webcast, giving you full contact and company information.

As long as the media placement is targeted and the subject is relevant to your audience, you can achieve high registration rates, a high number of attendees, and high-quality sales leads. Even if 10,000 people see the promotion of your webcast and 2,000 people register and 1,000 people attend, you can still achieve high ROMI and sales opportunities at relatively low cost in comparison to offline events.

We recommend that you put in place a data-capture form behind your registration link, so that registrants can give you their contact and company details. This also enables the system to send them automated webcast details such as time, date, location, and unique URL. Data captured should be used to update the marketing database CI with new contact data or for updating existing contact information.

- For best results, we recommend you localize your email invite and the registration form, whether that's using images of people from the local market, or writing copy in local language.
- You should also localize the data-capture fields, as well. For example, most EM countries don't have *county* or *state* so don't ask for this information because it doesn't exist. You will force your end user to submit random data (like test, or xyxyxyxy, etc.), or someone might end up entering his country into the county field, which will impact the quality of your data and segmentation—if you segment by country, this field may not be populated because people have updated the wrong field. This will make your data collection poor. Don't confuse end users by asking questions they can't answer.

Webcasts have clear and effective uses at every stage of the campaign, from awareness/acquisition, to nurture/consideration, to

purchase/development, to loyalty and retention. This makes a webcast one of your most flexible and enduring techniques. Goals for
each stage of the buying cycle include the following:

Goals for stage one: awareness/acquisition

- Raising awareness of your brand
- Launching a new product, raising awareness of a service/
  upgrade
- Capturing new contact data

Goals for stage two: nurture/consideration

- Contacts subscribe to your webcast from an email invite, website (your own or partner website or a third-party website), or
  online or offline banner.
- Webcast attendees can be followed up by telemarketing, either
  from a call center or account managers.
- Webcast registration, evaluation forms, and webcast questions
  and answers, all can be used to gather contact information and
  insight about your audience. This can be used for sales purposes and for follow-up e-campaigns.
- Evaluation forms can be used to ask attendees to evaluate your
  webcast at the end of the webcast. You might ask them to rate
  the subject, the speaker, or any other aspect.
- A webcast can build relationships with new contacts and
  migrate prospects in the ebocube commercial cycle to become
  warmer leads, and your sales force or local partners can make
  follow-up calls, aiming to make sales.
- Some webcast applications allow you to use the power of video
  conferencing; the speakers could set up webcams or go to a stu-
  dio and record and broadcast to viewers.

Through data capture, you can make sure your prospects details
are correct and up-to-date, again using online registration forms,
which ideally should feed your marketing database and reporting
tools automatically. However, if you use an independent provider, you
will need to do this manually.

Goals for stage three: purchase development

• Qualified leads (attendee/registration data) can form closed opportunities. You can use survey questions on the registration form to qualify registration and attendees as potential leads with BANT questions (i.e., asking registrants if they have budget, authority, or responsibility to purchase). Advise them of upcoming projects and time frames to understand what they want to buy immediately.

• You can follow up registrations, captured through online forms, with lead-qualification telemarketing followed by sales calls. By so doing, you're developing the prospect data into customer data and developing existing customer relationships.

Goals for stage four: loyalty and retention

• Webcasts can keep all your customers up-to-date and informed, from the comfort of their own personal computer, whether that's on the beach in Dubai, a deep forest in Serbia, or the hustle and bustle of Beijing or Shanghai. These can be quite small scale for a specific industry or account and managed by an account manager or person who speaks the local language. The content can be created by a local marketing agency or an in-house marketing team and can be created with the aim of promoting a specific solution tailored for a loyal account.

Event Costs

Imagine you're in Moscow, looking for the perfect location for your first event in an EM. First of all, you need to know where a good location is, so, as an event manager, you would probably have to fly to the country to inspect the event location or engage with a good local agency to do that for you, unless you have a local marketing team who will take care of that.

You'll need to negotiate a good price to rent the location; you'll need to hire a caterer for the local event; and you'll need to brand the event for the local market, order the localized giveaways, and arrange for the speakers to travel. Now suppose that 30% of your hard-copy direct mail invites bounce (providing you can measure that). Your speaker gets stuck in customs because his passport is stamped by a country that is not welcomed in that country politically, your branded giveaways are under suspicion, and your food offends the local culture. As attendees start to arrive, it's a challenge to capture all of their names even though you have 20 laptops set up because they haven't registered online and decided to turn up at the last minute, or attendees haven't brought their tickets/barcodes for you to scan. At the evening dinner, more people turn up than planned for and you have to bring out extra seating, but that's still not enough, and you suspect the two attendees who have turned up in jeans are at the dinner for a free night out, while some actual customers have not been seated! The event has not only been costly to your budget, but to your reputation.

Webcasts are cost-effective because

- You don't have to rent a location, facilities, or catering.
- Your company and speakers don't need to travel, so you don't pay for flights, accommodation, visas, and expenses.
- There are no giveaway costs, branding costs (except branding of your collateral), or event staff fees (unless you hire speakers).
- Attendee data is captured with online registration or login and then is automatically and instantly fed into the marketing database if set up through the registration process.

Webcasts allow you to target contacts across global boundaries and time zones. An online media plan consisting of multiple local media websites will get excellent reach in local EMs, supported by advertising on your own localized websites. Although physical events are still extremely popular in EMs, your prospective audience can't always travel due to logistics or costs, especially not for unknown brands. Attendees can choose to respond or not with the rest of the audience and can participate without feeling conspicuous. Physical events should be used strategically—for example, an "annual expo" major launch, sponsorship of an industry event, raising awareness to capture new prospects, retain loyalty, generate PR—rather than tactically (e.g., customer workshops).

Webcast systems can be automated to send reminders, one day before the event or even one hour or five minutes. For example, if the culture is relaxed and people generally have a good work-life balance, a webcast may not top their priorities. Also, the medium is still relatively new. However, if the content is valuable and targeted, response rates are likely to increase.

As an example, one of our first series of webcasts targeted small to medium-sized businesses with 20 to 250 employees, midmarket businesses with 251 to 500 employees, and larger enterprises of 501 to 1,000. Although the webcast was in English, the email invites were fully localized, including languages, copy, images, and most important, time zones. We did the following:

- Localized text for invites, translation done by local marketing teams in 15 languages
- Used English where it was an accepted business language (such as India or Saudi)
- Targeted existing data as well as newly purchased lists in 25 countries
- Broadcast across 20 different time zones to a global audience with no space constraints

Even though the webcast was broadcast in English, attendees had the option to submit their questions in local languages, and we had question managers in local countries answering questions in local languages in real time. Although you can target a wide audience with webcasts, in comparison to offline media such as TV and radio, you can be more targeted with the medium. With radio and TV, you can market to the audience that is expected to consume the media; however, with webcasts, you can target based on self-reported job titles, companies, company sizes, and firmographics. You can target contacts based on marketing history stored in your marketing database (e.g., respondent to previous webcasts or communications).

Overall, we suggest these techniques for ensuring webcast success:

- Pay attention to the quality of the user experience, from the initial registration, receiving reminder, and calendar invite, through to attending, dialing, and logging in, viewing the content, submitting questions, and completing evaluation forms.
- Test the webcast ahead of time by having someone on your team dial in to make sure the number is working for participants and speakers.
- Engage with a reliable webcast provider or install reliable applications; choose quality over price to avoid poor user or speaker experiences.
- Ensure your local speakers or moderators in local countries have a good-quality high-speed connection, preferably a wired connection as opposed to wireless.
- Ask that speakers call and log in an hour before the webcast to discuss webcast execution.
- Place the speaker where it won't pick up ambient noise.
- Inform speakers and moderators to close other applications, such as instant messaging, email, and web applications, especially if the application requires them to share their desktops.
- If you broadcast prerecorded content, let your audience know that questions will be answered by interactive chat online rather than by the speaker.
- If questions are answered in the local language, you can use question managers in local countries/regions as well as the domestic countries.
- After attendees have registered, advise them to view the webcast on a high-speed Internet connection in a quiet location.
- Allow your audience to select high- or low-speed viewing when watching the webcasts. If it's high speed, the viewer will usually get the full-screen version and higher-quality broadcast.
- If your speaker is using a presentation instead of being recorded, advise the speaker to speak a few seconds after clicking to the next slide, because delays occur sometimes as viewers' browsers refresh.
- The webcast tool should drop a calendar invite into registrants' email accounts after they've registered. The calendar should contain the webcast URL and event details.

- Set up your webcast application to send automated reminders before the event. You can arrange for automated reminders to be sent up to five minutes before the webcast starts, stating, "(Webcast is now starting.)"

- For "no shows," request that the webcast application provider host the content online so that they can access it as a VoD. At some point, you might want to post it on your website for all visitors to access, or email "no show data" with the VoD.

- You can produce podcasts by dividing the webcast content into short podcasts. Podcasts typically last for 10 to 15 minutes.

- Ensure the webcast team is logged in to the webcast and application and dialed in to the number at least 20 to 45 minutes before the webcast. This is a good opportunity to test the login details, the dial-in number, the quality of voice and web applications, and the content (video or presentations). It's even more important that you're prepared if the content will be broadcast live and not prerecorded.

- To ensure that all the expected attendees see the content from the start, when the webcast is due to start, take a few minutes to let your host introduce the topic, the application, and to welcome the attendees. It's a good opportunity and time to present how questions and polls will be dealt with on the webcast (housekeeping rules) and to let viewers know that there will be an evaluation form. This will allow late joiners to see the webcast content from the start. Joiners may be late in EMs due to login experiences, slow connections, or just because of cultural differences!

- If your moderators cannot answer all the attendees' questions in real time, perhaps because they don't have the answer or there are too many questions; they can follow up the question with an email response or phone call, which should be mentioned in the introduction to the webcast. You should include a opt-in check box on the webcast registration form (in the invite) for follow marketing e-communications.

- If the webcast is localized, we encourage that the host of the webcast (and the moderator) speak the local language. However, if you haven't got the budget to localize the webcast or to get a local speaker, ensure the moderators can answer questions in the local language, and have local characters set up on their keyboards. Moderators can be an employee, partner, or salesperson, as long as they have the answers and are comfortable answering in real time.

- Some webcast applications enable you to show your slides in any order (as opposed to a strict sequential order), which allows you more flexibility and control. If you want more flexibility to refer to previous or upcoming slides in the deck, this may be a useful function to look into or use, and it also helps if you are running out of time.

- It's good practice to email the link to the VoD to the attendees and no shows 24 hours (in an ideal world) after the webcast so that they can review the content or see what they've missed. You can use an automated system to speed up this process as part of your application, or you can edit the video (including the viewers' questions) and send the email out from your campaign tools, including one-to-one emails at a slightly later date.

- You can host the video on your public/partner websites using a data-capture form as a prerequisite to viewing the video to capture new contacts and potential leads. The video can be split into a podcasts and hosted on your public site. A podcast can be downloaded onto a PC or mobile device. Podcasts can be delivered as RSS feeds from your website, and you can allow people to subscribe.

Websites for Marketing in Emerging Markets

WWW stands for World Wide Web, of course. But, you can also think of it as a stand in for World Wide Wealth. A website is no longer a one-way channel or catalog. It can offer you huge competitive advantage if used to its full potential. There are limitless opportunities as long as your site is interactive; visitors should be able to leave comments, subscribe to articles, download material, and click to chat. Contacts in EMs can view your site from a number of devices, including laptops and smartphones.

A website is a measurable, trackable, interactive tool. At a minimum, it should include a beginning file known as a home page, or online "shop" window, and a collection of interlinked web pages that can be accessed through the Internet.

Web pages may contain text, images, videos, podcasts, blogs, forums, links to social networks, instant messaging/click to chat, downloadable whitepapers, video case studies, manuals, demos, RSS feeds, and other multimedia.

Your website may be used for e-commerce, depending on your product or service. Your site should be maintained and updated to keep visitors returning and to rank highly on search engines. Your website should be used to capture information, such as contact or company information, and feed your marketing database. Your website is also good for capturing user behavior through web analytics, and users can provide you with feedback through data-capture forms.

Without a website, your company does not exist in the new cyberworld of an EM. Without a localized website or localized key pages, your company is less competitive in the local markets. Local content and local websites create competition for local companies, and are important for search engine optimization. Your website is key to your ebocube strategy and will leave the competition miles behind. EM countries comprise more than three-quarters of the globe and have booming populations who are online now more than ever before. Your online communication can lead users to your site for more information and allow them to follow the stages as they move along the ebocube commercial cycle. It is made up of several components.

Microsite

A microsite is a temporary set of focused pages separate from the parent or primary company website, although they may link back to main website. The microsite is likely to have its own domain name, which should contain the activity name (as part of the promotion) and may be localized, as long as the characters are Latin. At the time of this writing, however, we know that Arabic characters will soon work in web browsers. The microsite domain may make reference to the company name (e.g., www.ebocubesumitt.com) or it may be a subdomain of the master domain (e.g., www.ebocube.com/sumitt), or it could be a completely distinct domain name.

The primary purpose of a microsite is to provide information focused specifically on a marketing campaign about a product, service or event. Such sites may be linked into a main site or not or taken completely off a site's server when the activity is scheduled to end. The parent site of a company contains broader information and is not activity/ campaign specific. The microsite is intended to achieve an objective in the ebocube commercial cycle for a specific campaign, which would be difficult to achieve with the parent website containing lots of different pages of information, which may overwhelm the visitor.

Campaign Landing Page

A campaign landing page, not to be confused with a web landing page, is a page that can be separate to your parent site and is designed to match offline or online communications as part of an integrated page. Its primary goal is data capture and promotion of a specific activity. It allows for design, copywriting, and a clear offer. The purpose of separating this from the parent site is to optimize results and to not dilute the message, because users may navigate the parent site going away from the CTA. A landing page may have no navigation bar at all. A data-capture form is in the form of a landing page. (The generic term *landing page* refers to the first page a person sees when linking to a website, which is different from a campaign landing page.)

SMART Objectives

Before you build a local site or redesign your existing site, create a microsite or a landing page and ensure that you have well-defined, documented SMART objectives (online brief covered in operations) outlining what these forms of media should achieve and the metrics you will use as key performance indicators of success. The ebocube commercial cycle helps you to define those objectives and to optimize, execute, analyze, and measure what your site can achieve as part of your ebocube strategy.

After you have your objectives, design your site with the user in mind. Too many websites are designed for companies as opposed to being designed for users.

Your website/microsite/landing page objectives should derive from the ebocube commercial cycle and your overall EM strategy.

Each time you devise a campaign that directs traffic to a landing page, you should have clear objectives in mind. A high number of visitors is a good sign, but you have to take them on a journey and close the loop on your marketing effort by capturing contact information and developing the contact.

Localization

Using a local website and local content will create competition for local companies and leave global competitors who are not localized miles behind. Localized content will improve search ranking, too, if users search in local languages.

Purchase localized domain names (e.g., www.ebocube.br, www.ebocube.cn).

A global gateway/filter on your .com home page should create a global gateway that allows visitors to be routed to pages for their local market. This allows users to navigate to their local site and relevant information, which is in the local language.

Purchase the local domain name and redirect users to the parent site .com localized pages (e.g., www.ebocube.pl will redirect to www.ebocube.com/).

A localized domain name is good for all of your marketing collateral. For example, if you promote www.ebocube.br and redirect to the parent domain with a localized section, the localized domain will be perceived better by local audiences and among local competition. (BR is the ISO code and domain name for Brazil.)

Web Content and Analytical Measurement Tools

Many user-friendly web content management systems (CMS) are on the market. CMS tools are used to control the content and the structure of websites. You should invest in a CMS tool that enables you to host rich media and interactive applications. A good CMS tool for EM should also support various language character sets.

Core to ebocube is measurement, which can be presented through the dashboard (as discussed in phase one). Web analytics can feed a number of the metrics in the dashboard depending on the defined campaign metrics, based on the ebocube commercial cycle objectives. For example, web hits may be a part of your operational view, whereas a regional/country pipeline generated through the Web will be in your high-level view.

Web analytics reports can provide unique insight into user behavior on your website. They can give you an understanding of usage of your site, including popular pages in the local country and localized pages versus nonlocalized content. Web analytics can let you know where traffic has come from (upstream traffic) and gone to (downstream traffic). Web analytics can help you identify marketing and sales opportunities and to maximize performance. Web analytics tools can show whether you're currently getting traffic from the EM on your .com site.

All stages in the ebocube commercial cycle can be achieved through your website (see Table 7.2). Your website needs to support the phases of ebocube commercial cycle. It is best to integrate your website with other forms of marketing communications.

TABLE 7.2   The ebocube Commerical Cycle Metrics Matrix—Website

Stage in the ebocube Commercial Cycle	Site/parent/campaign landing page Primary response	Secondary metric response
All Phases of the ebocube Commercial Cycle	Data submission Downstream traffic Upstream traffic Exit survey, customer satisfaction survey Information from forums of blogs Most popular pages (time spent and unique visitor)	
Awareness/Acquisition	Unique visitors/page New visitors/page Data submission Bounce rate Subscribe to newsletter/RSS Click on CTA or download (podcast/vod/whitepaper/case study/webcast link)	Click to chat
Consideration/Nurture and Develop	Click on CTA or download (podcast/vod/whitepaper/case study/webcast link)	
	Click to chat	Unique visitors/page
	Return visitors based on cookies	New visitors/page
	Data submission	Data submission
	Lead candidates/leads	Bounce rate

TABLE 7.2   The ebocube Commerical Cycle Metrics Matrix—Website

Purchase/Develop	Sales, e-commerce	
	Data submission	
Loyalty/Retention	Customer portal login usage	Unique visitors/page
	Return customers to site	New visitors/page
		Data submission

Awareness and Acquisition

Your website enables wide reach, and you can reach millions of people with your website globally, regionally, or by country. Internet users are choosing to look at you and are aware of your business if they've visited your site, so you need to measure the number of unique visitors, number of sessions (pages they have visited), and perhaps bounce rates (people who have accessed one page and logged off of that same page without visiting other pages).

You can increase web traffic and the number of people visiting your site in a number of ways. However, the ultimate aim of your site is to take people to the later stages of the ebocube commercial cycle (namely, consideration, purchase, and loyalty). Before you increase traffic, consider what you want the customer journey to be, and design your site so that it's easy for the user to accomplish tasks to meet your objectives and move along the ebocube commercial cycle. You might use specific microsites and campaign landing pages as part of your integrated campaigns. These are dedicated to your campaign and message and avoid dilution from your main parent site. Awareness can be generated for your company or brand, your products and services, events, public relations, and general company information.

Data Capture

Data-capture surveys can be used on your website. Your website is available 24/7 globally and offers a good opportunity for your company to capture data in an EM.

On your local pages, whether users access them through the global gateway or through a local domain, ensure data-capture forms are short and localized to achieve maximum results.

In the Middle East and India, English as a business language is acceptable. However, you could test variations of localized versus nonlocalized data-capture forms and measure which is the most successful for other countries or offer both English and a local language on a page or site. Videos and images are a great ways to raise awareness; you can link to videos (e.g., hosted on YouTube or a video server) from your site to raise awareness.

Data Capture and Raising Awareness

Incentives for information, such as free online whitepapers, newsletters, and demos, are a good way to feed marketing database prospect information and to refresh your customer contact data. This information should be easy to extract for the purposes of campaign segmentation and should be reported in your datacube.

Automated emails of welcome should be generated as soon as the visitor has submitted contact information and your system has verified it. Encourage the new contact to update preferences and permissions. This follow up will ensure the nurture campaign will be more targeted. If you're following up with existing contacts, thank them for their continued interest and include a link for them to update their permissions and preferences. These emails should already exist and be executed by the system.

You should encourage contacts to send links to colleagues via share-a-link or links to social network sites, but not all major global social network sites are popular in EMs. Keep your content up-to-date to encourage visitors to return to your site, and as a general rule, you shouldn't have out-of-date content on your site. Other techniques for you to use at this stage include giving visitors the option to subscribe to RSS feeds (Real Simple Syndication). This is an easy way to distribute content via the Internet. You can also encourage people to share pages on social media like Facebook or to "retweet" content on Twitter; the aim is to bring more visitors to your site and create a call to action. Typical content includes email newsletters, podcasts, blog content, and even links to sites. Your website can also use the following:

- External web banners to raise awareness and interest.
- Links to your site from related sites.
- YouTube can promote business videos along.
- Links to business social network sites, such as LinkedIn, or nonbusiness specific such as Facebook, Orkut, or Xiaonei (Chinese equivalent of Facebook), along with other social business networks. You should research which sites are popular in each region or EM, and track clicks on links using trackable, friendly URLs.
- Links from external e-commerce sites.

Search Engines

Search engines are used the world over. Google is the world's leading search engine. However, there are local search engines in EMs that you need to consider for web promotion. For example, in China, Baidu is the leading search provider (2010), and so your in-house team or agency will need to engage with them.

Invest time and resources to research the best local search engine to achieve maximum effectiveness in the region and country. In the following list, we identify just a few of the leading search engines in some EM countries:

- **China:** Baidu dominates.[1]
- **South Korea:** Naver (72.7%), Daum (11.5%), Yahoo! (6.2%).[2]
- **Bulgaria:** Google, followed by MSN, Yahoo!, Jabse.[3]
- **Czech Republic:** Seznam.cz (62.53%), Google (24.75%), Centrum.cz (4.84%),[4] Atlas.cz (2.58%), Jyxo.cz (0.42%).[5]
- **Russia:** Yandex (47.5%), Google (25.1%), Rambler (14.8%).[6]
- **Ukraine:** Google (51.3%), Yandex (31.5%), Rambler (8.7%), Meta.ua (2.8%), Mail.ru (2.6%).[7]

Your web content can also affect the ranking of your website on search engines. Just remember in this regard, EMs and businesses in developed economies are likely to search online for business solution the same way.

Once visitors have landed on your site, from whichever method they were driven, and have been tracked and reported, you can raise awareness using rich media, interactive methods, and downloads.

Demand Generation

End users who are actively searching online for products and services are in the consideration stage. You can use your site to move searchers from awareness to consideration by doing the following:

- Making it easy for people to contact your company, by including a phone number, or by enabling visitors to fill in their information for a callback, or via live chat.
- Providing incentives once they complete the requested forms.
- Posting customer testimonials using quotes or videos, or viral case studies.
- Allowing people to register for offline and online events. This will increase their consideration of your brand, product, and services and give you further opportunity to communicate.

Netmining allows you to adopt behavioral targeting to understand business users' interests. By anonymously observing user behavior through cookies over a number of days, your company can gain a deeper understanding of a visitor's needs and online tendencies and can serve people relevant and timely content online related to what they have searched for. For example, user x returns to site page y three times in one week, your company presents an online data-capture form making reference to her search criteria, or produces a pop-up online chat box. This allows you to recognize she is a potential sales lead who has demonstrated interest.

If you intend to send the potential lead straight to sales (i.e., bypass the call center), ensure the candidate has BANT (i.e., they have a budget, authority to buy, need/project and time frame for project) to avoid wasting sales time. If they do not have BANT, keep their data stored in the marketing database as data that can be nurtured and developed with further consideration campaigns.

Nurture/Consideration

After you have acquired data, you need to keep the contact "warm." If they've registered for a whitepaper on a specific topic, the next phase is to send the contact an awareness email on the topic. Make sure you have captured the data on the contact interested in receiving the download, and then send the contact an email related to the demonstrated interest to which the contact has opted in. Make sure you are tracking calls as well as emails and feeding responses to your marketing database and thus building a history, which is your contact intelligence. For a further discussion of this process, see Chapter 9, "Marketing Operations (mops)."

Customers need to see how easy it is for them to procure your product or service. If your product is low risk and easy to implement (for example, software that can be downloaded directly to an end user's PC) or a purchase (for example, downloading an ebook to Kindle from Amazon), websites are a good tool for e-commerce straightforward transactions; otherwise, they are good for lead generation and capturing contacts that can be forwarded onto sales.

For complex, high-risk products, buyers are unlikely to close a deal online, particularly in EMs where people like speaking one to one when it comes to sales or where trust is often built over time like in Asia. The best course is to direct them to a local partner or contact within your company, most likely the sales force. In EMs, people like to go to stores to feel and touch products and interact with a salesperson at the point of sale. A lot of EM countries like good business relationships, so once a contact is at purchase stage, he or she should be directed to a salesperson.

Purchase Development

Once contacts have made a decision to purchase your product or service, you want to retain their business as a loyal customer. You can do this by providing customers with the following:

- Logins to their own account through your website giving them personal offers.
- E-services that allow customers self-service elements online, which also save you money by reducing costs of customer service calls. To be successful and to ensure customer satisfaction, self-service sites need to be highly functional and localized for non-English-speaking users.

Customer benefits need to be exclusive to them to gain their loyalty (e.g., a preview of your latest product launch before the rest of the public finding out).

Customers can subscribe from their accounts to receive information with exclusive offers that can be delivered through RSS feeds or other online communication.

After you've defined your high-value loyal customers from your marketing database, using RFM (regency, frequency, and monetary) models, you might want to follow up with direct mail or gifts. At this point, you should have high-quality contact details for them, gained, for example, through invoicing systems or account manager relationships. Or, you can give account managers special links or emails that provide, only them, offers that they can receive online.

Benefits of Technology-Based Awareness

Cisco has saved billions of dollars annually leveraging Internet technology, allowing customers to have access to self-service support as well as creating partner web tools.

They update their customer support websites regularly with the latest presentations and other rich media and information, reducing print costs that would have been expended on brochures. Web enables e-support, so they also save on call center staff and customer service support costs. As well as saving money, the Web generates revenue for Cisco by creating sales opportunities by generating leads.

The Web also helps reduce environmental impact by allowing viewers to download content off of the Internet. Then it is up to them whether they print it. Your carbon footprint is further reduced by cutting out shipping and mailing.

Data Analysis

You can post surveys on your site and ask users what they think of your site and how it can be improved in the region or country. This provides valuable market research at low cost, with minimal effort (as long as the form is automated, which it should be). Use business rules to ensure the same users aren't targeted too often.

Website content can be analyzed and updated instantly. Therefore, if you have any news, contacts can read about changes as soon as they happen and respond in real time.

Through blogs, forums, and social media, your audience can share their authentic views, spontaneous reactions, and unfiltered personality, and you can view and respond in real time—this qualitative information doesn't feed a dashboard but is still extremely useful. This is a great way to obtain descriptive, primary market research and feedback. For example, blogs and collaborative media are extremely popular in China, as people use collaborative web applications to communicate and make their own news.

You can also enable live chat on your website to increase lead conversion or to provide customer services, reduce calling costs, and improve sales leads and customer satisfaction. You can conduct live chat as text from a developed economy to EM; the data is sent over the Internet, and it's free to communicate and instant.

Mobile devices such as smartphones increase reach because they make the Web that much more accessible. Devices are becoming more available and popular in EMs. For example, China is very advanced with the use of Mobile Web. In fact, in some locations outside of Beijing and Shanghai, it's easier to access Mobile Web than broadband. Always measure and analyze responses based on localizations versus nonlocalized and responses to different content, and test search engine optimization results in EMs and web optimization.

Web marketing is highly trackable for ROMI. It allows you to track web statistics to see how much traffic you get from the domain and opportunity pipeline, which can inform you what to keep active and what to shut down, or which content to remove.

Best Practices for Remaining Relevant

Creating web pages with local campaigns and localization is just the start. It's important to keep web content up-to-date and relevant so that users return and are engaged. This allows you to achieve a high search engine rank so that you can continue to generate prospects. Even multinationals have problems keeping their websites up-to-date, so keeping local content relevant is a challenge, but doable as long as you focus on what you can realistically manage and your A countries are first as a starting point for your web operation.

Ensure that you have the dedicated resources to maintain local pages or sites. You might want to maintain full sites for A countries and perhaps create just a few local pages for B and C countries. If you're targeting one EM country as opposed to several, you might have a button on your .com that allows users to convert popular or transaction landing pages into a local language. This is determined by your overall business strategy.

Be clear from the outset on your EM strategy and what your websites should achieve. This will improve the choice and amount of content. This focus allows you to improve the contacts' experience, capture quarterly results, and reduce masses of unnecessary content. Always keep your content simple and easy to navigate.

Design Practices

For all individual sites, without being inflexible or neglecting local insight through the web statistics (operational report), try to use standardized global information architectures, design, and wireframes. Templates and style sheets will allow you to do the following:

- Control information on your site.
- Be consistent (because the user may have used your .com previously). After all business users who travel expect consistency across the globe.
- Be cost-effective by having to spend less time on website design and development.
- Launch a campaign across EMs in multiple regions consistently. Websites designed sharing the same templates globally allow you to update your content quickly and easily in less time with less money.
- Brand with a consistent look and feel for all of your pages and sites. This will help you to establish a strong global brand identity.
- Standardize using style sheets to control formatting, including colors, fonts, layouts, sizes, or multiple sites using one master page and cascading elements. To improve efficiency, use Cascading Style Sheets (CSS) for the Web. (Remember this is not to be used for email!)
- Authorize members of you local team to have access to certain pages so that they can make up-to-the-minute changes.

Functionality over Design

Although design through rich media is important on your pages, it's more important that visitors to your web pages, microsites, campaign landing pages, and parent site can easily achieve their user goals through good *functionality* and *navigation*, which ensure a good user experience.

Use imagery and video, but keep the files small and make sure they still present well. Look at what other companies are doing. For example, Amazon's site is highly functional and successful, although the design is extremely simple.

Remember to identify and use keywords and key phrases on your home page to improve your search engine ranking. Keywords need to be written in local languages if businesses use local languages to search instead of English. Research which keywords or keyword phrases your target audiences are likely to use through your partners, local teams, sale force, or account manager. Use web analytics tools to understand which keywords are driving traffic to your site and make sure your browser page titles and page headings contain keywords, too.

Use static imagery on your site rather than rich media if you know that a region or connection may have a slow connection speed. Especially avoid using rich media images on your home page because users' first point of call may be your home page. A slow is experience is a bad experience.

Although Internet penetration in EMs is growing rapidly, and many businesses decision makers and influencers have access to the Internet, you need to consider that connection speeds will vary across EM regions. If possible, get your local team/partners to test pages on a local connection.

Search Engines, Browsers, and Links

Users in EMs may be using any number of browsers (e.g., Chrome, Firefox, Explorer, Netscape, and Safari), so research local browsers. Your site may display well on one browser but not on another, so test your site in different browsers and versions and optimize the average screen resolution accordingly.

Mobile Web can impact a viewer's experience of your site. Google and Facebook are optimized for mobile devices, but not all pages can be optimized for mobile screens, and it can be expensive for users trying to download rich media.

Work with your partners and local teams to research popular search engines. If you haven't got a local team, work with a local agency to get the research. Again, measure search results through your web analytics tool (operational dashboard).

Optimize the pages that are key to your users, such as contact details, information about your company, and partner/reseller locations.

Work with partners, resellers, and third-party sites (e.g., online newspapers), and request that they link to your site to improve your search engine optimization. Or add your link to related blogs or social networks yourself. New EM businesses will want to share information. Where better to let them do that than on your own website?

If you've offended the local culture, or your product or service isn't great, you might first find out about it through your blogs/forums, along with the rest of the world. Also, if people are writing in their local language, you might struggle to understand what they're saying about your business! Responding is a good opportunity to improve customer satisfaction and credibility.

Police the blogs and forums so that you know what content is being generated. Some negative content should be kept to improve the credibility of the user-controlled information. However, if the content is completely damaging, remove it and act on the feedback. If it's true, you can send communications or updates about your site informing users of any improvements or apologizing.

To achieve maximum impact with your websites, landing page, or microsite, follow this advice:

- Ensure that your website is interactive, or a two-way communication channel.
- Reserve country-specific domain names, such as .cn. If you want to establish yourself as a local player, a local domain name will help.
- On your .com site, create a global gateway that allows users to navigate to the local country site.
- Keep important information above the fold on your site, including your contact information and brand.
- Enable users to search easily so that they can find information quickly.
- Do not try to target several countries with localized websites at once because they are time-consuming to maintain and localization is expensive. Create localized sites based on A, B, and C country analysis. Test the success of them based on web analytics.
- If you don't have localized images of people, use product images or graphics for services rather than using images of people not from the local country.
- Include a legal footer giving full details of your registered company, which will improve trust; if you have a local office, use that.
- Ensure that web utilizes a Secure Sockets Layer (SLL) certificate if you're offering low-risk sales on your site or collecting any data/sensitive information.
- Allow users to subscribe to RSS feeds or email newsletters so that you can move them along ebocube commercial cycle and acquire/refresh data.
- Use the local language for conversion particularly (i.e., transaction pages or data-capture page). Ensure any survey forms are short and user friendly.
- Research local search engines. Don't rely on Google or Yahoo! for all of your search traffic.

- Keep content fresh and up-to-date to improve search engine optimization and to ensure return users.
- Promote your site offline, too, to improve maximum results.
- Use microsite and landing pages that can be switched off when campaigns have ended so as not to overload your main site with too much information.
- Localize key important pages, such as transaction pages, even if you can't localize the entire site.
- Use a global template that can be replicated by region.
- Your landing page should be neat, easy-to-read, and use space between content.
- Place the CTA above the fold.
- Repeat keywords from your campaign on your landing page.
- Keep the campaign landing page separate from your site and remove the primary site navigation, because you don't want to confuse users who are there to follow up the primary CTA. (You can link back to your parent site; however, this shouldn't be the main CTA, just an option.)
- Make sure the customer finds the offer easily; it should be featured in your email campaign, banner campaign, or other promotion.
- Offers should be relevant to your target audience, to persuade them to part with contact and company data.
- Collect contact and company information from visitors who visit your campaign landing page. (If you do not collect information, you are missing an opportunity to acquire names to build your marketing database and to generate potential sales leads.)
- Capture data to track the success of your overall campaign.
- Data-capture forms on websites, landing pages, and microsite must be short, contain mandatory fields, and be localized with the option to use English (because many EMs employ English-speaking expatriates).

Endnotes

[1]Multilingual-search, "GLOBAL SEARCH REPORT 2007," http://www.e3internet. com/downloads/global-search-report-2007.pdf.

[2] Ibid.

[3] Ibid.

[4] Ibid.

[5] Ibid.

[6] Ibid.

[7] Ibid.

8

Web Banners and Integrating Offline Channels into Your ebocube Strategy: "Offline Isn't Dead!"

Upon completion of this chapter, you should be able to

- Describe the efficacy of web banners
- Understand the importance of events to marketing strategies in emerging markets
- Identify why, when, and how direct mail should be used
- Discuss the role of telemarketing in emerging market strategies
- Distinguish above-the-line communication channels from other emerging market media

Web Banners

Web banners are a form of Internet advertising and should always be part of an integrated campaign. They're graphic images and come in various sizes. Banners can be created with animation. (This works well in emerging markets [EMs] by engaging audiences.) They can be used to encourage users to click through to a predefined website or campaign landing page. Banners can also be used on your internal site for key promotions.

Web banners can be used throughout the buying cycle. They will increase consideration, by getting visitors to click through to campaign landing pages, which should match the campaign collateral used for the integrated campaign. Landing pages should be optimized for campaigns. In EMs, there should be an offer, especially if a visitor has gone to the trouble of clicking your banner. Banners can be used for loyal customers, too; however, the message will be unique to customers with special offers.

Data-capture forms can be embedded behind banners so that when end users click them you can update or refresh the marketing data record. Before engaging an agency to buy media placements on the Web, work with partners to clearly define your campaigns objectives and the user interest. Research to determine where users should land when they click the link, what the follow up should be, and how much traffic you expect to click through. Make sure you have resources in place to follow up the data before placing the banner.

Even though you might achieve a high click-through rate and a high amount of traffic to your site for the duration of the campaign, this doesn't necessarily mean you've achieved your objectives. A high number of visitors can sometimes be perceived as a good thing because it shows that you have raised awareness, but you need to understand the contact's interest once he or she arrives on your landing page. If you have a high bounce rate (people exit your page immediately after arriving) coupled with high traffic, this can be deemed negative. Take users on a journey. You might want to plot what that looks like on paper. Take them to a data-capture form, or at least a download. This should be predefined as part of your integrated campaign goals and objectives.

Your banners may be more effective or deemed suitable if they are placed on local third-party websites. In some countries, website owners might not accept banners that are not localized, or the banner might look strange if it is not in the local language. In any scenario, images should reflect the local culture. This will increase click through to your localized website or microsite campaign landing page. Local media agencies will also be able to advise you on costs and where your competitors are advertising, plus the traffic for certain sites. The benefits of effective web banner strategy include the following:

- Gather data captured
- Piggybacks from established, tested popular sites in local markets with established traffic
- Be localized to EMs
- Partner with local media websites
- Allow you to be compelling to local markets
- Build brand awareness
- Include phone numbers or other direct response information
- Measure and track which website gives you the best results
- Measure which websites attract the most visitors
- Improve future campaigns based on data collection
- Test same banner on different websites
- Test offers and incentives
- Can be creative
- Can reach global markets

As with any media, make sure that the timing is right. You don't want to buy banner space during a local holiday, for instance, when traffic tends to dip.

You can use web analytics tools in your banner ads to track click-through rates yourself as opposed to relying on agency statistics. If you use your own data-capture form, include tracking priority codes (ebocodes) to check which banners have generated data (discussed Chapter 9, "Marketing Operations [mops]"). These can be measured against metrics in your dashboard, and contact data can have codes stored against them in your marketing database. This enables you to establish which campaign and communication medium they responded to (as discussed further in Chapter 9).

It's important to know what you can measure and what metrics mean as a result of your marketing efforts. Table 8.1 shows metrics that should be considered with web banner and social media websites.

TABLE 8.1   The ebocube Commercial Cycle Metrics Matrix—Banners and Social Media Metric in Relation to the ebocube Commercial Cycle Stage

Stage in the ebocube Commercial Cycle	External web banners and social network	
	Primary response	Secondary metric response
All Phases of the ebocube Commercial Cycle	Number of impressions on external site	
	Number of clicks	
	Data submission on banner or landing page	
	Bounce rate on landing page	
	Follow up on landing page CTA (download/data submission)	
Awareness/Acquisition	Number of impressions on external site	
	Number of clicks	
	Data submission on banner or landing page	
	Bounce rate on landing page	
	Follow up on landing page CTA (download/data submission)	
	Unique visitors to campaign landing page (new/returning)	
Consideration/Nurture and Develop	Click on CTA or download (podcast/vod/whitepaper/case study/webcast link)	Number of impressions on external site
	Click to chat	Unique visitors/page
	Data submission	New visitors/page
	Lead candidates/leads	Data submission
		Bounce rate
Purchase/Develop	Sales	
	Lead candidates collected through banner or site converted into sales	
Loyalty/Retention	Click through for customer offers plus follow up	

Awareness and Acquisition

If your campaign aim is awareness, you're likely to collect the minimum data, because people will not yet know about your products/solutions/services, although they might be aware of your brand. At this stage, you might only request an email address and opt-in permission as a starting point.

Use offers on your banners to entice contacts to give more information (e.g., free whitepaper, subscriptions to newsletters, click for a demo, free trial, or a free latest trendy gadget). As always, this data should feed your marketing database. This is a good way to capture prospect information and to refresh your customer contact data.

Ensure that data that you capture is stored in your database and that your marketing database can handle/store local characters. This information should be easy to extract for the purposes of campaign segmentation and should feed your datacube report.

As soon as the visitor has submitted contact information, and your system has established it through the database, an automated email can be sent either welcoming the new contact or giving the new contact the option to update preferences and permissions. This ensures the nurture campaign will be more targeted. If it's an existing contact, you can thank contacts for their continued interest and include a link for them to update their permissions and preferences. These emails should already exist and be executed by the system. The email may also further communicate the campaign advertised by the banner.

Consideration and Nurture

After you've acquired the initial data, you need to keep contacts interested. If they've registered for a whitepaper on a specific topic, the next phase should be to send that contact an awareness email on the topic. Before capturing data, the next step of the user journey should be predefined. For example, capture the new name, and to nurture the contacts, send them an email related to the demonstrated interest, as long as they've opted in.

Purchase and Development

Web banners used as part of an integrated campaign can be used to develop a customer into a loyal segment through up-sell and cross-sell promotions. The banner ad message may read, for example, "Upgrade your software." Data captured through banners can be developed by further communication such as email or telemarketing. If BANT (budget, authority, need, and time) questions have been answered and captured through the online banners, contacts should be directed to the call center or sales or account managers or partners for further qualification. Data captured should be validated by the survey. For example, the survey should let contacts know that contact details are invalid. After the data has been passed through the marketing database, data should again be validated, rejected, or passed on (to ensure data passed to channels is clean).

Retention and Loyalty

On your own site, you can have a separate login area for customers, and when they log on, you can use banners (e.g., "Upgrade your software, –10%") for your loyal segment or for customers you need to retain. This can be maintained by matching a landing page to the marketing message, which in turn creates a good customer experience.

Offline Methods

Marketers can continue to use offline methods as part of the awareness stage and should include a call to action (CTA), an optimized campaign landing page, or a dedicated microsite. It should include a user-friendly, localized URL. These methods may include the following:

- Print media with a CTA directing people to your site, including direct mail, industry newspapers, magazines, and so on. Classified advertisements in well-known newspapers in EMs do receive good reach, although buying media space might not appear highly sophisticated.
- Outdoor billboards in EMs are extremely popular. Some are digital, and with an online CTA, you can capture responses, and you can include a free phone number.
- Events/sponsored events—capture data for follow-up email campaigns.
- TV and radio advertising and sponsorship of programs/events—again use online call to actions ("go to www....Today!").

The landing page of a campaign referenced in offline ads must be specific as to what you want the user to do. For example, if you want to direct the contact to your parent site, be clear as to what you want the user to do. Otherwise, you could end up with a high bounce rate, which would be regrettable, especially after you've gone to the trouble of attracting thousands of visitors. To ensure users find what they are meant to find, you might use a campaign landing page separate from your website or a microsite, especially if you have a lot of information to share and the additional site is justified through return on marketing investment (ROMI).

In the consideration stage, you might also use a (toll) free phone number; however, it's expensive to encourage large numbers of people to call you at the awareness stage. The primary aim of awareness is to raise the profile of a company's brand/product/service and to get as many people in your target audience to see the communication. You can measure how many people have seen this by providing uniquely tracked friendly URLs per communication (e.g., ebocube.com/promotion). Therefore, you might just put the phone number on your website so that people who are in the consideration stage can call. Alternatively, you could put a data-capture form onto your landing page and call back candidates with BANT questions; or you can host a live chat during which any visitors can speak to your agents in real time.

There are a number of offline communication methods, and when used with online efforts, they can improve campaign effectiveness and objectives, although offline elements can be reduced greatly because of online possibilities. Traditionally, marketing communication made offline vehicles the primary delivery system and integrated online in a support role. Today offline is integrated and can be core to your business communication.

Offline communications, from events to telemarketing, should be executed and tracked through tracking tools, with the results feeding to your CI database, and they should be combined with online elements that are key to the execution.

Events

In EMs, in particular, people like to attend events and have face-to-face interaction. You will be expected to sponsor, exhibit, create, and speak at events. However, you cannot be at every physical event—this would be an ineffective use of budget—so online elements should be used to support your event and reduce your ROMI risk.

There are two main metrics that you should measure and track in the stages of the ebocube commercial cycle for events. The first is the number of registrants for your offline event (registered through online site). That is a key metric to measure because it indicates what you can expect (in terms of attendee numbers)—don't be surprised if for some EM countries, you get a spike in registrations days before the event! Naturally your attendee number will be lower than the number of registrations; you might get a 40% drop of rate because not every contact who registers will attend your event. It's a characteristic for developed-economy events but even more expected for emerging markets.

The second key metric is the number of attendees. This number is important because your aim is to turn those attendees into qualified sales leads to generate revenue for your business and automatically return on your marketing spending or to add new names into your database from attendees if the event is more geared toward awareness.

These two metrics should be carefully measured as objectives derived from the ebocube commercial cycle; however, the *purchase and development* stage should supersede these metrics if your event objective is loyalty or purchases. You would like to see lead conversation (how many attendees have been converted in to qualified leads) and finally deals that have been closed by the sales team as a result of this offline event. The same thing applies to your loyal and retained segment, but because they are existing customers, the way you analyze them is through the number of up-sell/cross-sell deals.

Awareness and Acquisition

Exhibiting, sponsoring, or speaking at industry events or your own events can help you to establish your company/products or services in EMs.

Data acquired at events is likely to be accurate and of high quality, provided that the data-capture process is efficient. This is your opportunity to enhance your marketing database and capture data for EMs. Ensure that you're prepared to collect the correct data fields that can be stored in database, sent to a call center or sales force to verify the data, and then reported in the dashboard. You might also capture business cards through competitions offering cool gadgets as prizes.

Prior to your events, send out your "save the date" email to your contacts, if you have any, to drive contacts to the event landing page or microsite where they can register and you can capture registration data to begin the process or developing contacts interested in your proposition, which can later be sent to sales for follow up.

Consideration and Nurture

Businesspeople may attend your event because they're aware of your company/brand/product and want real-life interaction and confirmation with your company and assurance of your brand. If people see you at an industry event, they might consider your brand even further and have your company in mind when making purchasing decisions.

Purchase and Development

Events are great opportunities for salespeople to network, turn contacts into customers, and initiate deals.

Retention and Loyalty

Loyal customers will expect you to invest your time and effort with them at exclusive and highly tailored events, whether physical or virtual (for example, through TelePresence). Events give your company and sales teams a great opportunity to strengthen established relationship with high-value customers in EMs. After you've defined your high-value loyal customers from your marketing database, using RFM (recency, frequency, and monetary) models, you can invite them via email to exclusive events to increase loyalty, such as executive breakfast meetings. Generally for huge accounts that purchase regularly, account managers will know who they are also, and they may be your company's strategic accounts! These may significantly impact your company's profits if lost, or perhaps these accounts and your relationship with them impacts your company strategy. You might have an individual "strategic marketing plan."

Direct Mail

Hard-copy postal mail or glossy brochures are still widely circulated. They should be saved for high-value customers who want to receive offline personalization or for physical events for one-to-one distribution. Events also provide sales teams with the opportunity to discuss sales.

Table 8.2 shows metrics relevant to direct mail communication. They should be reserved for high-value customers who want to receive offline personalization or for physical events with one-to-one distribution. Each piece of direct mail/brochures should open opportunities for data capture and further discussions with sales teams.

TABLE 8.2 The ebocube Commercial Cycle Metrics Matrix—Direct Mail in Relation to the ebocube Commercial Cycle Goals

Stage in the ebocube Commercial Cycle	Direct mail Primary response	Secondary metric response
All Phases of the ebocube Commercial Cycle	Bounce rate	
	Data submission	
	Response call/text back/email/click through to site	
Awareness/Acquisition	Response call/text back/email/click through to site	Bounce rate
	Data submission	
Consideration/Nurture and Develop	Number of lead candidates from response channels	Data submission
Purchase/Develop	Sales captured from response channels	
	Lead conversions from response channels	
Loyalty/Retention		

Track and move the contact along ebocube commercial cycle.

Awareness and Acquisition

Direct mail can support your email marketing case when you have a full, valid, and verified postal addresses but no email address against a contact record. You can capture an email address or lead by sending direct mail with an online CTA (a short and easy-to-remember URL) so that contacts will remember it when they go online.

End users are redirected to a data-capture form when they go to the CTA after typing the URL in from the direct mail into their Web browser. On this form, they can submit contact details, providing a valid email address as well as opting in for your communication and specifying preferences for communication from your business. To increase data submission rate, you can offer an incentive, which is popular and excepted in encouraging contacts to submit their data.

Purchase and Development

The online communication methods mentioned earlier in this chapter and in previous chapters provide more cost-effective results for the commercial cycle. They're cost-effective in comparison to traditional offline communicatinions channels and can have a greater impact in achieving ebocube commercial cycle goals because of the versatility of the mediums. Also, a significant factor in any lead-generation campaign is responding quickly and effectively to allow for timely and aggressive follow up, either by a pre-engaged call center, account managers, local partners, or a local sales force. Follow up within at most three days after the initial communication has been delivered. Recipients tend to forget what communications or offer was sent and may become "cold" again.

Retention and Loyalty

As mentioned previously, there are challenges in getting high-quality data in EMs. Sending direct mail can be expensive and inefficient because you cannot ensure delivery or easily measure open rates or bounce rates. Save direct mail for high-value, loyal customers. High-value customers are defined as having a high RFM value, and they should be in your retention segment of your database, the segment that will increase profits. Although email is still a good channel to communicate, direct mail can look more formal and engaging.

Telemarketing

Calling contacts in EMs is more welcomed than telemarketing in developed economies because contacts aren't used to telemarketing and many businesses do not do that in EMs, yet.

This method of communication involves salespeople or marketers contacting businesses by phone. It may be outsourced to a call centers in EMs using highly trained agents who can speak the local market's language/dialect as their mother tongue and who understand the business environment. Call centers should use automated systems that feed the dashboard and your marketing database, or call centers can have their own reports, but ideally you want one centralized dashboard.

Telemarketing can be the highest cost form of direct marketing, but it plays a core role as part of integrated campaigns in lead/demand generation and as part of the buying cycle. It can be used to support the development and purchase objectives of the ebocube commercial cycle in support of online communication or as follow up to further qualify potential leads.

Telemarketing can be used to target prospects and customers, including account-managed businesses to increase penetration of their accounts. If targeting account-managed companies, it's of paramount importance that the account managers be consulted prior to the telemarketing activity to protect their relationships and opportunity pipeline. Account-managed contacts should be flagged in your marketing database, and when setting up campaigns through campaign management tools, you should predefine, through the system, where responses should be routed (i.e., a further-qualification call center or directly to a salesperson). If they're named account responses (e.g., registrant to webcast or any data-capture form), they should be sent to account managers to be followed, up and if not, they should go to a call center to be sold to or further qualified and then passed on to a partner in the EM to close the sale.

Telemarketing can be supported by online efforts, and agents can advise people to look online for information. Contacts can also request a call back online. The components of telemarketing include the following:

- **Inbound:** Lead qualification (i.e., BANT or consideration/ purchase phase), enquiry resolution and escalation, and free phone number and follow up to email/web forms.
- **Outbound:** Lead generation (demand generation, develop-ment), lead qualification (nurture/development of data increase contact consideration). Calling a list that has been emailed on your campaign, or calling a contact that has requested a call back leads to nurturing. Call contacts to find out whether their status has changed, especially if they mentioned in a previous call that they may have a project in three months.

Table 8.3 shows the ebocube commercial cycle metrics as they pertain to telemarketing.

TABLE 8.3   The ebocube Commercial Cycle Metrics Matrix—Telemar-keting Metrics in Relation to the ebocube Commercial Cycle Goals

Stage in the ebocube Commercial Cycle	Telemarketing Primary response	Secondary metric response
All Phases of the ebocube Commercial Cycle	Invalid phone num-bers	
	Number of lead candidates sent to call center for further qualification	
	Lead candidates rejected	
Awareness/Acquisition		Inbound calls to call center from a trackable source

TABLE 8.3   The ebocube Commercial Cycle Metrics Matrix—Telemarketing Metrics in Relation to the ebocube Commercial Cycle Goals

Consideration/Nurture and Develop	Number of outbound calls
	Number of leads generated
	Number of inbound calls to the center
	Lead candidates sent to call center
	Lead candidates closed
	Total leads
	Number of open lead candidates
Purchase/Develop	Conversion of lead candidates to sales
Loyalty/Retention	Number of up-sell/cross-sell

Account-Managed Calls

Account managers will make calls to their account managed contacts when they think it's appropriate. Marketing can advise recipients via direct marketing to contact their account managers as a CTA. Account managers should log responses or sales to direct mail/campaigns in account management tools, which should feed your dashboard on results. This all depends, of course, on the account being profitable enough to be account managed.

Above the Line

Above the line includes television, radio, cinema, magazines, newspapers, PR, and billboards.

Above the line will not be the core of your business-to-business one to one, targeted marketing in EMs. It will be more of a support role and is likely to be used to raise awareness. Above the line is less targeted than direct marketing.

If you do want to use above the line in EMs, track responses by using a friendly URL directing users to an online campaign landing page to track responses or phone numbers as CTAs. Several friendly URLs can be set up for the purposes of tracking. For example, if you use two publications, you might have two unique friendly URLs and track which one has been clicked the most. Use two uniquely tracked data-capture forms, to measure which publication has directed the reader to a web page or produced the best response rates or leads.

A high response rate doesn't determine the quality of responses or potential leads, and therefore your campaign landing page should contain a data-capture form that enables you to assess who has seen your campaign and allow you to follow up.

You can also track above the line by providing a free phone number. (In EMs, free phone numbers are still not the norm and so can work well.) Determine how you want to follow up responses and what the customer journey should be; this is also based on your budget.

Table 8.4 shows relevant metrics for all above the line activates such as TV, print, and outdoor—these activities should never again be labeled "awareness" without metrics to justify the claim!

TABLE 8.4   The ebocube Commercial Cycle Metrics Matrix—Print, TV, and Outdoor Metrics in Relation to the ebocube Commercial Cycle Stage

Stage in the ebocube Commercial Cycle	Print/TV/outdoor Primary response	Secondary metric response
All Phases of the ebocube Commercial Cycle	Response call/ text back/email/click through to site	
	Number of lead candidates from response channels	
	Sales captured from response channels	
	Lead conversions from response channels	

TABLE 8.4   The ebocube Commercial Cycle Metrics Matrix—Print, TV, and Outdoor Metrics in Relation to the ebocube Commercial Cycle Stage

Awareness/Acquisition	Response call/ text back/email/click through to site
Consideration/Nurture and Develop	Number of lead candidates from response channels
Purchase/Develop	Sales captured from response channels
	Lead conversions from response channels
Loyalty/Retention	Log in to customer portal/calls to account managers or call center

9

Marketing Operations (mops)

Upon completion of this chapter, you should be able to

- Describe the function of marketing operations
- Link mops to feeding the dashboard—closing the loop
- Understand the key role of mops in your marketing campaign
- Understand how to use a budget planning online tool
- Recognize the importance of an online brief
- Identify challenges with database management
- Discover how to test campaigns
- Distinguish trackable versus non-trackable aspects of your marketing
- Understand how to use ebocodes to track responses in CI
- Start planning how you to execute, track, and measure your next integrated localized campaign in an EM and measure ROMI
- Discover how to close the loop

Figure 9.1 shows the ebocube model with the mops phase highlighted. The mops phase shows how to budget, plan, execute, track, and measure fully integrated marketing campaigns, online and offline elements, feed the dashboard with meaningful metrics, and update your company database CI represented through the datacube. This is how you will close the loop on your marketing efforts and come full circle.

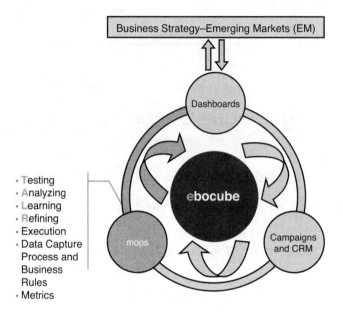

Figure 9.1   The ebocube model, phase three: mops

mops Defined

The marketing operations department/role/function (mops) involves using tools to support campaign managers, such as segmenting contact data, selecting lists, coding, and implementing localized integrated online campaigns of all complexity and sizes. The mops team is formed of campaign specialists who work in execution, reporting, and analytics. Their role involves being objective and analyzing campaign performance through dashboards and providing marketing intelligence to improve campaigns or for internal customers in larger organizations, like marketing campaign managers and product owners. Alternatively, in small companies, this is also the role of the marketing manager, executive, and so on.

These marketing experts use various tools to execute, report, and work closely with campaign managers from the onset of the campaign strategy and planning all the way through to return on marketing investment (ROMI) and analysis. Contact and company data along with operations are key to making marketing managers' campaigns successful, effective, and measurable. mops team members (employees or external vendors) know how to execute and track campaigns and how to prove they work, how to leverage online communications for maximum ROMI, how to select data from the marketing database, and how to track and measure results to prove marketing in EMs. This is the essence of the ebocube model. We expect the technology used for electronic customer relationship management (eCRM) and marketing in EMs to change quickly as the communication channels and devices for receiving messages continue to evolve and more sophisticated techniques are required to achieve the campaign goals.

mops is a developing discipline, and many companies are still establishing processes, technology, and infrastructure for mops. It's an operational discipline that leverages processes, technology, resources,[1] and metrics to run the marketing and CRM function as a measurable contributing function to the business by formalizing and organizing campaign planning, tracking, execution, and reporting. It reinforces your internet marketing strategy and tactics in EMs with defined processes and established reporting.

mops establishes a campaign process so that you do not need to redefine a process every time you run a campaign. This saves money and resources and reduces waste by capturing results effectively in a planned, organized method underpinned by technology and automated processes.

mops provides structure and reporting, and will help to nurture a healthy relationship with related functions by creating transparency of the campaign process and providing meaningful data through reports in the dashboard, thus enabling collaborative working. mops moves marketing from a speculative function to a solid quantifiable function by providing process based on logical thinking and structured campaigning and by producing meaningful marketing results represented through clear reports: the dashboard phase one.

mops supports marketers; the systems/tools should work for them, and not the other way around. The best practice is not to force marketers to use business models and technology, but to adapt them and make them work for them to support their experience, knowledge, and skills in this new digital and what can sometimes seem like complex world. The business benefits should be established before designing processes and investing in tools and operations.

Why mops?

Marketers are under increasing pressure to prove ROMI for their campaigns, especially during the global recession/financial crisis. Budgets are scrutinized and cut due to financial pressure. EM countries are new markets, and executives and CEOs want to see the financial results for marketing in these regions in particular and in real time.

mops is fundamental to the running of the ebocube and enables you to do the following:

- Get better visibility of your campaign effectiveness through measurements and results shown in the ebocube dashboard.
- Learn more about EMs and what works and what doesn't.
- Get the most from your EM marketing budget. EM marketing can show ROMI via tracking and updating the ebocube dashboard to request more funds internally or through partners.
- Feed your business strategy from the learning and business intelligence available in the dashboard.
- Save money, by organizing and structuring marketing, increasing revenue through learning and pulling activities that do not work.
- Target valuable segments with effective campaigns based on historical data and learning.
- Plan, track, and measure closed-loop campaigns from the planning and budgeting phase through to execution and reporting.
- Manage and improve your company and contact database by enabling you to set up processes that help you to efficiently

acquire, nurture, and develop contact records in a structured and organized way.

* Manage online tasks in the campaign's work flow and structure work and project manage complex global localized campaign's elements easily and efficiently.
* Analyze, learn, and refine your campaigns.

Web Applications

mops is supported by technology and web-based applications can be used to support and execute the processes of planning, budgeting, campaign execution, tracking, and reporting. Not only do these tools increase speed to market, they also enable global collaboration with virtual teams (internal teams/partners/agencies) and allow all users access to web tools, which support mops and provide real-time reporting.

mops tools can be used for the following:

* Planning and engaging employees and teams (online brief)
* Campaign management tools (execution and tracking of actual campaigns)
* Measurement and reporting (the dashboard, including the datacube)

mops is a closed-loop process that consists of the following (see Figure 9.2):

* Planning (phase two of ebocube formalized in an online plan)
* Budgeting (phase two of ebocube formalized in an online plan)
* Campaign online engagement (phase two of ebocube formalized in an online plan)
* Setting up the campaign
* Execution
* The dashboard (reporting, feeding strategy; phase one ebocube)

Figure 9.2 demonstrates the processes in mops: Phase one and two consist of analysis, evaluation, and planning; phase three is the execution stage! There are a number of processes and tools to be utilized here to support the process.

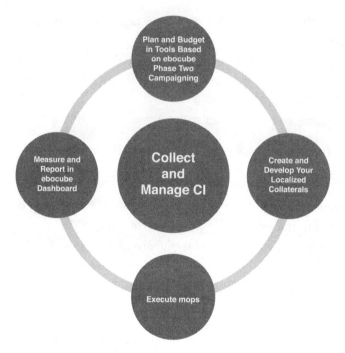

Figure 9.2   mops closing the loop—process

Market Attractiveness

After you've decided on the most attractive markets in terms of size and profitability, using the market attractiveness matrix (attractiveness versus your capabilities) and any reporting available from the ebocube dashboard, plan your campaign with a proposition in line with your company's overall market development strategy. Then you will use the datacube to review and analyze your marketing database, and then plan your campaign for the next business cycle.

Budget Tracking, Planning, and Allocation Process

As part of your overall business plan, you will have a budget for EM marketing budget management that centralizes marketing budget, partner funds, and cost data while feeding dashboards to pro-vide real-time visibility into marketing ROMI. Utilizing online appli-cations for EM budgeting is pivotal to your marketing investment returns measurement and for reviewing how budget was allocated to various activities, allowing budget allocation and tracking of each marketing activity as part of the overall integrated campaign. The tools enable you to control and track your budget allocation periodi-cally; you can specify and track all the budget information for the campaign. Marketing budget management tools will help you accu-rately plan marketing spend and attribute that spend to specific pro-grams and campaigns. Today, too many organizations still track marketing budgets in Excel and try to manually track ROMI.

A marketing budget management tool should allow you to see at any time how the budget has been split between regions, countries, and even particular marketing activities. You should be able to check associated ROMI for spending in the ebocube dashboard quickly and easily and look at things such as cost per acquisition of new contacts in database and cost per lead.

The key goal is to get management to see spending as the cre-ation of the sales pipeline produced as opposed to expenses. Your budgeting tool should feed into a ROMI system. That is, the ebocube dashboard and ROMI should be linked to specific campaign activities to identify what has generated financial results. It needs to be in the system to be organized, to be integrated with execution tools, and to feed reporting tools without manual intervention. This is how you prove your marketing effectiveness and ROMI in EMs.

Budget data (see Figure 9.3) can be entered hierarchically in your budgeting tool, starting for example with a total amount for a global campaign, which is split by countries and country activities. This breaks down budget information, and at the same time in report-ing you can "roll up" to the total amount spent for a campaign and look at total ROMI, which you can also break down.

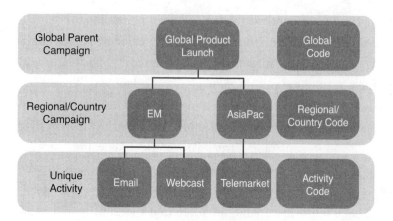

Figure 9.3   The ebocube cascading the budget through the budget tool

You may also get a total fund for a region (see Figure 9.4), which you can break down by country, activities, and communication media mix.

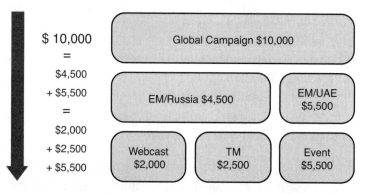

Figure 9.4   The ebocube budget cascade fund breakdown

Figure 9.5 shows ROMI for budget breakdown. This is demonstrated in the dashboard and shows ROMI, which is captured and broken down by a budgeting tool. ROMI is demonstrated in terms of financial values such as leads, sales opportunities against the investment campaign objectives for the last two quadrants of the ebocube commercial cycle, purchase/development, and loyalty/retention.

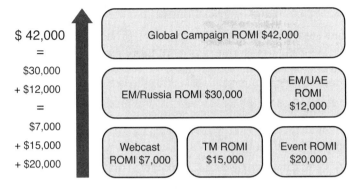

Figure 9.5   ebocube reporting roll-up

Budgeting

A unique budget code is passed and tracked through various integrated systems, which include the following:

- Plan and engagement (online brief)
- Execution (campaign management tools)
- Measurement and reporting ROMI, opportunity and sales (dashboard)

In your marketing database, budget codes should be linked to (feeding campaign codes) and stored against contacts (against transactional history) so that you can determine how much marketing budget is expended against a contact/segment in your customer intelligence database. This will give you visibility on all of your activity results, including ROMI, opportunity pipeline, and sales related to your initial budget.

If your budget isn't tracked through these operational systems, you will need to use a manual process, which could lead to inaccurate reporting and might provide incorrect reporting or ROMI—processes like budgeting should be automated.

There can be various budget codes created so that you can track campaigns at various levels; this is referred to as cascading or rolling up. A global parent campaign/regional budget is likely to be the highest level in your reporting hierarchy (depending on how you have set up your tool) in the ebocube dashboard. Related sub-budget codes, associated with media mix or incentives, can be rolled up to the parent budget code (i.e., total amount spent). A parent campaign may include budgeting for a global/regional or country level.

Sub-budget codes are related to the media mix, incentives, and individual activities for your overall campaign. This can be tracked and reported on an individual, granular level. Your dashboard should allow you to roll up and report to the parent budget code or drill down to subactivity budget codes, and thus you should have a hierarchical view of your budget spend and ROMI. The activities created under the parent budget code in your system should allow you to roll up to the highest level of budgets in your reporting tools.

A unique name for your budget code referencing the campaign name will help your company's business leaders to instantly recognize a campaign once it's finally reported in the ebocube dashboard; the code enables the system to transfer the data or information efficiently and effectively.

A budget code name should follow a specific naming convention, making it easy for the person reviewing the results in the ebocube dashboard to identify the campaign or activity quickly. These names should flow through engagement tools to execution to reporting. In addition to the code, names help humans to recognize campaigns and codes help system transfer related data, codes, and names, which can be used to query the ebocube dashboard easily. For example, you may use a budget code to query the results of specific campaigns. This pertains to parent budget codes and sub-codes.

If you have the resources to launch and follow up a campaign globally, you need to budget for the global campaign. You'll need this unique code if you're launching a product, service, or brand across the globe, including in EMs. You should track all the related ROMI to the overall global campaign, from all related activities.

Your global campaign code and global campaign name will be tracked through all of your campaign execution systems and measured and reported on through your ebocube dashboard.

In the high-level view of the ebocube dashboard, you'll find financial results such as sales, opportunity pipeline, and leads. You can break down results by the region/country, which is why you need to create a region/country budgeting subcode.

In your operational view, you can track all activities executed under this code on a granular level, such as open rates across the world or an EM.

Campaigns can be tracked by country or region. If your resources or budgets are small or simply your campaign is relevant to only one region via a local campaign, the high-level code will be on a regional or country level, and all related activity results will be rolled up to this code in your reporting.

It's important to input your budget in terms of how you want to be able to break down or view reporting (by country or region) so that your system should allow you to enter a country or regional field. This in turn will generate a budget code, which will feed your reporting systems. Your regional and country code/name will be tracked through all your campaign execution systems and measured and reported through your dashboard.

Budget per Activity

Budget activities are split by your media mix (communications channels) and incentive/offer, and each activity is given a unique budgeting code linked to the parent campaign, for tracking all spend and for reporting purposes.

You'll need budget activity codes to track ROMI split by communication channel in the dashboard and to report on the cost of the incentive and on the ROMI generated. This should also feed your operational view of the dashboard and high-level view of the dashboard.

This will allow you to determine which communication channel and incentive from your integrated marketing campaign has been the most successful, operationally or overall in terms of ROMI.

Your activity budget codes will feed and be tracked through your campaign execution system and measured and reported through your ebocube dashboard.

Online Briefing and Reporting

An online brief will make your life easier by enabling you to manage multiple campaigns in different countries and engage marketing teams such as data, telemarketing, creative, and execution, giving you visibility of planned activities and phases of campaigns and elements executed in a structured and organized central web application.

The brief enables you to do the following:

- Define activities that need to be tracked and how they should be reported.
- Engage your execution teams internally or externally, speeding up the flow of communication and achieving collaboration and enabling a record.
- Customize for partner or agency. (For example, they may have read-only rights, instead of administrative rights, and so they cannot edit campaign briefs.)
- Track progress on campaigns and timescales.
- Project manage campaigns effectively (campaign management) and monitor how many campaigns are running.
- Document in one place, through a web application. This can reduce email going back and forth and conference calls between various teams while planning, executing, and tracking campaigns. This will reduce overcommunication or oversized mailboxes by sending heavy files to each other—these should be uploaded to campaign management files.
- Have help buttons, forums, and shared knowledge capabilities or other forms of collaboration.

- Build an online communications plan for your campaign, specifying objectives and each individual communication channel (e.g., event/webcast, or variant/phase of a communication such as an initial email, reminder email, thank-you email). All communications needs to be executed, tracked, and reported.
- Specify data segments that will need to be tracked and lists that will be pulled.
- Engage the data team.
- Engage localization creative and copywriting teams and external vendors. They don't necessarily have to have the tool—they may receive email notification only.
- Engage with the campaign execution team and external vendors.

Creating an online brief is the second logical step in the mops process; it should be mandatory that your budget code flows into this briefing web application or is entered into the brief manually. This should populate campaign information into your brief, including costs. The budget code will flow from your budgeting tool, through the brief, campaign execution tools, and finally to your ebocube dashboard reports per campaign and related activities.

The budget code should also pull through related information into the online brief such as region and campaign name as well as budgeted amount. This will give marketers information about the budget related to the specific campaign.

The online engagement brief should inform relevant teams when the job has been logged ready for execution. For example, it could enable the data team to have visibility of jobs from a central brief. This is a central place for marketers to request data and for the data team to understand what data should be extracted from the marketing database and how to segment the data, such as regions or countries, industry sectors, test segments, or data sources (i.e., internal or third-party data).

This briefing tool should be an interface to campaign management execution tools. This reduces the step of populating another tool with instructions for the execution of the campaign.

Your online brief should include options to select all the trackable communication channels possible, including the following:

- Email
- Event
- Direct mail
- Print
- Banner
- Web marketing (including on social network site)

Your brief should also allow you to enter the incentive used or offer, which should also have budgeting information stored against it. Offers may include the following:

- Whitepapers
- Gifts
- Offline Events
- Online Events

In the ebocube dashboard, tracking and reporting can be specific to any of the previously listed communication channels. Execution is structured by this plan, which formalizes and documents phase two of ebocube.

Your online brief should include all the trackable data segments you want to measure. You can track decision makers' responses separately from those who are not decision makers, for example, but you need to request this in the online brief, as follows:

- Verticals
- Job titles
- Accounts
- Interaction with previous campaigns

Automated notifications can be sent to stakeholders managing the campaign, including call centers, agencies, and third-party partners. Notifications should let stakeholders know when activities are planned, when they need to act, and when activities are overdue or if they've been executed.

Customer Insight

Your marketing database is not just a contact database, it stores all the marketing and sales transactions against each individual contact. Marketing and sales history is stored against contacts that have been targeted with a campaign and executed through the tools as part of mops.

Sales information can be fed through sales tools or account management tools (for example, Salesforce.com). Financial information can be fed through accounting or invoicing systems. Customer service or call centers should also feed customer insight CI with their contact transactions and updated information. CI is fed by multiple sources and databases to create one full picture of your contact on contact and company level (firmographics).

Customer insight is an industry term used to refer to the collection, deployment, and transactions against contact information that allows a business to acquire, develop, and retain their customers.[2] This includes transactional history and any marketing history stored against a company or contacts. CI is an operational system for storage of all information related to contacts, as well as companies rolling up to account levels, such as a company's account with your company.

CI is fed by multiple sources such as sales, lead management tools, or company websites that use data capture, data-capture forms on emails, or any online reporting linked to a contact (e.g., opening an email, financial systems, and many other sources). A database or CI is a live entity and changes constantly; all updates are done in real time to maintain accuracy. Your database should be refreshed with new feeds on a regular basis to keep it up-to-date.

CI should have many of the efficient initial cleansing steps and business rules applied for any new entry. Every new entry needs to be validated; therefore, business rules play key roles here. Based on those rules a new entry is recognized as a new or existing contact, actual or suspect entry (like test test test—false information self reported by responder). Business rules in your database help to keep it clean and accurate; however, wrongly defined business rules may damage the quality of your data. We've seen cases where good, high-quality data loses its quality after being uploaded to CI!

Business rules include validating contact information when it's loaded and ensuring that duplicates are not created.

Company data and contact data are fundamental to the ebocube business model. We will not go to deeply into the technical aspects of data management, but we will introduce the fundamentals of your database management or CI and some basic rules that impact your execution. The datacube is typically presented in a tabular format or graphs and can be split by many variables (e.g., countries, region, or company size).

Data is the core, the lifeblood for your marketing business-to-business (B2B) activities. You can't talk to companies on a one-on-one highly targeted level with your great offers if you don't know who you're speaking to. Your marketing database, which the industry refer to as CI, is the biggest asset your company can have right now when penetrating businesses in EMs. With "clean" up-to-date, accurate data, you can win market share over your competitors even if your proposition is not as good as theirs. It's the core to contacting and reaching the correct people globally, with the correct offer at the right time. Contact records data and company data cannot be managed without an effective data warehouse that can manage international language characters. You must make sure that your data warehouse operation system supports international characters. You will be dealing with multilanguage data entry, and you must bear in mind that language characters are different from language characters in the English language. The best way to check if your system work properly is for you to upload a sample (even 10–15 records) to your warehouse and extract it back to compare to the original file uploaded.

For example here is an original record (full postal address):

Łukasz **Dworski**

Żabia Góra

Ul. Kębściowa 14

POLSKA

And after extractions back from the system (corrupted):

≤ukasz **Dworski**

ɲabia GdΔ³/₄ra

Ul. K♦Γb≠ciowa 14

POLSKA

If you run specific activities intended to improve the quality of your data (for example, a survey to gather missing fields of information), the datacube is the platform where you can review results and the health of your data. It's a snapshot before and after your campaigns, showing the improvement in data quality (e.g., improvement in number of complete fields of information).

Before you start planning your contact data strategy and utilization of the datacube, it's very important to understand the fundamentals of contact database management and to measure quality before improvement activities. Once you work on improving a segment of data, CI will continue to be updated from new sources, so you have to be able to identify the results of your data-cleansing exercise without results being skewed from new records coming in.

Ideally, your marketing database or CI should be stored in once place and be managed either by an in-house team or by one vendor. Multiple vendors or data splits into different systems create many potential issues, including list data requests, service level agreements (SLAs), and vendor management, to bigger issues such as data mismatching, duplications, or lack of consistency in contact records (e.g., one contact may be opted out in one system but not in the other creating risk).

Your Data Warehouse (CI)

You need a robust data warehouse that supports many variables, language characters, firmographic information, and information about the customers' sales and marketing transactions or marketing history. The system should be designed and built to store data captured and to categories data so that it can be easily extracted for segmentation of lists for campaigns and organized to be reported meaningfully in the datacube. For example, answer fields in the database may include company name, industry/sector, first name, and last name; answer banding should be standardized where possible. There should be standardized industry names (either in the local language or English) and standardized bandings for companies, such as 20–249 employees for a small to medium-sized business (SMB). This, for example, will enable you to extract all companies that fall into this banding or the SMB segment for campaigns. Basically, data needs to be categorized systematically. This also needs to be taken into consideration when data is captured: Question fields must match answer fields in your database.

"Why do I need a database? I can manage my contacts in a spreadsheet. It's easier, quicker, and friendlier."

During our careers in B2B marketing, that was a question asked, believe it or not, by some marketing managers! There are thousands of important reasons as to why you need a centralized marketing database, and a spreadsheet will never replace these benefits, and this is a subject for another book.

Let's answer the question with other questions: How can you manage dynamic opt outs in Excel? How can you track marketing history in Excel quickly and efficiently with high accuracy? How will you identify customers versus prospects without feeds from transactional systems? How can you log budget/spend information per campaign against a contact? How will you identify account-managed customers or prospects, sites related to accounts, and contacts associated to companies? How can you manage the frequency of campaigns targeting contacts in Excel or other corporate governance, such as excluding competitors or employees from communications? How can you track and exclude contacts/businesses that are in the process of buying a product or solution without feeds from your sales lead management tools?

Imagine if all of your account managers or sales teams also created their own lists in Excel, and imagine trying to consolidate this data for marketing purposes. It would be impossible to implement a campaign based on the phases of the ebocube commercial cycle by developing your loyalty segment based on recency, frequency, and monetary (RFM) value scoring. Generally, advanced segmentation based on marketing/transactional history and response data wouldn't be possible. How would you implement RFM modeling and continue to identify high-value customers that drive profits for you in EMs?

There are always challenges with data maintenance, and managing your database with an Excel spreadsheet isn't only risky, it's inefficient.

Challenges with Data

We are very familiar with meetings where either the first PowerPoint slide or any other slide starts with "Data Issues" as a title. We can't tell you how many meetings we've attended where the topic of "data issues" has arisen. Marketing stakeholders complain that there are a data issues for EM countries, when we query them about the data issue. The solution might not be clear, and some marketing stakeholders can't identify the issue they need to solve. They may blame poor data for bad results, and if there is poor visibility on results because mops hasn't been implemented, data can be an easy scapegoat. To solve data issues, you have to identify the problems clearly. The only way to identify problems is through the datacube, which can be presented through different views, depending on who is going to use it. You can establish fields of data that are missing in the data hierarchy by starting from head office/parent site down to subsidiary sites, to contact information, establishing where you have gaps and inaccuracies of invalid data.

You've got a database in your pocket. Have you ever sent a group text message to your contacts via your mobile phone and found out that some text messages were undelivered according to the delivery report you've set up to track messages? Your mobile phone SIM card can store contact data: first name, last name, mobile number, email, and perhaps land number. However, this data might be inaccurate because your friend, for example, has moved abroad, updated her number, switched to another service provider, or her last name might have changed because she got married. You might have even stored her name or number incorrectly. Consider all these challenges with a database! Your mobile phone typically holds 100 to 150 contacts. Now imagine if you had 1,600 contacts, 16,000 contacts, or even 16,000,000 records for contacts, including transactional and marketing history, all stored in a database.

Prepare yourself for challenges when maintaining and gathering data for EMs. You'll never have an entirely accurate, up-to-date, and valid set of records in your database, although you should aim to manage and maintain it as well as possible, There is no such thing as clean data! Contacts move on, records become obsolete, or sometimes inaccurate data is loaded into systems. For example, when you complete an online survey, does your mobile number ever happen to be 12345678910? We even found out that Mickey Mouse lived in an EM once when we were reviewing data extracted for a telemarketing campaign!

Self-reported data can also pose a problem. For example, an employee who works for a multinational may report the number of employees in his site office rather than global company. Therefore, you might send an SMB campaign to a contact working for a multinational. It probably isn't the contact's intention to do this, but it happens. Also, contacts may fill in their company name as, for example, Petrochemical International, whereas the existing company record in your database is Petrochemicals PLC. Therefore, it might be difficult to match or link this contact to a company or existing account or contact record, which will affect your data list segmentation and marketing and may even create duplicate records. Of course, you can take many measures to reduce such problems. It's important to consider this because when you're looking at your datacube report and you notice you have 13,000 contacts who are not matched to a company or site, you know how to improve this situation with your data team and marketing campaigns. We say, "Police data entry!" If you work for a small business, your database is likely to be smaller and easier to manage. However, these issues will still exist, just on a much smaller scale. You might also manage data and campaigns, and therefore it's even more important that you're aware of such challenges. Point of capture for data is crucial to maintaining a clean, reliable database.

Emerging Markets: One Post Code, One City

In many countries in EMs, whole cities may share a postal/ZIP code, if they have any at all, which can make it difficult to build and improve the quality of a database. For example, in the United Kingdom, small areas, such as streets, are split by unique postal codes. It's easy to gather full addresses, companies, and even contacts who relate to these postal codes. Because of multiple postcodes in the United Kingdom, companies are technically able to build databases and keep them accurate. By using local post offices and Royal Mail services in mature countries, you can keep your data base clean and accurate. This isn't the case in EMs.

A Google search on a postal address does not work so easily in an EM. Where direct marketing has been running for awhile, there are services set up to find addressees (and to look for associated emails and a list of contacts who have given permission to be contacted).

Merge-Purge: The "Perfect" Contact Record

The majority of database matching is based on the merge-purge technique. This is a technique that merges all duplicated or incomplete information from different sources related to the one, same contact record and creates only one near-perfect contact record. For example, if two records of incomplete data (see Figure 9.6 with a contact matching example) enter a database, business rules are applied and will merge this contact into one, reducing the number of duplicates and keeping the most accurate and complete record.

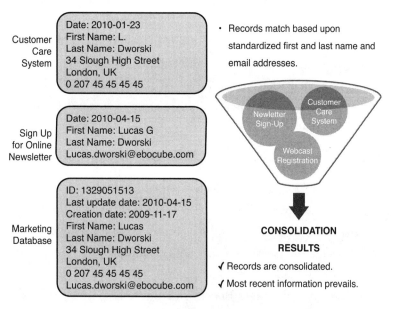

Customer Care System
Date: 2010-01-23
First Name: L.
Last Name: Dworski
34 Slough High Street
London, UK
0 207 45 45 45 45

Sign Up for Online Newsletter
Date: 2010-04-15
First Name: Lucas G
Last Name: Dworski
Lucas.dworski@ebocube.com

Marketing Database
ID: 1329051513
Last update date: 2010-04-15
Creation date: 2009-11-17
First Name: Lucas
Last Name: Dworski
34 Slough High Street
London, UK
0 207 45 45 45 45
Lucas.dworski@ebocube.com

- Records match based upon standardized first and last name and email addresses.

CONSOLIDATION RESULTS

✓ Records are consolidated.
✓ Most recent information prevails.

Figure 9.6   Contact matching consolidation

Matching depends on the business rule set up in your database. It's usually defined by the mops department. Business rules may work in combination and specific order (e.g., first matching is applied by email address and name match; secondary matching is name, postal address, and phone number). The matching process can be simple, based on one attribute-value match, like first name and last name (see Figure 9.7). It can be also more complex (see Figure 9.8) combining more attributes—values like phone number, name, and postal address.

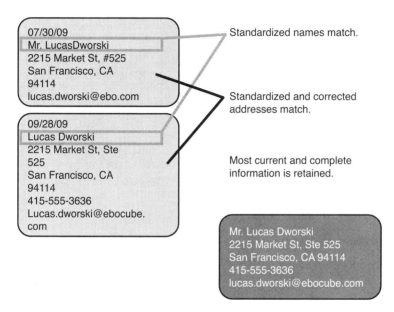

Figure 9.7   Name-matching example

Your database will need to support international characters/different languages for EMs.

Business rules may, of course, prioritize and overwrite sources of inputted data. For example, the latest input may be treated as the most accurate and will overwrite existing information.

You might also set up trusted sources. For example, any input from financial transactional, invoice, or shipping systems overwrites postal addresses or online data and self-reported submissions. End users submitting data from an online form may submit false data to acquire the incentive quickly or to achieve their goal quickly. Financial systems must have accurate and correct postal addresses to be able to handle financial transactions as well as shipping and delivery

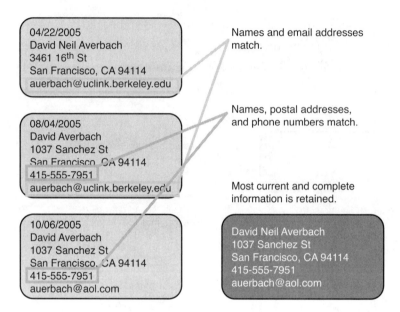

Figure 9.8   Complex matching example

in EMs, and therefore financials system are more reliable as an accurate and trustable source of postal addresses (site addresses) as opposed to self-reported data from online data captures because the data needs to be accurate for payment purposes, and at that stage the relationship is solid.

As marketers or e-CRM managers, you should have an understanding of your database because it is key to the success of your direct one-to-one campaigns in B2B targeted marketing for EMs. Even if you have a database team, you shouldn't work in silos or without knowledge. You should have a basic understanding of the database, capturing data and storage. And because it's you who will be creating and approving data capture, you should know what's mandatory or not when creating data-capture forms that are going to be used on your website, email, webcast registration, and so on. If you're going to provide postevent data to be uploaded into CI database, you must make sure that it doesn't work against the database's existing answer attributes. Remember, if you collect information you cannot store, you've wasted your efforts and customers' time.

You don't want to capture data that can't be used or stored, and you want to make sure that your marketing activities are improving data quality.

Marketing, Campaign Execution Tools

The execution tool can be set up or programmed through the online brief information. Some execution tools require you to input the execution instruction or to "schedule a campaign" and upload email created. If the briefing tool can do this, you've streamlined the process. Remember, technology should work for you, the busy marketer.

Your execution tools are used for email fulfillment, creation of data-capture forms and event registration forms, generating tracking codes, creating vanity URLs, and all the technical code required for tracking and measurement of campaigns. There are many providers on the market with complete suites for campaign management and execution.

Marketers can also use these tools to set up trigger marketing. For example, contact is automatically targeted with a specific action (e.g., sending thank-you emails) when end users complete a related specific action (e.g., submitting a data-capture form). These actions may include registration or information request. These are vital opportunities to interact with customers and differentiate yourself from your competitors and move the contact from one stage in the ebocube commercial cycle to the next. Follow up can be automated based on responses.

Sales management tools are not as sophisticated as marketing campaign management tools and are limited in their marketing capabilities in terms of campaign execution, tracking, and measurement. Although they are good for account management communication, they're not designed for mass targeted mailings and complex data segmentation.

ebocodes: Marketing Tracking Codes

Marketers have used promotional codes for years. For example, a piece of offline direct mail may contain a printed code, and when the recipient calls to enquire, the call center agent or salesperson will request the promotional code to track which piece of communication the caller is responding to. This code is then stored against a contact record in a CRM system, showing which communication the contact has responded to, thus building up a contact's profile with marketing history. This enables the marketer to report on results (i.e., responses), manually, and to spend more on communications, which will produce further results, targeting the responders with similar communications that they previously responded to and were interested in. The Internet is able to do this function without human intervention. Responders don't need to mention which campaign they are responding to because this can be measured through ebocodes.

An *ebocode* is a simple, powerful way to track the responses produced by a particular list or form of communication. An ebocode is a numeric or alphanumeric program code generated by campaign application tools. They should be programmed to be linked to the budgeting code and carry the campaign information. They are used to store every marketing interaction against a contact in the CI database, improving customer dialogue and helping to push contacts through the ebocube commercial cycle through effective CRM. They also update the ebocube dashboard with unique response results, such as leads generated by campaigns and other results linked to segments of data or at the most granular level (namely, individual contact).

ebocodes are used to track campaign responses by contacts or segments of data. They track when respondents have responded to communication channels. A response may be opening an email, registering data through a data-capture form, or attending a physical event. A response can be matched against an ebocode that is stored against the contact from the segment of data targeted with the communication. For example, if clicks or open rates are measured, this can be linked back to the contact against the ebocode. Analyzing data with ebocodes will change the way you manage your messages: It will help you to make your email marketing effective and reliable, because you know which emails your contacts are most interested in and which lists or contacts are the most responsive.

For example, a contact is part of a campaign and is selected in a segment of data that has been sent an email. When the email has been executed, the contact record is updated with an ebocode (action taken against the contact) through campaign execution tools. In other words, when an email is sent, the contact opens the email, clicks a link, and this is reported against the ebocode and stored against the contact by programming software. Popular campaign execution tools do this for you. You do not really need to understand the technicalities, just how to use the tools to track and store campaign information against a record. In addition, you need to realize that you are building marketing history against a record that can be used for further marketing efforts:

• Your email may contain a link to data-capture form.

• This form should contain the same tracking ebocode stored against the contact that has been emailed, so that when contacts fill in response information to the survey, it updates the CI with new information, and you can check which list or segment has produced a response in the form of data capture.

• By completing and submitting this data-capture form, contact records will be "marked" based on ebocodes as a positive responder to your campaign in CI. (That will be done automatically by integrating your campaign management tool with the CI database.) This process allows you to segment and target, very quickly and clearly, all responders to your specific piece of communication. You can target those responders with the next logical communication or action within your campaign, moving them along the ebocube commercial cycle—for example, sending follow-up communications or pushing contacts to call centers for further qualification (if it's the purchase stage) or directly to account managers.

- ebocodes are assigned to different segments of data.
- The rule of assigning ebocodes to different segments is very simple. You just need to ensure they're segmented in data segmentation tools and allocated unique names—for example, viewer of previous webcast or attendee to last year's seminar.

CI should also recognize that this is a response against a specific campaign and communication method. This starts to create marketing history and enables you to follow up. You have various options. For example, you could request all data from participants who attended a previous year's online event (an ebocode is stored against responders) and send them an email for this year's forthcoming event. Or, you could request all the contacts that registered for last year's event through an online form and send them an email on the upcoming event.

How you collect the data is not static, and you might have multiple ebocodes for a single campaign. For example, you might split the target audience data between a technical audience and a business audience. Utilizing two ebocodes will enable you to track whether best responses (e.g., opens or clicks) have been generated from the technical audience or business audience. Responses data can be stored against contacts in CI against the ebocode. The ebocode will contain information on the campaign activity and details, such as communication media used or budget associated with a campaign.

Without ebocodes, you would get a blending of metrics or response data so that variations in response by segments wouldn't be identified. For example, if an email is sent to three different segments with a data-capture form, response sources to the data-capture form can't be identified if the data forms are not "tagged" with ebocodes. Therefore, you could not identify which email segment created the highest response rate in terms of data submission. Or, if the segments were not attributed ebocodes, you wouldn't be able to easily report in your operational dashboard which contacts were linked to high open rates or clicks or which contacts targeted with certain communications have resulted in leads.

Leads who have responded to a call to action (CTA) by submitting data are entered into a database and reported in your ebocube dashboard. The campaign-related ebocode is also entered into CI, and later receives credit for an eventual sale. The exact dollar value of the deal can then also be assigned to the communication channel and segment.

ebocodes created by execution tools and attributed automatically to data segments have to be unique. As long as the same campaign-tracking ebocode is not associated to more than one segment, you are in good shape. If not, you will not be able to identify which list performed the best.

ebocodes: Web Traffic and Offline Data Sources

When visitors arrive at your site, you can use a data-capture form. When the form is submitted, a unique ebocode for that form should also be submitted to your database along with the contact information. Again, if they are a lead, you can attribute the web form to this in your ebocube dashboard.

When you capture data offline (e.g., a business card at an event), ebocodes can be created and responses can be uploaded, into CI against the codes, by manual input so that you can easily and clearly identify attendees of this specific campaign event in CI and again attribute leads to the event in reporting tools, which are passed to ebocode information.

Another example is an inbound call center may receive a call. The caller provides a promotional code provided on the marketing communication, which helps the call center agent to identify the communication the contact is responded to. The call center agent loads response data to the database campaign against an ebocode created through campaign management tools. This enables you to track marketing history against each contact in your database. You can also base future marketing activity and segmentation on ebocodes based on marketing history, which is their main advantage. For example, as a marketer, you might want to target anyone who has responded to an inbound phone number provided on the communication piece.

Measuring Different Media Channels

To track offline response data to offline promotional vehicles such as newspapers, magazines, direct mail, radio, and TV promotion, you can use a unique web URL per media channel, which redirects to a data-capture form when responders click it. For example, a reader of a specific newspaper comes to your URL, which redirects the reader to a data-capture form, www.ebocube.com?id=12345. In this case, the ebocode 12345 would be placed in the data-capture link, which will flow against the contact response in your marketing database and help you to identify a lead related to a communication channel in your ebocube dashboard.

Programming ebocodes: Directing the Response in the System for Follow Up

An ebocode may also contain information or a label, programmed from execution tools, which may be used for further campaign follow up. For example, it's possible to direct a response to a webcast to a call center or to sales lead management tool by programming this information through the campaign management tool that generates the ebocodes.

ebocodes are like a barcodes on your luggage at the airport. When you fly, the marketing execution system will recognize the contact's destination location and will know whether to push it to departure or arrival area through CI or simply put it on hold (i.e., you are transferring to another flight).

The whole idea of ebocodes is that it puts a label on the contact record so your database (CI) will recognize the marketing action, and it will push the contact to the correct destination (e.g., account management tool, call center).

For example, if it's a response to your lead-generation campaign, the contact should be pushed to a call center for further qualification. What the ebocode does is recognize the destination (call center) and check each contact record to see if there is a positive answer to lead-scoring questions—for example, BANT questions (i.e., responder has indicated that they have a budget, authority to purchase, need, or project with timeframe). If the answers are positive, CI pushes those contacts to a call center or allocated account manager; if not, those contacts stay in CI without further actions.

The CI database will follow the instructions you have provided in the programmed ebocode.

Additional Tracking Codes: Parent, Child, and Cookies

A parent code is related to the overall campaign code and is usually related to a budget code for information, such as 1234. In the ebocube dashboard, this will allow you to pull an overall report on campaign unique responses (e.g., overall leads per campaign regardless of response channel).

A child code may be related to the parent code (e.g., 1234_1), but is assigned to a unique piece of communication or specific segment of data that has generated the result. This enables you to pull contact data that's part of a whole integrated campaign and create a hierarchy of results, thus allowing you to drill down to details for results or roll up to overall campaign results regardless of response communication channels.

Any communication channel that you execute through ebocube should be assigned a unique ebocode for tracking response data, whether that's offline media or online. This will help you to track responses broken down per communication channel. It will allow you to report unique responder per communication channel or segment, and most important, feed CI with marketing history per contact to follow up.

ebocodes used to track the results of marketing to data segments help to identify the following:

- Which segments are more responsive, so that you can measure behavior such as clicks or read emails, or you can check responses in the form of data submission down to a contact or list.
- Which communications they are more responsive to.
- Which segments need to be de-marketed. If contacts have not responded, you can stop marketing to them or market to them in a new way. The metrics in your dashboard will show you who hasn't responded. However, it might not be so clear in helping you to identify why they haven't responded. It's up to you to try new communication, propositions, and ideas.
- Campaign and transactional history against a contact who may have attended an event or who opened an email to register with your site.
- Data-level input to help you to target customers more successfully with future campaigns. For example, you might want to target everyone who registered and attended a webcast in a specific city in an EM with a follow-up piece of communication.

Contacts that have been targeted for a specific campaign should be suppressed for unrelated campaigns or messages running during the same period. This can be based on ebocodes and suppression rules. For example, if a contact has been called in the past 30 days, that contact should not be called again.

Tracking without ebocodes

You might be interested in seeing how many visitors you get to your site, but you might not want to capture individual responses/data. You might just be concerned with total visitors. In this circumstance, you might want to track unique visitors with cookies. You do not need ebocodes to do this. However, if you want to capture information from the user and load it to CI, you should capture with an ebocode in the link to identify the source of data capture. The ebocode will identify campaign action response and can be set up to automatically trigger a welcome email.

Or, you might be interested in seeing how many people click various friendly/vanity URLs you set up, which may be advertised on printed or offline material. Friendly URLs are short, memorable URLs created for marketing campaigns, and responders can enter them into a browser. For example, you use two URLs in print media: one in newspaper x and the other in newspaper y. You want to see which one will get the most hits or generate the highest unique visitors. Therefore, you can set up two friendly URLs (e.g., www. ebocube.com/promo or www.ebocube.com/advert) and check which URLs receive the most viewers and therefore which paper generated the best results for your campaign. Friendly URLs will not be set up to capture data, but you can redirect these URLs to data-capture forms that can be tracked with ebocodes to feed your database with contact information or leads. Your ebocube dashboard will also show unique visitors to each link per newspaper, and show unique responses per newspaper, which are captured and associated to tagged individual data-capture links.

Whether communications are sent directly from your company to the recipients or through partners marketing to end users depends on how you structure your operation and track and feed information into the ebocube dashboard.

If you are using an agency to implement ebocube, select a trusted innovative partner who is willing to be trained on ebocube and any tools and can understand what is required in terms of dashboard results, CI enhancement and values, and the importance of your customer base and marketing. They will need expertise in online marketing, reporting, and powerful software solutions. You might choose to develop applications for your partners so that they can track, measure, and analyze campaigns in your ebocube dashboard.

TALR (Test, Analyze, Learn, Refine) Case Study: Campaigns

mops allows you to test, analyze, learn, and refine each element of your integrated marketing campaign in EMs, which is extremely powerful. You can test elements of a campaign on a small sample of the data before you target all your data. For example, you might test an email or different communication channels in conjunction with your actual campaign.

Through testing, you can learn about EMs and measure the success of your campaign in the ebocube dashboard. Learning allows you to improve effectiveness, response rates, and ultimately, lead generation. You can improve your marketing campaign to correspond with the information you receive. Online data is easier to track compared to offline. With offline, you must rely on customer feedback, whereas with online you can test in the background.

Testing enables you to send two different test email variants to two data segments to see which generates the highest response rate or best results. The emails may vary in terms of different subject lines, localizations versus nonlocalized images, calls to action being placed in different areas, and special offers used. For decades, this has been a classic method in direct mail, where companies split their contact mailing lists and send different version of direct mail to different recipients.[3] A/B testing is also popular on the Web, you can for example show different page versions to different visitors and monitor which page works best.[4]

After you have completed your test and analyzed the results, identify areas for improvement and refine your campaign based on what you have learned. Marketing excellence in EMs is achieved by learning and development rather than execution habits and assumptions, which will continuously generate the same results if not reduce success rates.

The ebocube Dashboard

Information needs to be gathered and mapped in an organized way to your ebocube dashboard. Our objectives are not to instruct you how to (technically) build your dashboard here, but to help you to understand the metrics you need to determine and articulate your results. These methods are not fixed and are likely to change as technology and communication methods advances. You need to build your business case and provide it to the IT team. Then IT will run the project, test it, and build it.

The ebocube dashboard is something that will develop over time. You need to know the business logic behind it rather than understand the technological processes. There are complex solutions, but you can just start by using an Excel spreadsheet to start accumulating data on your campaign from your standard execution reports, although long term you ideally need an automated tool for accuracy and to capture data from multiple sources. Define the column titles first or what you aim to prove. Part of the design of your dashboard involves selecting the data sources that feeds it. Design also involves defining a simple user interface, navigation, and the three user views: high-level view, the operational view, and the datacube.

Before you start to execute your marketing activities through mops, ensure you define your dashboard. The ebocube dashboard should be defined before you start building the business processes to feed it with the information.

The ebocube dashboard is ideally fed by many different automated operational systems, including partner execution tools, agency execution, and in-house execution tools. Systems also include marketing budgeting tools, campaign execution tools, web analytics tools, sales tools, and the marketing database, to name a few. The ebocube dashboard can be customized in many ways, so you have to define what you are measuring to make it work effectively for you.

The dashboard should link sales and marketing results to the budget. This is enabled through the way you have coded your campaign. ebocodes enable you to tag responses to individual contact levels, allowing you to report on unique responders on a granular level. You can also roll up to your overall campaign results by looking at the parent campaign code. You need to define what you want to see in the ebocube dashboard so as not to overload it with meaningless information that might hinder decision making.

There are many ways to bridge the gaps between marketing results and tracking those through execution and mops. Although technology and method of reporting will evolve very quickly, the Internet and EMs promise to be the future for business growth for at least another 20 years. Your business/marketing strategy should be to penetrate EMs with the ebocube model.

ebocube's a flexible and easily adaptable model can work for various business segments, regardless of size and vertical structure and can help you to define your strategy. The model elements can also be localized with local languages and integrates well with localized applications/systems. You can target A, B, or C countries, although A countries are the most attractive in terms of revenue and market size.

Define your profit and sales objectives in terms of your budget and resources for sale follow up. The majority of your campaigning will be through online communications. Set parameters for prospects, such as customers who have previously purchased products or services through email campaign management applications. Forty percent of your campaign efforts should be spent on data.

Example of ebocube Campaign: Datacube Review

Because ebocube is developed for B2B marketing, your datacube report will need to cover company site information as well as contact data. You target and sell products to companies; however, you communicate to contacts in those companies. So, you need to analyze two views in your datacube. First, you need to start with the higher-lever view (the company level), and second, the contact level. This will help you to determine which companies you can target, sites, and then contacts available to communicate to. To get the full picture and to identify gaps in your data, you need the two views: company and contact.

The datacube should represent all the data that your company has access and rights to for EM. The datacube may represent data provided to you by a partner or in-house data as well as any external sources that you have permission to use. Ideally, all data should be stored in one place (CI), allowing data-matching techniques to work effectively (but we know that in some circumstance we can't do that because of legislation or other limitations).

The ebocube company was born in 2001, and CI data grew organically through multiple marketing outbound activities capturing data in EMs, but also through inbound marketing (website subscriptions) and data acquired on ebocube.com. We used the datacube to review the data available for our A country segments and campaigns.

Communication channels are impacted by data available to marketers, such as how many marketable email addresses are available, valid phone numbers, and direct mail addresses. This is illustrated in Figure 9.9.

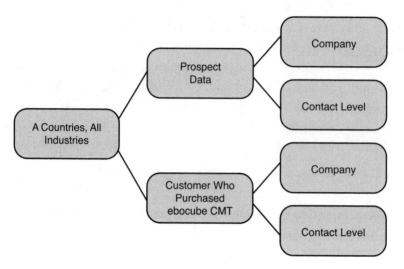

Figure 9.9   Hierarchical structure of data extraction

Using a hierarchical structure, you can request that data be pulled on various variables. Per the chart in Figure 9.9, we wanted all companies in our "A countries" (parent and sites) split by prospects and customers who had previously purchased from us. Then we extracted the data for the purpose of launching new ebocube dashboard application.

We discovered that we had very few valid contacts with marketing contact information for SMBs for all countries and verticals, but high-quality and -quantity contact data for enterprise and midmarket, as ebocube was originally created for large organizations.

The data segmentation is highlighted by the datacube at contact level, shown in Figure 9.1.

Briefing the Campaign Online

We created the campaign briefing tool to document ebocube commercial cycle objectives and to program campaign execution tools. The data was segmented into separate cells for the purpose of marketing and tracking, using ebocodes, and for sending different creative variants and different targeted offers to the individual trackable cells.

TABLE 9.1   Datacube View of Contactable Records for Data Segmentation for Campaigns

Communication Channel	Email	Telemarketing	Direct Mail
Data segmentation			
Decision maker	16,500	14,300	12,800
Influencer	10,000	12,700	12,500
Technical role	3,500	9,000	4,300
Business role	23,000	18,000	21,000
Opt in	22,350	24, 600	23,200
Last interaction less than 2 years	17,800	20, 100	14,000
Last interaction more than 2 years	8,700	6,900	11,300
Total for each channel	**26,500**	**27,000**	**25,300**

The segments were tracked with ebocodes and data captured and marketing information was set up to be fed against contacts in CI.

First step of our campaign: awareness and data acquisition

- Raise awareness of ebocube applications
- Acquire new contact data for existing companies
- Acquire contacts for SMB companies
- Update and refresh existing contact records across all segments and countries
- Improve data completeness against existing records across all countries and business segments

We used the following: communication channels/media mix, e-mail, web banners, online and offline press, and telemarketing as follow up.

Second step: emails blast

We created emails variants for the target audience identified in our database as having emails. The offers at the awareness stage were a whitepaper. We used a technical variant for the technical audience and a business variant for the business audience. We included a data-capture form behind the whitepaper, tagged it with an ebocode to track data responses against the email segment, and then used the data-capture form with the minimal fields to track who downloaded the whitepaper and so that contacts could send us their most up-to-date data.

Before launching the final email, we decided to test responses to sample data through A/B testing. After A/B testing, we analyzed the variants with the highest response rates and used the best performing emails for the relevant segments.

We used web banners with unique and individual tracking (for visitors and response captured data) placed on the following:

- Home page per country pages for ebocube
- Popular pages on our website
- ebocube.com events page
- Third-party sites (local resellers/partners [using tracked vanity, friendly URLs to see which generated the best responses] on local social network social media used in EMs)

We placed data-capture forms on our web banners, using a different ebocode per banner so that we could recognize where data (submitted) feeding CI originated (i.e., web banner x, part of campaign x, date, and so on). This also enabled us to show unique responders in the operational view of ebocube dashboard.

Press: We used online and offline press communications

All forms of communication above had a unique trackable vanity URL that linked or redirected to a data-capture form. We used the same offer on the banner as placed on email to ensure consistency (i.e., a free whitepaper). The ebocodes on the surveys fed contact data in CI. The campaign landing page also fed CI with response information against new or existing contact records. Once the form was completed, end users were redirected to the campaign landing page to claim the offer, and the next steps were as follows:

1. If end users submitted their details and downloaded the whitepaper off of the microsite, a follow-up email was sent to them inviting them to a webcast.

2. If end users did not open the email or follow our call to action, we sent them another email after a week with a different subject line and shorter copy.

3. If the end users received the follow-up email but still did not respond to the campaign, we de-marketed to these contacts and released them for different campaigns.

The offer at the consideration stage is a webcast sent by the system. At this stage, the banners, press adverts, and microsite are still live. Remember, you are constantly capturing data and pushing contacts through to the consideration phase.

If you have a low response rate at this stage, you will need to consider the offer (incentive), the proposition, creative, and the message or the data used. Perhaps the message is too complicated for your segment. You might want to change the offer. The creative aspects of your campaign may not be compelling. For email, check delivery rates and also check emails to make sure they are valid.

Telemarketing

You might post a free phone number on the microsite, which routes to the call center, and use a separate message to inform recipients to call their account managers directly, if they have one.

If a caller is qualified as a lead by the call center systems, this will be logged against CI and the ebocube dashboard (lead generated). The call center will log the lead and call against a system-generated tracking ebocode so that the leads can be identified to the campaign. Then contact data is stored with marketing information to form marketing history in your CI marketing database.

Lead candidates who call their account managers directly should be logged in to the dashboard against the campaign name, and this should be fed by sales tools.

You can also report on clicks from uniquely measured vanity URLs placed in the press, or on web banners, tracking the number of unique responders (i.e., those who submitted data to the banner or email).

Customer Journey: A Case Study

When contact submit their data through the data-capture form in the awareness acquisition phase, a follow-up email is sent, inviting them to a webcast aimed at generating consideration for our proposition (i.e., ebocube).

Actually, two webcast invites are sent, and all variants are localized for the countries. One webcast is technical and will be sent to respondents who downloaded the technical whitepaper. (The ebocode which was used to track whitepaper downloads and data submission will be used to pull the data.) The second webcast is about the business benefits of ebocube, and is targeted at respondents who downloaded the whitepaper responding to data and with a business job title.

Whoever has not registered to the webcast is sent a reminder ten days before the webcast and then again three days before the event. Registrants will have an email calendar invite dropped into the recipient's calendar.

All registrants are sent a webcast reminder three days before the event and an hour before the event is due to start. This is automated by many webcast hosting tools.

The webcast registration form, at consideration stage, uses lead-qualification questions, responses are captured, and all data is sent to CI.

Any lead candidates captured through the webcast registration, who answered positive to the BANT/lead-qualification questions, will be sent to the call center for further qualification. However, if they're recognized through business rules as being account managed, they will be routed to a lead management tool for the appropriate account managers or sales personnel to follow up. The lead candidate numbers will also feed to the ebocube dashboard.

If overall you have a low response rate at this stage, you will need to consider the event. Perhaps the message is too complicated on your email variants for your business and technical segment. You might want to change the offer. Reasons for low response are that the creative campaign may not be compelling, the timing of the webcast may not be convenient, or you just found out it's a public holiday in your target market.

After the event has taken place, you are then ready to move into purchase and development, which includes the following:

- Registrants to phase two can be sent to the call center to be further qualified as leads or to partners to be sold to.
- The call center will again ask BANT questions, as asked on the webcast registration form, and verify registration contact details provided via the webcasts data-capture form, ensuring data is valid.
- Top leads should be sent to be closed by the sale team or by partners or account managers dedicated to prospects or customers.
- Account-managed or named accounts should bypass the call center, because they have established relationships, and go straight to the account management tool to be followed up for sales opportunities. This is based on CI business rules, which should suppress account-managed leads flowing to the call center, which should be informed by your campaign management tool.
- Poor leads should be released out of governance for new campaigns so that contacts can be targeted with a nurturing campaign. The call center should give them a follow-up call at a later date if specified by the responder.
- Until a lead is closed by an account manager or partner, these contacts should not be marketed to unless the account manager/partner has closed the lead down. This should be reported on in their lead management tool, which should update CI and the ebocube dashboard either as a logged sale or a rejected lead—the number of rejected leads will indicate the quality of marketing leads.

Sales will either close the sale or reject the lead or update record information.

Banners, press advertisement, and microsites are still live, raising awareness and capturing data, and responders are now being invited to the video on demand (VOD, a recording of the original live webcast). Again, these new contacts are requested to fill in a registration form that includes lead-generation questions.

The campaign duration should last until objectives are reached, or can be pulled if proving ineffective (i.e., showing poor results) in your dashboard. Or, you might pull certain elements, instead of the whole campaign. For example, you might stop running a banner advertisement on one third-party website because the cost does not justify the results.

mops is an emerging function in marketing. It will help you to plan, budget, track, execute, and measure your campaign in EM in an organized way.

Using TALR (testing, analyzing, learning, and refining) for your campaign, you can test elements of your campaign and report on them before sending all of your contacts the message and thus improve results.

What Next?

Set up a planned campaign using a brief with SMART objectives, track your media responses and use, capture data, and push contacts through to the consideration phase. If data isn't being captured or responses are low, maybe the campaign should be stopped or you should look at which elements are not working, which should be measured individually. This can be review in the operational view of the dashboard.

Test a select sample of data and use two creative variations for an A/B test to see which email generates the best responses.

Perhaps send a webcast invite to new contacts who have shown an interest in the awareness and acquisition stage of your campaign (perhaps by downloading whitepapers or submitting their basic contact data). Again, they will need to register by filling in lead detail questions to view any content, and the whole integrated campaign should be planned, including follow up.

Information collected from lead candidates should feed the dashboard. Closed deals need to be logged by account managers or partners and reported in the dashboard.

Create the next element of the overall campaign by targeting your high-value segment (RFM segment). These will be customers who have previously purchased and are loyal to your brand.

Develop newsletters to keep customers informed; this will keep them loyal, but also keep them buying more through information.

If you're not reporting already, you need to start creating your dashboard to show your results. Carefully plan how you will do this—even if you only have a few metrics, try to tell your story to generate results even if you are just starting out with a spreadsheet.

We are more than sure that some of the dashboard elements are already in use at your company and supporting your marketing cases in your organization. It might be sophisticated, or it might be as simple as a spreadsheet where you track your activity, marketing spending, and potential (estimated) or actual revenue. You can use existing systems/reports and infrastructure. All of us as marketers want to show the results of our efforts, but it's not possible without the dashboard light because you will be working in the dark.

The previous generation of marketers used to say: **"Half of the money I spend on advertising is wasted; the trouble is I don't know which half"** (according to John Wanamaker).[5] Today, in this innovative, global-information century and with the ebocube business model, that excuse is obsolete. Because of marketing operations and the ebocube dashboard, we all know which part of our budget is being wasted.

The time is now.

Thanks for reading,

Lara and Lucas

Endnotes

[1] Marketing Operations 2.0: Mobilizing Marketing for a Web 2.0 World, "Marketing Operations," http://mopartners.typepad.com/marketing_ops_at_work/2009/05/marketing- operations-mobilizing-marketing-for-a-web-20-world.html.

[2] Wikipedia, "Customer insight," http://en.wikipedia.org/wiki/Customer_insight.

[3] Use it.com, "Putting A/B Testing in Its Place" http://www.useit.com/alertbox/20050815.html.

[4] Ibid.

[5] Wikipedia, "John Wanamaker," http://en.wikipedia.org/wiki/John_Wanamaker.

References

Useful links/information on developments EMs:

- **The World Bank Group**, http://www.worldbank.org

  The World Bank is a source of financial and technical assistance for emerging markets—this is a good source of information on some of the projects being invested in.

- **World Fact Book**, https://www.cia.gov/library/publications/the-world-factbook

  The World Fact Book provides information for countries all over the world, covering politics, economies, social issues, and history.

- **"China becomes third largest economy,"** article on http://www.ft.com/cms/s/0/8d9337be-e245-11dd-b1dd-0000779fd2ac.html

  The FT has a dedicated online section on emerging markets.

Useful links for Internet statistics globally:

- **Internet World Stats's "Email Marketing Basics and Glossary of Terms and Definitions,"** http://www.internetworldstats.com/articles/art060.htm

- **International Telecommunications Union's "Global ICT Developments,"** http://www.itu.int/ITU-D/ict/statistics/ict/

  Both are fantastic resources for global Internet usage statistics and growth rates, including mobile Internet, from around the world.

Useful links for online definitions:

- **Marketing Sherpa**, a dictionary of "rich media" terms, http://www.marketingterms.com/dictionary/rich_media/
- **Wikepdeida's "Microsite,"** http://en.wikipedia.org/wiki/Microsite

Readers will find useful definitions for the online world from Marketing Sherpa, as well as Wikipedia, which is an excellent up-to-the-minute online resource.

Links to interesting research on mobile Internet:

- **Portio Research Ltd**, "Slicing up the Mobiles Services Revenue Pie," http://www.portioresearch.com/Slicing_Pie_June08_Limited%20Edition.pdf
- **Nielsen Mobile**, "Critical Mass: The Worldwide State of the Mobile Web," July 2008, http://www.nielsenmobile.com/documents/CriticalMass.pdf

When we began writing in 2007, we found these research reports helped us to appreciate the role that mobile Internet services and marketing will play in the future and in EMs.

Useful links to mops information:

- **ANA (Association of National Advertisers)**, "ANA Marketing Accountability Task Force Finds Few Follow Best Practices," 2007, http://www.ana.net/news/content/600
- *Marketing Resource Management: The Noble Art of Getting Things Done in Marketing. Efficiently*, by Romek Jansen and Frans Riemersma (2009).

Both resources were useful in helping us with discussions about marketing accountability and the developing discipline/function of marketing operations.

INDEX

C

calendar functionality, 48
call to action (CTA), 224
campaign briefing tool, 274-277
campaign landing pages, 125, 200
campaign management, CRM and, 75-78
campaigns, 113-115
  considerations for, 152-153
  email, 156-158
  incentives, 154
  lead-generation, 132
  loyalty, 142-143
  online communication, 154-155
  optimizing, 145-146
  planning, 116
  SMART, 158
    managing email, 158-159
Caribbean, 14
case studies, customer journey, 278-280
CEE (Central and Eastern Europe), 12-14
chief marketing officers (CMOs), 85
child codes, 267-268
China, 11, 24
  mobile marketing, 172
  Mobile Web, 211
  outsourcing, 23
CIS (Commonwealth of Independent States), 20-21
CMOs (chief marketing officers), 85
CMS (content management systems), 202-204
co-branding, 50-51
collaboration across borders, 45-49
color, campaigns, 152
commercial cycle, ebocube model, 63, 69-70
Commonwealth of Independent States (CIS), 20-21
communicating with customers, increasing satisfaction, 137-138
communication
  online, 154-155
  timing
    email, 170-171
    mobile email, 171-173
company culture, 35-36
competition, global competition, 25
conferencing tools, 47, 49
consideration
  events, 228
  SMART, 161-162
  web banners, 223
  webcasts, 192
  websites, 208-209
consideration stage, 140

consumer brands, 50
contact data life cycle, 69
contact level, data cube, 110
contacts, 125, 152
  data life cycles, 117
  merge-purge, 258-261
  nurturing prospects, 131
  planning, 116
content management systems (CMS), 202-204
conversion rates, 93
cookies, 267-268
CRM, campaign management and, 75-78
CSS, email, 180
CTA (call to action), 224
cultures, 143
  researching, 147
  time zones, weekends, and work schedules, 151
currency exchange rates, 153
customer insight, 251-253
  data warehouses, 254-255
customers
  case studies, 278-280
  communicating with, increasing satisfaction, 137-138
  developing, 132
  loyalty, 142-143
  retaining, 132
  RFM (Recency, Frequency, Monetary), 136-137
cybersurveillance, 179

D

dashboards, 33-34, 81, 84-85
  business intelligence, 85-86
  designing, 100, 105
  ebocubes, 271-272
  financial results, 86-87
  marketing operational dashboards, 94-96
  operational view, metrics, 96-100
  phase one, 71-75
  views, 88
    high-level dashboard view, 89-94
    operational view, 89, 95-96
data
  acquired data, quality of, 129-131
  challenges with, 255-257
    merge-purge, 258-261
    postal codes, 257
  data capture, 121
  email, 127
  getting into emerging markets, 118-120
    data capture, 121
    data-capture forms, 123-124
    homegrown data, 120-121

FINANCIAL TIMES

In an increasingly competitive world, it is quality
of thinking that gives an edge—an idea that opens new
doors, a technique that solves a problem, or an insight
that simply helps make sense of it all.

We work with leading authors in the various arenas
of business and finance to bring cutting-edge thinking
and best-learning practices to a global market.

It is our goal to create world-class print publications
and electronic products that give readers
knowledge and understanding that can then be
applied, whether studying or at work.

To find out more about our business
products, you can visit us at www.ftpress.com.